T0632784

PENGUIN BOOKS

BEYOND THE FLOWER

Judy Chicago is an internationally known artist, writer, feminist, and intellectual. Her published works include the *Holocaust Project* (the companion book to the traveling exhibition), *The Dinner Party*, and *Through the Flower* (available from Penguin). She lives in Belen, New Mexico, with her husband, photographer Donald Woodman, and their bevy of cats.

PHOTOGRAPHY COORDINATED BY
DONALD WOODMAN

PENGUIN BOOKS

Beyond the Flower

The

Autobiography of a

Feminist Artist

Judy Chicago

PENGUIN BOOKS

Published by the Penguin Group

Penguin Books USA Inc., 375 Hudson Street, New York, New York 10014, U.S.A.

Penguin Books Ltd, 27 Wrights Lane, London W8 5TZ, England

Penguin Books Australia Ltd, Ringwood, Victoria, Australia

Penguin Books Canada Ltd, 10 Alcorn Avenue, Toronto, Ontario, Canada M4V 3B2

Penguin Books (N.Z.) Ltd, 182–190 Wairau Road, Auckland 10, New Zealand

Penguin Books Ltd, Registered Offices: Harmondsworth, Middlesex, England

First published in the United States of America by Viking Penguin,
a division of Penguin Books USA Inc. 1996
Published in Penguin Books 1997

1 3 5 7 9 10 8 6 4 2

Copyright © Judy Chicago, 1996
All rights reserved

Photographs by Donald Woodman, copyright © Donald Woodman, 1996. Other images from the
Through the Flower archives. Reproduced by arrangement with Through the Flower.

THE LIBRARY OF CONGRESS HAS CATALOGUED THE HARDCOVER AS FOLLOWS:

Chicago, Judy.

Beyond the flower: the autobiography of a feminist artist/Judy Chicago;
photography coordinated by Donald Woodman.

p.   cm.

Includes index.

ISBN 0-670-85295-3 (hc.)

ISBN 0 14 02.3297 4 (pbk.)

1. Chicago, Judy, 1939– .   2. Artists —United States—Biography.
3. Feminism and art—United States.   I. Title.

N6537.C48A2 1996

700′.92—dc20

[B]   95–25812

Printed in the United States of America
Set in Garamond No. 3
Designed by Kate Nichols

Except in the United States of America, this book is sold subject to the condition that it shall not,
by way of trade or otherwise, be lent, re-sold, hired out, or otherwise circulated without the
publisher's prior consent in any form of binding or cover other than that in which it is published and
without a similar condition including this condition being imposed on the subsequent purchaser.

To my staunch network of friends,

without whom the artist—and her art—would have been lost.

And to my mother's tattered Thesaurus,

relic of my childhood,

which I retrieved when she died and I'll retire now

that I've finished this book.

Contents

Introduction

I began work on this book sometime in the late fall of 1993, while residing in a modest house in a semirural area of Albuquerque. For the last few years, I have been living here with my husband, photographer Donald Woodman, and an assortment of cats. People often imagine that I live a rather glamorous existence, and it is true that there are times when I am whisked to art openings or shuttled from book signings to media appointments, then dine at expensive restaurants, courtesy of business tabs or generous friends. And there have certainly been long periods when I was at the center of large projects, surrounded by assistants and the hum of a busy studio.

But this is not the case now. In fact, after more than three decades of artmaking, for the first time I am without a real studio. Instead, I have a room that might best be described as a study, where I have been spending most of my time writing. When I started this manuscript, I was thinking about putting down my paintbrush permanently, primarily because I was being plagued by the nagging questions: What is the point of having struggled to create what is now an immense body of work if most of it is to sit in storage or—

if in museum collections—go undisplayed? And why make any more?

During most of these years, I have been married (though not to the same man). Nevertheless, I have always spent a lot of time by myself, maintaining a rigorous work schedule that I rarely interrupted for anything or anyone. I have lived an existence focused on art, punctuated—for at least the last two decades—by intense bouts of exercise and, recently, attending to the needs of our six cats. Mully, the eldest, died last year, and recently we added Trio to our roster of beloved felines. Until this three-legged but rambunctious animal attached himself to our household, my favorite had always been Sebastian, an adorable black and white creature with a short tail, the result of having had it run over and therefore amputated when he was age one. The reason I mention him and the others—the long-haired and handsome Romeo; fat, black Inka; scrawny Veronica; and half-wild Poppy—is that during the time we have lived in this house, Donald has been away most days and I have been more alone than usual, with only the kitties for company.

Strangely, a little over twenty years ago I started writing my first book—*Through the Flower: My Struggle as a Woman Artist*—in a small house in the very same neighborhood. I was then married to Lloyd Hamrol, a sculptor. We lived in Los Angeles but spent one summer in Albuquerque while Lloyd built a site-specific installation at the University of New Mexico and I made lithographs at the Tamarind Lithography Workshop. I would arise each morning at 5:00 A.M., write from 5:30 to 7:30, then go to the print shop. At the end of the day, I would emerge from the cool, temperature-controlled studio into the intensely hot, dry New Mexico climate and the strange clicking sound of cicadas.

It would have never occurred to me then that I would end up settling in the Southwest, where I have lived since the mid-1980s. Nor could I have envisioned being away from painting for such a lengthy period of time. Neither would I have imagined that—rather than writing sporadically or around my fixed studio hours, which is what I have previously done—I would spend so many uninterrupted days sitting at my typewriter. And even though this is my seventh book (a fact that cannot be more surprising to anyone than it is to me), I have written it for the same reason I wrote *Through the Flower*. In both instances, I hoped to resolve some of the conflicts I was experiencing in regard to my life as an artist, these recent feelings even more vexing than the ones that motivated me to write my first autobiographical book.

I initially took up writing during the early 1970s, at the beginning of the Women's Movement, which opened up many options for women of my generation, the most significant (to me) the possibility of being myself as a woman artist. This was something that had seemed utterly out of the question during the time I was coming up as a young artist in the entirely male-dominated art scene of Los Angeles in the 1960s.

In order to be taken seriously as an artist (my singular goal at that time), I had felt obliged to disconnect from my natural aesthetic impulses as a woman. With the advent of the Women's Movement, I felt permission to discuss this as well as the discrimination I had experienced during the first ten years of my professional career. Before the Women's Movement burst into being, I had often tried to talk about the dreadful sexism of the art world, the response to which had invariably been some disparaging comment like: "What are you, Judy, some kind of suffragette?" But when I read the early feminist literature, I realized that I was not alone—not in my experiences and not in my anger—which I became determined to communicate, preferably through my art.

I had been searching women's history for clues about whether other women might have struggled with problems similar to my own in the hopes of finding answers that might be useful to me. I had also begun to lecture about some of these issues and to grapple with how to change my own artmaking mode—without sacrificing its transformative quality—when I wrote my first book, which was inspired by Anaïs Nin. (In fact, I keep a beautiful photograph of her on the wall of my study, which I frequently glance at because I am again following the advice that she gave me at the time.)

I met Anaïs at a party in L.A. By chance, she had just read an essay I had written for *Everywoman,* a feminist journal, in which I first took up some of the questions that would be more developed in

Through the Flower (though I had no thought of writing a book when I did this piece). My article was published while I was teaching at Fresno State University, where I had gone for a year to establish an art program for young women students aimed at providing them with an art education that would (hopefully) allow them to develop as artists without doing what I had felt compelled to do—that is, deny my female identity. In addition to wanting to create this program, I also hoped that by helping my students work openly with female subject matter, I might be able to find my way back to my own impulses and also summon the courage to express them openly.

This was to be no mean feat (my own effort, that is; the students took to it like ducks to water), though at the time I did not realize how formidable a challenge it would be. Going to Fresno jump-started this process, one that turned out to be extremely scary and also risky, as there was no precedent (that I knew of) for either the educational program I had initiated or my aesthetic goals. Unquestionably, one reason I felt compelled to go to Fresno was in order to be away from the male-dominated atmosphere of the Los Angeles art scene. It would not have been at all conducive to what I wished to do, which was to think, study, and experiment with new ways of being an artist.

At any rate, when Anaïs and I met, she invited me to visit her, an opportunity I leapt at because I admired her. This was the time at which she was coming to prominence after years of having had her work ignored. I had read her first published journals and identified with both her struggle and some of her ideas about the female artist. When I arrived at her airy house in the Silver Lake area of Los Angeles, I found myself immediately confiding my feelings, fears, and aspirations. In a rush of words, I stated that I desperately wanted to be myself as a woman artist but didn't know how to integrate my artistic and female selves. I then explained that I had begun studying the history of women's art and literature, looking for personal reinforcement while also looking to see whether there was such a thing as a unique female perspective, an issue we discussed at this and later visits.

At this time, Anaïs said something that took me totally aback. She suggested that I write a book, that it was a way of working through such dilemmas; she added that in her opinion, I had definite literary talent. Even now, I can remember thinking: "She ought to know." I shall be forever indebted to her because writing that book helped me clarify my aims, allowed me to share my somewhat confusing experiences as a woman artist, and unexpectedly brought me an enlarged audience for my work, along with the realization that there was a larger potential viewership for art than I had presumed.

However, becoming a writer was not easy for me, even though I had always been able to express myself both visually and verbally. But from the time I was young, I was entirely focused upon becoming an artist and hence had given no thought to pursuing a literary career. Far more daunting than honing my writing skills was that it seemed that writing a book would mean radically departing from the role of artist as it was defined then. During the time I had been at UCLA finishing my master's degree in art (the same period I was attempting to establish myself professionally), I had discovered that artists were expected to assume a posture suggesting that they were both inarticulate and dumb.

The following story seems to suggest the attitudes that prevailed at the time. During a visit to L.A., a young and extremely intellectual New York critic paid a call on an important collector. Lounging around the opulent furnishings of the collector's large and sunken living room were some of the city's most outstanding artists (all male). In an effort to make an impression, the critic commented: "This scene reminds me of a Delacroix," to which one of the artists replied by asking caustically, "Who the fuck is Delacroix?" His query was met by peals of laughter by the artist's colleagues, all of whom knew exactly to whom the humiliated critic was referring and why. (As I had become friends with some of these guys, they were only too happy to share this story with me, including the fact that both the ambiance of the room and their postures were indeed, as the critic had pointed out, reminiscent of one of Delacroix' paintings.)

In an environment such as this one, in which I was trying to make my way, it seemed that writing a book would definitely collide with the general expectation that artists should be seen and not heard, particularly if one was of the female gender. Numerous—and hurtful—comments from men in the art world had already taught me that

I was viewed by most of them as overly aggressive, probably because of my insistence that my work be taken as seriously as that of my male colleagues. I felt anxious that by writing, I might appear even more threatening, an unsettling prospect because, more than anything else, I wanted to be accepted in the art community.

Despite the many risks involved, my drive to be myself was so intense and my need to communicate my experiences so pressing that I went ahead in the hopes that I would find some resonance in terms of what I had been going through. During this period, I was altogether convinced that my difficulties were entirely the consequence of my being a woman, a premise that was, at least to some extent, correct. What never occurred to me at that time, however, was that some of my discomfort in the art community grew out of the fact that I had quite a different set of values than those which predominated. But I think it best to limit my remarks in this introduction to my perceptions and actions then, allowing my dawning recognition of my divergent orientation to become evident as I report upon my developing comprehension—and acceptance of this—in the later pages of this book.

At the moment, my primary purpose is to explain how I first came to write *Through the Flower* and why I am now picking up that tale, left off in the early 1970s. In this volume, I intend to describe some of what has occurred since then and how it could have happened that I came to the point where I was thinking about giving up art. The prospect of putting down my paintbrush made me altogether miserable, as it has been creating art that has provided meaning to my life. But to tell the truth, I couldn't figure out how or why to keep churning out more projects or art objects that seemed to just pile up in storage—or, if in collections, remained largely out of view. What made this problem even more perplexing was that whenever my work was shown (innumerable times over these years), people would continually tell me how seeing it had "changed their lives."

This contradiction seemed particularly poignant in relation to my most well-known work, *The Dinner Party*, a monumental multimedia, symbolic history of women. Despite the fact that this piece has traveled around the world, been seen by nearly one million viewers, and is being featured in many art history texts, it—like too much of my work—has spent years locked away in crates in one or another warehouse. Because I could not resolve the issue of how to continue being an artist in the face of what appeared to be ever-greater storage bills, I thought it might be wise to once again follow Anaïs's directive and see if I could write my way through this perplexing quandary. Also troubling was that I found myself being haunted by something that she had told me about in relation to her own work.

During one of our visits, Anaïs shared a recurrent and distressing nightmare. She was on her deathbed when suddenly a figure appeared, hovering over her while whispering into her ear, "Anaïs, it was *all only a dream.*" "No," she would reply, rising up from the bed, "my achievement as a writer is real." Falling back into the death swoon, she would hear the voice reiterate, "No, Anaïs, it was *just a dream!*" I can vividly remember my response at that time, which was that— given the burgeoning Women's Movement—this nightmarish vision of hers was merely a relic of bygone days when women's accomplishments were neither recognized nor honored. After all, as I reminded her, her work was finally being both published and celebrated.

Yet at the point at which I began this manuscript, I found myself experiencing the same feeling of insubstantiality in terms of my own work. Fortunately, Anaïs's advice of so many years ago has proven just as important to me in the 1990s as it was in the 1970s. Writing this book has allowed me to achieve some clarity about what brought me to such a low point as to think about giving up art altogether and also what I might do to ensure that such a dreadful nightmare as hers remains only that—a bad dream. But this has been an extremely painful process, as there has been much that took place during these last twenty years about which I had never really thought.

In preparing this manuscript, I read over the personal journals that I have kept since 1971. I must admit that I was shocked by the person revealed by what was very intimate writing, words written with no thought of publication and hence incredibly unself-conscious. With some distress, I was forced to recognize that behind the facade of the self-assured public persona that I have become and even the confident artist in her studio was another, more haunted figure, one so excruciatingly sensitive that she recoiled at any but a loving comment and suffered terribly at the inevitable insensitivities of even those who cared about her.

What did I do with this seemingly constant turmoil of emotion? The answer became obvious as I worked on this book: The feelings fueled my incessant drive to create. In all likelihood, had it not been for the problems I have been describing—about feeling thwarted and frustrated in terms of all the art that I have already made—I would have just gone on generating images without ever having taken the time to evaluate my experiences of these last two decades, a process that, however difficult, has proven invaluable. However, throughout this period, I have longed for my studio; it has been agonizing to be separated from my artistic life. But it seemed so pointless to continue making art if the work I had already done had no solid place in the world.

It required more than two years and the writing of this book to resolve this quandary. As there are many pages between this introduction and that resolution, allow me to comment upon how odd it seems that I took up the continuation of *Through the Flower* in such close proximity and in such similar living quarters to those I occupied (however briefly) when I rather unknowingly began a literary career. When I wrote my first autobiographical work, I did so in the hopes that others might find my experiences informative, even insightful in terms of their own struggles.

After its United States publication, that book was issued in England, Germany, and Japan, and it will soon be put out in China (which thrills me no end; imagine my life story being relevant to women there). This worldwide distribution helped build an international audience for my work. It also produced letters from readers around the globe whose grateful responses suggested that continuing the account of my life might again prove to be of some value to others. In this book, I intend to briefly review my childhood and my early professional years with the perspective of maturity, then chronicle the last twenty years and reflect on what has occurred during this time.

Before taking up the saga of my last two decades, I would like to explain the titles of these two autobiographical books. Along with

being the name of my first book, *Through the Flower* was the title of
my 1973 painting. It is also the name of the nonprofit corporation
that has helped to support and exhibit my participatory projects since
the late 1970s. The phrase itself refers to my earlier efforts to move
through the confines of female role—as symbolized by the flower—
into an enlarged space, something I believe that I have now achieved.

The title of this book, *Beyond the Flower*, refers to my more recent
struggle to forge and express an expanded perspective, one that I consider to be more inclusive than my previous views, which, as I mentioned, centered almost entirely on issues of gender. My primary aim
during these last two decades has been to move out into an expanded
sense of myself and the world from the base of my feminism, steadily
enlarging my perspective and reflecting this through my work. However, the process of moving "beyond the flower" has been a rather
significant challenge, one reason being that it has required coming to
terms with my own power in a world that fears and demonizes female
power. As a result, I now realize that I have not always been able to
adequately explain my motivations, my point of view, or my philosophy. Moreover, I assumed that these were self-evident, especially
through my art. But the degree to which my work, along with my
person and my intentions, have been consistently misunderstood and/
or misrepresented has shocked me.

Having recently reread *Through the Flower* in preparation for the
task of writing this sequel, I must admit to being somewhat taken
aback by its unabashed honesty. It is not that I don't intend to be
equally candid; I do. It's just that the confessions of a mature woman
will, I am sure, be somewhat more discreet and also deferential in
regard to the feelings of some of the people with whom I've been
close, something that I failed to do before. Moreover, now that I am
more of a public figure, I have come to cherish the intimacy of my
private life.

I shall therefore ask for the indulgence of my readers if I do not
disclose all that some may know of my many intellectual detours or
my too numerous romances. If I have omitted something that is
known to have occurred, it is because the person has asked me to or
because I decided that it would have distracted from the more im-

portant task of examining what has happened to me in order to understand something of where we women are in history. I have always stood somewhat apart from my career, viewing it as possessing a larger, symbolic significance in that I believe it reveals what many women of talent can expect to encounter in the late twentieth century as they endeavor to do what all gifted people wish to do: that is, try to practice their talents to the best of their abilities.

BEYOND THE FLOWER

Chapter One

How Judy Cohen Became
Judy Chicago

*F*rom the time I was a child, I always had a burning desire to make art. In fact, I started to draw when I was barely able to talk. My preschool teacher had told my mother that I was gifted, and when I look at some of my childhood drawings—which were prized and saved by my mom—I can see what prompted the teacher to make this assessment. At a stage in which most children are making stick figures and colored blobs, I was doing drawings such as "Fun in the Sun." This now-faded picture, featuring a girl jumping over a rock, demonstrated a talent for conceptual thinking that would be considered unusual for any four-year-old child.

My mother, who had been a dancer herself and maintained a lifelong interest in the arts, encouraged my artistic ambitions. When I was five, she borrowed a friend's membership card to the Art Institute of Chicago so that I could attend the free classes held in the museum auditorium. Then, despite my family's fluctuating and often limited finances, my mom always managed to find a way to pay for the more rarefied classes at Junior School, where I went each week until I left Chicago to go to college in California.

Almost from childhood, my artistic life felt more real to me than any other aspect of my existence. Every Saturday, I would take the Number 53 bus from our home on the North Side, near the lakefront, which dropped me off right near the stone lions that flanked the steps to the museum. I always felt as if I were entering another world, one in which I could totally lose myself in the creative process. I would emerge from the cramped classes in the basement with a sense of satisfaction that I came to crave. I would walk up the wide stairway leading to the light-filled galleries, often spending the rest of the day there.

I loved wandering among the paintings and sculptures to study the millions of colored dots that together form Seurat's *Déjeuner sur la Grande Jette* or to marvel at the luminosity of Monet's paintings of haystacks in the changing light. Standing in front of the ribald images by Toulouse-Lautrec, I traced his use of reds and noticed how the viewer's eye is made to move around the entire canvas. As observant as I was, however, the one thing that I totally failed to notice was that nearly all of the art at the museum was by men. But even if I had noticed, I doubt that I would have been at all deterred from my own aspirations.

I cannot remember when I first decided that I would be an artist when I grew up. I know that I spent countless hours by myself drawing, and I became the official school artist almost as soon as I entered grammar school. I illustrated yearbooks and decorated the gym for dances, activities that continued in high school, though by my teens my life circumstances were quite different. The one constant throughout these years was my ambition, which was to become a famous artist, to be part of the glorious art history I saw represented at the museum.

I have always, from my earliest days, had a strong sense of myself, which was encouraged by my parents. Years later, my mother told me that she had always known that I was different—"special," I think she said. For in addition to being artistically talented, I was also extremely bright. In the environment in which I was raised, these twin traits somehow afforded me such special treatment—from family, friends, and at school—that I never once encountered the notion that, given my gender, my aspirations were either peculiar or unobtainable.

My parents were Jewish liberals, with a passion for the intellectual life and seemingly endless energy for political activism. Some of my earliest memories include going to the union hall with my father, where I'd eat hot dogs while listening to him deliver some rousing political speech. He was a Marxist and a labor organizer, and I derived from him a lifelong passion for social justice, the belief that the world could be changed and, equally profoundly, that I could trust and be unconditionally loved by a man. I also learned that the purpose of life was to make a difference, a goal that has shaped my existence.

I can still see my mother and father dancing together in our living room, for theirs was a love marriage, which was quite evident in the way in which they interacted. Music, especially blues and jazz, forms a backdrop for many of my childhood memories because my parents had a vast record collection. I was raised amid record parties for various causes, including several for the Spanish Civil War. People of all races mingled in our second-floor apartment to engage in near-constant political arguments. Moreover, there was an expressed commitment to equal rights for women, something I not only heard stated but saw demonstrated by the way in which my father always made sure to include the women in these lively discussions. Moreover, I saw it manifested in the way he treated me.

To say that my father adored me would be an inadequate description for all the love and attention he showered upon me, and I cannot emphasize enough the pivotal role he played in my development. Because my mother was employed full-time as a social worker and later as a medical secretary, it was my father, who worked nights at the post office, who was home when I awoke from my afternoon naps. He would gently place me on his lap and begin to play a series of games that he had invented to train me in logic, mathematics, and, most important, in values. (The details of these games escape me, as I was only two or three when they started, though the results have stayed with me throughout my life.)

I can vividly recall my father at the center of the many conversations that raged in our house, patiently explaining one or another political theory to the assembled group. To make him happy I had to perform intellectually, which I started doing as soon as I could talk.

The few remaining family members and friends from this period still remind me of certain "Judyisms," the precocious comments I produced in order to gain my father's approval, which he repeated to all who would listen.

There is a common misconception that females are severely discriminated against in traditional Jewish families, but this was not my experience. My father, Arthur, was the youngest of ten children, "nine of whom were living," as my Grandma Cohen (his mother) used to put it. Her husband, my grandfather—who died the year I was born—had been a practicing rabbi, the twenty-third in an unbroken tradition. It had been expected that my father would follow in his footsteps, but he rebelled against this assumption even as a child when he refused to go to *cheder,* or religious school.

My mother came from a small family, one that was scattered and lacking in presence during my early years. But my childhood was punctuated by many raucous Cohen family affairs. Given that the family was so large and that most of the relatives lived in and around the Chicago area, there were numerous opportunities for large and noisy get-togethers, especially at the Jewish holidays and, oddly enough, at Christmas, which was usually celebrated at our house. Though there was never a tree, various aunts and cousins would bring stacks of inexpensive presents, which I would excitedly hand out to people in our front room as my father called out their names.

The Cohen family seemed to speak to and about each other constantly. Because my own household was one in which the life of the mind held sway, I always felt somewhat separated from what appeared to me mostly trivial concerns, although I definitely enjoyed the sense of love and connection of family events. My father was particularly close to his sister Enid, the one nearest in age to him. She and her husband, Willy, who first drove a taxi and later opened a liquor store, lived nearby when I was born. We spent a lot of time with them and their two children, Corinne and Howard, both of whom were a decade or more older than me. Many years later, Howard, who would become like a brother to me, would often remind me that he had known me since the time I was only a bow on my mother's pregnant stomach.

My father's various siblings all had differing relationships to their

Jewish heritage, a few maintaining religious observances but most turning their backs on the Orthodoxy in which they were raised. My mother once told me how she'd asked my father if he wished her to learn kosher cooking, which was prepared every Friday night at his mother's house. He shuddered and replied that he always got a stomachache after these meals. This response may be said to be a metaphor for his relationship to Judaism generally, for like many second-generation Jews, he (and my mother) basically rejected all things Jewish. As a result, I learned less than nothing about Jewish history and culture from my parents.

However, they were always quite clear that we *were* Jewish and that this was something to be proud of, though they never explained exactly why, except for my father's frequent references to the long tradition of rabbinical service in his family. He also spoke of an ancestor so illustrious that he had bequeathed his "blue blood" to all of his descendants, including me (though of course my father made no mention of women's traditional exclusion from the rabbinate).

The Vilna Gaon had lived in Vilna, Lithuania (hence his name), in the eighteenth century. I would later discover that Vilna had at one time been referred to as the "eastern Jerusalem" because of the long tradition of Jewish life and learning that had flourished there. It was part of the Pale, a section of Eastern Europe that had gone back and forth between Polish and Russian control. All of my grandparents had come to America from this area, which included Latvia, birthplace of my maternal grandfather. As a child, I asked my father about these countries, only to be told that "they didn't exist anymore." This declaration came back to me and made me both angry and sad when, many years later, I traveled there in search of the Jewish heritage that I had been denied.

But even if I was ignorant about my Jewish background—knowledge that I would one day yearn for—with hindsight, it becomes obvious that I was raised in a household shaped by what might be called Jewish ethical values, particularly the concept of *tikkun,* the healing or repairing of the world. I was taught to believe that working to achieve this transformation is what life is all about and that material possessions are utterly unimportant. I can still recall my father pointing to all the books and records in our house and saying "See these, these are the only riches that count."

I am convinced that my father really didn't want another child, but my mother became pregnant despite his stated objections. My brother, Ben, was born in 1945, in an environment very different from the one that had spawned me. Moreover, he was born with a vestigial stomach, which meant that he had trouble ingesting food. Consequently, being hungry, he cried all the time.

I remember one night at dinner when his wails became too much. I turned to my father and begged him to do something. "What am I supposed to do?" he asked as he pulled off his belt. "Shall I beat him until he stops crying?" "NO!" I shouted, dissolving into tears. I was stunned by my father's threat, for I myself had never been hit—not by him, nor my mother. In fact, my parents had always expressed indignation about the one person we knew who beat her child—one of my cousins on the Cohen side.

When I was in grammar school, my father was investigated for his political beliefs. It was the early days of the Red Scare and McCarthyism, a period that would cast a pall of fear over everyone with left-wing sympathies. A cloud of despair settled over our household as my father, forced out of the post office and the union work that he loved, began searching for a way to make a living. Though he worked for a while as an insurance agent, it was the start of what would be a slow but steady decline.

Sometime later I began coming home from school in the middle of the afternoon to find my father sitting in the living room in his favorite velvet chair, smoking and staring vacantly into space. When my mother came home from work she would become furious, but instead of saying anything, she would put on blue jeans and begin to clean the house. She never explained what was going on; all she would say was that my father was at home because he didn't feel well. But I would often hear them arguing, usually about money.

By the time I entered puberty, I felt as if I were living several different lives. There was school, which was always easy for me. In fact, most of the time I was bored, so I consoled myself by reading the contemporary fiction that lined our household bookshelves. By the time I graduated from grammar school, I was well acquainted with such American writers as Dos Passos, Fitzgerald, and Hemingway, and I was starting on the Russians, beginning with Dostoevsky. (My high-school teachers would not believe that I had already read these writers and would therefore not accept book reports on what I was actually reading. Instead, I would filch book reports from the condensed pieces in the *Reader's Digest,* which seemed to satisfy my doubting educators.)

Then there was the private drama at home that was so baffling to me. I could see my father failing but I didn't know why. I sensed my mother's anger, which she refused to talk about. My recollections of Ben are that we were not all that close, though my brother later reminded me of the many hours we had spent together contentedly playing Monopoly. However, we had very different childhoods, so that our memories were not at all the same. Certainly, there were some times when our family life became what it had once been: for example, all four of us going to visit my Grandma Cohen, and my father, Ben, and me playing games on the streetcar on the way there.

Finally, there was my art life, which, as I have mentioned previously, was already more real to me than anything else. Certainly, it provided me a retreat from the events in my life that I found so confusing, especially since it was at about this same time that I began to be classically trained, which was quite time-consuming. Manuel Jacobson, my teacher for many of my years at Junior School, did not believe in starting such training until a child was at least eleven years old, so as not to inhibit the creative impulse. But once this age had been reached, one began rigorous training in anatomy, still-life drawing, and study of both human and animal bones, the latter through regular drawing trips to the Field Museum of Natural History. Mr. Jacobson was quite encouraging to me, although he often pointed out—with some quiet frustration in his voice—that my drawings never seemed to fit on the page. (I suppose one could say that being too large for the picture frame might be considered a harbinger for what would be in store for me in my adulthood!)

When I was thirteen my father, who had been suffering from a mysterious stomach ailment, went to the hospital for an operation. Ben and I were sent to stay with Aunt Shirley, one of my father's sisters. We remained there for several days, with no word from our mother. Finally, Aunt Enid came over to tell me that my father was "very sick." "He couldn't die, could he?" I asked tremulously, thinking that she would answer "Of course not." Instead she said "Yes," and walked away. A few days later he died, apparently from kidney failure after an operation to remove part of his stomach, which had been eaten away by ulcers.

Over the years, many people have insisted that my father really died from cancer, though no one would admit it. But according to my mother, my father died of a combination of unpredictable circumstances, not the least of which was his having had peritonitis as a ten-year-old, which caused him to spend almost an entire year in bed; he was supposedly the first person to have recovered from this disease before the advent of penicillin. Unfortunately, one of the consequences of his many supine months was that his organs had become matted together with adhesions, a discovery that was made only on the operating table. At that point there was no choice but to go ahead with the surgery, even though there was some doubt that he had enough healthy tissue to withstand the stress of the operation.

There was never any discussion of my father's death, and Ben and I were not allowed to go to the funeral; it was not for us to weep together as a family. It was as if my father simply walked out of our life and, with his departure, the three of us became entirely alienated from each another. At night we would sit down to dinner together with my father's palpable absence filling the room, my mother's refusal to discuss his death a wall between us. To this day I cannot understand what possessed her to shut us out like she did. Who knows? Maybe her own grief was so unendurable that she felt she would be destroyed—or would hurt her children even more—if she allowed herself to express her own feelings or ask us about ours.

Perhaps she was attempting to protect us, though there was probably no real way of shielding either of us from the trauma of our father's death. I was left grief-stricken beyond imagination and totally dazed by the loss of my most beloved parent. But I believe that Ben was affected even more, though the full and paralyzing effects would not become apparent for many decades. He and I became even more distant, perhaps separated by the sorrow we could not share. And for many, many years, I was deeply and bitterly enraged at my mother because in my estimation and for whatever reasons, I felt that she had totally failed both me and my brother at this terrible time.

Moreover, not only had we lost our father, but most of the Cohen family members seemed to disappear from our lives. Some of my aunts apparently blamed my mother for my father's death, primarily (and irrationally) because it had been her doctor who'd performed the operation. In fact, this might have been the reason for my mother's decision that Ben and I not attend the funeral. Perhaps she'd been afraid that we would be forced to witness something unpleasant—like an aunt accusing my mother of "murder" (which actually did occur).

This dramatic alteration in our extended family structure was also precipitated by my Uncle Willy being shot to death during a robbery at his liquor store a mere eight months after my father's death. My poor Aunt Enid lost the two people closest to her within such a short period. And as I tell this story I find myself thinking about my mother, and I feel my heart breaking for her. Not only was she widowed at forty, left with little money and two young children to support, but, as the result of a botched anesthetic during a hysterectomy she had around this same time, she began to have epileptic seizures. These could only (and barely) be controlled with phenobarbital, since she was allergic to all other medications on the market. I wish that I had not been so young and so unable to feel sympathy for her at the time. I understand now that she must have been suffering even more than Ben and I.

Shortly before my father's death, he and I had a conversation that left an indelible impression upon me. He had apparently promised my mother that he would not tell me that he was a Communist (I referred earlier to his being a Marxist, which is more accurate, as he ceased to be a party member in 1939). I do not exactly know why my mother extracted this pledge from my father, though I would imagine that, as this was the 1950s and anti-Communist fervor at a high pitch, she was probably frightened.

Perhaps my father, with some sense of how ill he was, wanted to be sure that he would be the one to explain his political views to me.

He spoke with me a short time before he left for the hospital. Even though I distinctly remember talking with him, I cannot completely recall everything we discussed, most likely because even now, more than forty years later, I still become quite choked up when I think about it. At one point he asked me if I knew what a Communist was, to which I replied, "I think so." Then, despite his vow to my mother, he told me that he himself was a Communist and asked whether I believed that all Communists were "bad," as I was being taught in school. (The "Weekly Reader" at this time featured comics in which monstrous yellow Communists were pictured bayoneting handsome American boys.)

It was almost as though I again became the young child who desperately wanted to impress her daddy with how smart she was. I cast about for an answer and finally replied that people like him *couldn't* be bad because they were only trying to make the world a better place. He smiled, which made me feel that my reply had satisfied him—though later, after his death, I went over this conversation again and again to see if I had somehow failed him and that was the reason he had died. With a child's logic, I believed that I was somehow responsible, a conviction that lodged deep within me for quite some time.

Another—and ultimately more far-reaching—effect of this interchange was that from then on, when it was time to look at the "Weekly Reader" in school, I found myself in possession of a secret: that my father was one of these dreaded Communists. This was something I puzzled over for a very long time and eventually concluded that I would have to choose between my own experience of my father and what the world would have me believe about him. I shall always be grateful for my dad's wisdom in initiating that conversation with me. As a result, I learned a crucial lesson: I had best trust my own judgment because other people's assessments could be very, very wrong.

I do not wish to give the impression that I was not a very confused girl after my father died. In fact, my teens were something of a blur. Although outwardly I seemed to be functioning well—continuing with my art classes and doing fine in school—my life was a mess. My mother and I were fighting almost constantly, the consequence of some teenage rebellion on my part, made worse by her continued refusal to discuss anything related to my father's death. Any attempt on my part to broach this subject seemed to result in her having a seizure, which (I am chagrined to admit) used to embarrass me terribly, especially if it took place in public.

I took refuge in my art life and also with my cousin Peggy, the daughter of one of my father's sisters. She and her husband lived near the University of Chicago, where they attended classes and taught part-time. Peggy would meet me after class at the Art Institute and we would go by subway to her house on the south side, where I would spend the weekend. We would engage in intense discussions about my father, by whom she, like some other cousins, had been inspired. For some reason I found these talks comforting, if only because, at least for short periods of time, I could remember him as he had been when he was alive.

One other strong memory I hold from my teens is of my boyfriend, Tommy Mitchell, a sweet and quite good-looking guy. He had a swell car, a '53 turquoise and white Chevy, in which he would pick me up after my Saturday classes at the Art Institute. Thinking back on the fact that this was the mid-1950s—at the height of what would later be called the "feminine mystique"—it seems somewhat remarkable that he never uttered a word of protest at my insistence that I couldn't possibly see him until after class since my work came first. Tommy was also memorable because it was with him that I first experienced orgasms. Being well-behaved, middle-class teenagers, intercourse was unthinkable to us. Instead, we would pet and dry-hump on whatever sofa we could find. The then-prevalent idea that women didn't *need* to come was one with which I was unacquainted, both at that time and later. I took my right to sexual pleasure for granted, and I was shocked when future boyfriends were not always so accommodating as Tommy.

One could say that I got through high school almost without noticing that I was there. Years later, some classmates (encountered by chance) mentioned their impression that I had thought myself "too good" for them, what with my artistic passion and seemingly advanced intellectual interests. Had they only known how mixed up and sorrowful young Judy Cohen actually was, perhaps their perceptions would have been different. For my part, the most important aspect of high school was getting through it in order to go to college.

I had been debating whether to attend the Art Institute, the University of Chicago (which had a joint program with the Institute), or UCLA, which was known to have a good art program. My mom's sister, Dorothy, who lived in Los Angeles, had offered to let me live with her and her husband, Herman, should I choose to go to school in California. Had I received a scholarship to the Art Institute—which I expected and thought I deserved—I would probably have chosen to go there. Instead, I decided it might be best to "Go West, Young Woman."

Shortly before my departure for California, Paula Levine, a girl who lived across the street from me, was killed, along with most of her family, when their car was hit by a train at a blind crossing. Paula, who was two years my elder, had been my best friend throughout our childhood. As a result of this tragedy, when I left Chicago I took with me two important traits: the determination to make something of myself and an acute awareness of the fickleness of fate.

If I were to meet this young Judy Cohen today, say, on the train taking her west, how would she appear to me? She was small, not more than 5'3", slim but with a slightly stocky bent, the result of her father's genes, which seemed to produce a body type featuring a somewhat thick midriff along with negligible hips and backside. She had cropped hair (common then for people with overly curly tresses) and wore glasses, which she often removed in an effort to avoid being viewed as "four-eyed." Her earnest manner and direct mode of expression gave little indication of her troubled heart. Somehow, the "free spirit" she had been as a young child had managed to survive the traumas of the intervening years. She still breathed the rarefied air of the "higher purpose" and had little patience for mundane concerns. All that was important to her was to become a famous artist and to make a difference in the world.

Soon after starting college at UCLA, I met Lloyd Hamrol, a fellow art student two years ahead of me. He was my first date in California and he was soon quite smitten with me, possibly because he had never met any female who seemed so sure of herself, nor so determined on a future as a successful artist. We dated on and off, though in my somewhat snobbish view, he was not intellectual enough. My tastes ran more toward the black-turtleneck type, commonly referred to as "beatniks." I also liked tall, lanky, smart black men, like Leslie Lacy, a philosophy student at USC whom I met at an NAACP meeting. It was with him that—after some awkward attempts—I lost my virginity.

After six months at the home of my aunt and uncle, I moved out and into a succession of apartments with a changing roster of female roommates. I adored college and was quite lucky to have been placed into a gifted students' program, which allowed me to substitute stimulating upper-division courses for less advanced beginning classes. My innocent manner and assumption that I had every right in the world to be respected for my intellect made me oblivious to the stares of male students and the somewhat indifferent responses of my professors when I would ask to be called upon in this or that academic class. If the teacher continued to ignore me, I would just wave my arm around in the air until he really had no choice but to acknowledge me, then answer my question.

At the end of my sophomore year, my mother and brother moved to L.A. They settled in the Fairfax area of the city, which is full of modest Spanish-style residences and apartment buildings. My mother got a job as a medical secretary and my brother enrolled in Fairfax High School. I was furious about their arrival, thinking that they had followed me when all I had wanted was to get away from my family. Years later, my mom told me that they had moved out west in order to establish residency so that my brother would be eligible for the low-cost but high-quality education of the California university system.

By then I was living with Jerry Gerowitz, a charming, brilliant, though mixed-up and rebellious young man, whom I would later end up marrying. Soon after my mother and brother got settled, I announced that I was leaving with Jerry for New York. After hitchhiking the whole way—unimaginable today, given the level of random violence—we ended up living in a cockroach-infested apartment on East Sixth Street.

I painted every day between eight in the morning and two in the afternoon, establishing my work hours as an inviolate time, a pattern I have maintained ever since. In the afternoon I taught art, first at the Henry Street Settlement, then at the Police Athletic League in the early evening. After work, Jerry, who had some kind of a part-time job, and I would hang around with artists and musicians, as the area in which we were living was filled with numerous creative people. Unfortunately, too many of them seemed to spend more time discussing their respective crafts than practicing them. I tired of this scene after just a year and decided to return to California and resume my studies. Jerry followed several weeks later.

Shortly after our return to L.A., I was diagnosed with a bleeding ulcer, which forced me to spend almost a month in the hospital. Somehow, I realized that my illness was related to the still-unresolved grief over my father's death. This prompted me to go into therapy, where I would eventually work through the many conflicted emotions I had brought with me from Chicago.

Jerry and I were married in 1961 at the county courthouse. I believe that my mother and brother attended the ceremony, but to be honest, I do not remember; I know that I visited them on a regular basis, though relations between us were less than wonderful. In 1962, I graduated from undergraduate school Phi Beta Kappa, having taken so many philosophy and literature classes that I found myself rewarded in a way no other art student had ever been. Jerry and I were relatively happy together, establishing an equalized relationship at a time when such a thing was still unusual. I assumed that he should do half the housework, and he complied. We had one argument about it when he left his dirty socks on the floor. I flipped, yelling something about how my having a cunt did not mean that I was his maid.

In 1963 Jerry was killed when his car went over a cliff on the twisting road leading to our house in Topanga Canyon. Our friend Janice Johnson found his body. She reported that it was covered with ants, which left me with a lifetime aversion to this particular insect.

Jerry's death precipitated a period of deep mourning, which, thanks to my therapy, helped me openly grieve for my young husband and, at long last, for my dad. It also helped me uncover and then recover from the guilt I had internalized about my father's death.

After Jerry died, I moved into a small house in Santa Monica, which had a separate building that I used as a studio. I spent most of the next year—my second in graduate school—trying to translate my sorrow into images and coming to terms with what was an exceedingly premature awareness of the fragility of life and my own mortality. As I described it in *Through the Flower,* I resolved to "build my life on the basis of my own identity, my own work, my own needs"—those few things I knew that I could never lose. My art became my focus, my solace, and my reason for living. At the time I still had absolutely no idea that building such a life was at all unusual for a person of the female gender.

The art that I created during this period—both paintings and sculpture, as I had a double major—was extremely expressive and also biomorphic in nature, full of visual references to female biology, which seemed to come to me quite naturally. This imagery caused some of my instructors to make wisecracks about my "wombs and breasts"— which, to tell the truth, I hadn't even noticed as such, so unself-consciously did I employ these forms. But their reactions made me feel extremely uncomfortable, as if I were doing something wrong. After my master's show (which featured some of this work), I simply abandoned most of it in the studio when I moved out of the house in Santa Monica.

By the time I left UCLA I was a twenty-three-year-old widow with a different name—Gerowitz—taken not out of wifely duty, no way. When Jerry and I were wed, young proto-feminist that I was, I had kept my original surname, altering it only after noticing—while doing the "gallery stroll" every Saturday afternoon, which is what all the "cool" art people did—that there seemed to be too many other artists named Cohen. I soon exchanged one seemingly patriarchal name for another, my then young husband's seemingly less common. But after Jerry died, people kept mistaking me for the daughter of his parents; not that I didn't like them. I did. It was just that two years of marriage hardly seemed sufficient reason to carry someone else's name for the rest of my life, especially when he disappeared under such unfortunate circumstances.

The upshot of all this was that I felt as though I did not have a name that suited me. Still, I had become somewhat known under this marital appellation, particularly after I started showing at the Rolf Nelson Gallery, one of the best spots in town. Rolf, whose outrageous manner belied a truly sensitive soul, started calling me Judy Chicago, due in part to the strong Windy City accent I had retained, but also because he thought it suited the tough and aggressive stance I had felt obliged to take in order to make my way into the macho art scene that was L.A. in the 1960s. Rolf tried to convince me to take this name professionally, but I went only so far as to use it in the phone directory. This was, in fact, an "in" thing to do at the time, as there were several artists with "underground" names.

By then I had begun hanging out with a number of prominent L.A. artists, all of whom were male. In an effort to be accepted as one of the boys, I actually went so far as to wear boots and smoke cigars, which I detested. I also began to excise any remotely female imagery from my work, an act that seemed essential in order to gain entry into what was an entirely male-dominated art community. About this time I also decided to go to auto-body school, where I learned to spray-paint, a skill that would provide me with the ability to fuse color and surface in many media, which would become one of the hallmarks of my work.

I am sure that one of the reasons I took up spray-painting was to prove myself to the guys, who were influenced in their work by the gorgeous lacquered surfaces that grace motorcycles and race cars. This was the time when the "finish fetish" style dominated L.A. art, especially as it was practiced by an artist named Billy Al Bengston, who became somewhat of a mentor to me. It was from him that I learned not to pay much attention to reviews. His advice was to count the column inches and the number of pictures, disregard whatever it was the critics wrote, and go on working, a position to which I adhered throughout most of my career.

Although Billy Al and his colleagues were not exactly supportive of women artists, they treated me with a modicum of respect, probably because they could see that I was talented, worked extremely hard, and was determined to be taken seriously as an artist. That was my singular goal, and everything else was secondary, including my personal life. For example, if I were not finished with my studio work at the end of the day, I would cancel any social engagement I might have made in order to complete the task at hand.

Early on I had been introduced to the idea that being taken seriously as an artist was more important than anything else, even economic success. Since my upbringing had instilled in me the idea of working for a higher purpose, it was easy for me to accept this canon, which was highly promoted among artists then, before marketplace values came to dominate the art world (one consequence of which has been that the notion of art as a spiritual pursuit was relegated to the sphere of the "quaint"). But what about money? you might ask. Higher pursuits aside, how did I earn a living?

The answer is that even though I was as poor as a church mouse, I looked around at my male artist friends to see how they made do, soon discovering that they lived by a system that might best be described as the "something will happen" school. This meant becoming accustomed to never knowing how one would pay the next month's rent, all the while hoping either that one's gallery would ring up to say a work of art had been sold or that some other equally providential event might occur. And as it was considerably easier to get along on next to nothing back then, I was able to scrape by, by adopting this rather insecure and anxiety-producing system, which was supplemented by part-time teaching (on weekends or at night, so as not to interfere with my daily studio hours).

Over the years I have often been questioned about my relationship to money, perhaps because I ended up building a large audience for my work among people outside the art world who are unfamiliar with the way art is customarily financed. Within the art community, artists are rarely interrogated about how they pay for their work, as I inevitably am. It was during the 1960s that I first learned—from my male colleagues, who actually taught me quite a lot—that one has to generate the money one needs in order to create. This means that, unless one is wealthy, some form of patronage is essential, be it one's family, dealer, or friends. I have been quite fortunate in that I have been able to acquire a number of patrons, some financially beneficent, others more modest in their means and hence their support. Many of them have remained loyal for years, becoming part of the ongoing network to whom I have dedicated this book.

The first of these were Stanley and Elyse Grinstein, whom I met in 1965 at an art party. Soon afterwards they paid me a visit, as they had expressed an interest in seeing my studio. By then, I was living in Pasadena with Lloyd Hamrol, my friend from UCLA who had become a sculptor. He and I had pooled our resources and with another artist, Llyn Foulkes, had rented a 5,000-square-foot loft in Pasadena. Our studio and living quarters were in what had once been a bank building, on top of what was then a vacuum cleaner store. A large staircase went up to a series of small offices, along with some large undivided areas that we had carved up into three huge work spaces. Lloyd and I had converted some of the offices into living quarters, though these lacked some pretty basic amenities. As a result, we had to cart our dirty dishes from the waterless kitchen to the bathroom to wash them, then take them back, both trips made with a "borrowed" shopping cart.

When Stanley and Elyse came over, we served them refreshments, then went into our respective studios to look at our art. By then I was making large-scale sculpture, some of which involved considerable expense. The importance of patronage came home to me at this time, primarily because Stanley and Elyse began to help me with materials. As if to emphasize what it meant to have such support, a huge box was delivered to our studio a few weeks later. I opened it to discover that the Grinsteins had sent us a complete matching set of dishes, having obviously noticed that the plates upon which we had served them snacks were ragtag, to say the least.

It seems important to point out that even if the male-dominated nature and mode of the artistic dialogue made it difficult for a woman to be fully accepted, L.A. was still a good place to be in the 1960s, as the art scene was booming. Critics and curators prowled artists' studios, including mine, largely because it was centered in an area in which many artists lived at that time. The only trouble was that I soon began to encounter what can only be described as prejudice. One critic, for example, while acknowledging my talent, would often tell me that I "couldn't be a woman and an artist too." I was told that I was a "bitch" when, to my mind, all I was doing was expressing my opinion. I was also called "castrating" and a "dyke" (a terrible aspersion then). I was hurt by these accusations, so much so that I would sometimes take to my bed, forcing myself back into the studio only by chastising myself by saying I had to toughen up.

I somehow knew that what I was experiencing was sexism, though there was absolutely no way to discuss this. I kept thinking that as my work got better, things would change. Instead, it seemed that the better my art became, the more resistance I met. It was at this time that I did a piece called *Rainbow Picket,* a series of multi-hued forms that rested against the wall to create a spectrum of color bars (later shown in "Primary Structures," a major show at the Jewish Museum in New York). Shortly after the work was completed, one of the most important people in the Southern California art world stopped by our studio. I invited him to see the sculpture, which I felt quite proud of. But as soon as we got into my space, he deliberately turned his head, refusing to even look at the piece—and, worse, going over to a work of Lloyd's that he'd seen numerous times.

Years later I ran into this man at some art event and we somehow got into a conversation about this exchange. He tried to defend his action by telling me that he had been disconcerted by the fact that my art seemed considerably stronger than that being done by many of my male peers. He went on to say that at that time women in the art world were assumed to be either wives or groupies, devoted to the care of the men. Therefore, he stated, when confronted with my work and my expectation that it (and I) should be dealt with in the same way he would have related to my male colleagues, he felt compelled to avert his eyes, as if he had seen a lady publicly lift her skirt and display her bare thighs.

As this period is one that is covered in *Through the Flower,* I shall refer my readers to that book if they are interested in more information about my reaction (devastated) and other events of this time. My main purpose here is to explain how I happened to change my name. To put it bluntly, I became increasingly pissed off by the ongoing rejections, put-downs, and misperceptions. Worse, I watched my male artist friends being offered one opportunity after another, while I had to struggle for even the smallest amount of recognition. By the end of the 1960s the Women's Movement had begun, and I read the early literature with something akin to existential relief. These writings not only reinforced my belief that what I was facing amounted to blatant sexism, they also gave me the courage to speak out. In 1970 I gave my first public lecture about "my struggle as a woman artist" in the Grinsteins' living room.

I sometimes joke that in these early days of the Women's Movement, we had not yet discovered (or invented, as the case may be) our own forms. Therefore we borrowed some, notably from the Civil Rights Movement. Perhaps inspired by the radical stance of the Black Panthers, I decided to publicly "divest" myself of the name Gerowitz in favor of Judy Chicago, which of course was already my underground name. My name change, which was done legally, took place in conjunction with two exhibits, both in Orange County. Jack Glenn, the owner of a rather prominent gallery in that area, was planning to hold a show concurrent with one at Cal State Fullerton. At this latter space, viewers were to be confronted with a large sign proclaiming my new-found freedom from male dominance, ostensibly achieved through this new moniker.

During this period my male artist buddies were all prone to very macho announcements and posters in relation to their own shows, something Jack suggested spoofing with a picture of me in a boxing ring, the very one in which Muhammad Ali trained. Jack had a sweatshirt made for me emblazoned with my new name, rented boxing gloves, and somehow got hold of some man-sized athletic boots. We trooped down to the gym, where we were greeted by some shocked boxers who were training there. The resulting picture, which was printed and sent out to supporters of the gallery, ended up as a full-page piece in *Artforum,* then the most influential of all art magazines. One result was that for many years, pugnacious male artists around the country asked me if I wished to "fight." I would also see this image posted in the studios of many women artists whom I visited during the 1970s. Although I was quite unaware of it at the time, it seems that numerous women artists were having experiences similar to my own. I guess that the boxing ring ad marked the moment when women all over the country came out fighting in an effort to somehow effect a change in the intense discrimination of the art world.

I do not know how Lloyd felt about all this, as we never actually discussed it. I expected him to be supportive, and he was. We had gotten married, which meant that, as my husband, he had to sign the legal papers concerning my name change, which he did uncomplainingly while I rather vocally protested such sexist laws. My family said nothing at all about it. I was seeing my mom at regular intervals, though our relationship was still quite strained. Ben had been at college in Berkeley, but he was already back in L.A. by this time. In fact, he and his girlfriend, Goldie, lived with Lloyd and me in Pasadena for some two or three months. I sensed that Ben harbored many resentments toward me that he refused to talk about, and years later he admitted that he had felt utterly abandoned when I left Chicago, which told me that he was far more attached to me than I had ever realized. When he and Goldie broke up a short time later, he decided to take up residence in Japan, where he would find himself as a potter.

Nor did my Chicago relatives ever comment upon my name change. By the time it was accomplished, I had begun to go back to Chicago on a regular basis, inspired to do so by my cousin Howard, who had sought me out after years of separation. Strangely, he had ended up marrying a woman with whom I had attended high school, though this took place some years after we'd both graduated. Arleen and I were like polar opposites during our teens: She was a gorgeous member of the May Queen court, and I was an unfashionably attired artist and intellectual. Nevertheless, we would discover that we had much in common, and she, Howard, and I became very close.

Chapter Two

What Is Feminist Art?

*B*y the time of my (very) public name change, I was living in Kingsburg, a small town just south of Fresno in California's agricultural center (some would say "navel"). But Judy, you might inquire, didn't you just indicate that you and Lloyd had been recently married? Indeed we had, although even before the ceremony—held in a park in Santa Barbara and witnessed by numerous friends—we had been living separately, though not as far apart as we would be during the upcoming year. Some time earlier Lloyd had rented his own space in Pasadena, about half a block up the street from our formerly shared studio. At the time, this seemed a good idea.

In 1970, I gave up the Pasadena studio to move two hundred miles north of Los Angeles. I had accepted a full-time teaching job at Fresno State University, primarily because I wanted to set up an all-women's art class. In order to feel free to accomplish what I had in mind for this program, I felt obliged to be away from the pressures of urban life and particularly the L.A. art scene. I wanted a chance to test my ideas, first outlined in *Through the Flower,* about establishing something I called Feminist Art education, a term that didn't exist until I invented it. My intention was to see if such an educational process might lead to a new kind of art, that is, Feminist Art. I defined this as art in which distinctly female subject matter would be both central and unabashedly expressed.

This was the kind of work I wanted to make myself, a goal I didn't yet know how to achieve. As a result of all that I had done in order to be accepted in the male-dominated art world, I had gotten quite far away from my innate impulses. I had begun to wonder what kind of art I might have made had I not been discouraged from the images I had created so unself-consciously when I was younger. At the same time, I did not wish to repudiate my carefully wrought artmaking methods but, rather, to find a way to reconnect this expertise with the subject matter and aesthetic impulses I had eschewed after graduate school.

My presumption was that young women at the beginning of their college art training would not yet have gone through this same process of disconnecting from their natural tendencies, the seeming consequence of a rather widespread approach to teaching art that emphasized form over content and, at least during the 1960s and 1970s, excluded gender issues altogether. I hoped that by providing my students with the permission to develop as artists without having to deny their womanhood—which had been required of me—I would be able to offer them a unique type of education while also being able to recapture this same ability for myself. The main explanation for my insistence upon an all-female environment was that the teacher as well as her students would thereby feel safe to pursue what was an entirely unprecedented undertaking.

Another reason I wished to teach only women was that I wanted to address a problem that was prevalent at the time. The preponderance of undergraduate art classes were filled with female students, although few of these students were successfully completing graduate school and making their way into professional life (given the number of young women showing today, I assume that this has changed). Thinking that perhaps my own experiences might be of some value, I wanted to try offering an opportunity for young women to develop away from the presence and, hence, the expectations of men. The chairman of the art department at Fresno State seemed quite sympathetic to my goals, though I am not sure it wasn't more a matter of his wanting to add my name to his faculty roster, since by then I had something of a name on the West Coast. At any rate, he went along with just about everything I asked, including my requirement that I teach only in the late afternoons, so as to preserve my studio time.

I had rented an old supermarket in Kingsburg and turned its main room into a clean white studio, the back space into a spray booth, the meat locker into my office, and a small storage area into my living quarters. It was here that I would create two series of large sprayed paintings, the *Fresno Fans* and *Fleshgardens*. In these images I would attempt to fuse flesh and landscape references, trying to make my almost entirely abstract form language more intelligible. At the same time, I would also experiment with other more overt types of imagery—both abstract and representational—and various media, including photography, film, and printmaking.

I also planned to undertake a more focused research project into women's history. I had already begun studying women's art, literature, and autobiographical writings in an effort to discover whether any of my predecessors had experienced and/or documented struggles similar to what I was then going through. The next step was to be a systematic though totally self-guided investigation, including the ferreting out of all the information I could find about women artists. I wanted to read the entire works of such major women writers as Jane Austen, the Brontës, and George Eliot. I also wanted to investigate the history of feminist thought.

It seems important to point out that there were no women's studies courses then, no body of contemporary theory, and little analysis, except what was left over from the first wave of feminism, which had pretty well subsided after World War I. At the time I started teaching, I began to receive invitations to lecture about my work at various places around the country. On such trips I always tried to arrange some extra hours to visit used-book stores. Judging from the heaps of inexpensive volumes I found by and about women, there was little or no interest in this subject then. I also discovered treasure troves of material in the local library, including some insightful feminist writings from the end of the nineteenth century that had never even been checked out.

Though Kingsburg was only a three-hour drive from L.A., it seemed a million miles away, which is one reason it had attracted me. Its small-town atmosphere (there were only three thousand residents) provided me an almost unimaginable level of psychic space for what might be described as a rather risky vision quest (risky in that I was pretty much on my own and doing something unheard of then). It was there in that converted supermarket, surrounded by the unmistakable odor of cottonseed oil from the nearby processing plant, that I painted and studied and realized that women have a heritage so rich it took my breath away.

What a revelation—and a relief—to uncover the lives, words, images, and ideas of so many talented women. I felt extremely validated by learning about their experiences, reading their writings, seeing even inadequate reproductions of their art, and studying their ideas and philosophies. It seemed that countless women before me had stumbled over similar dilemmas; had asked the same and sometimes even more profound questions; and had arrived at answers that were not only illuminating for me but would, I was convinced, be vitally useful to others.

Although this information inspired me, it also enraged me, because I could not believe that all these seemingly important contributions of women had been omitted from the mainstream of culture, be it in art, literature, history, or philosophy. My discoveries intersected with the values of my upbringing—which had emphasized the possibility of radical transformation—and led me to conclude that the only real solution to the problems I was facing lay in the creation of an entirely new framework for art: one that *included*, rather than *excluded*, women, along with women's ways of being and doing, which, I was convinced, could be quite different from men's. I would soon come to realize that numerous women throughout history had espoused this same notion. The problem seemed to lie in the fact that women were everywhere under the thumb of men and therefore had no room to be completely themselves, in their lives or in their art.

I discussed much of this in *Through the Flower,* and since then I have encountered some rather bizarre interpretations of my ideas. It has been suggested that I believe all women's differences from men to be innate. This is not at all my opinion: Some differences are probably the result of some indeterminate combination of nature and culture, the exact character of which cannot be discerned at this moment of gender-acculturated history. But it has just always seemed obvious to me that, given such realities as birth, lactation, and maternity, not to mention vulnerability to sexual abuse, there are certain experiences that are unique to women. Bringing these into the art dialogue *openly* was what I was after, both in my own work and that of my students.

The teaching methods I brought to Fresno evolved out of the part-time teaching I had done during the sixties. Even then my definition of a teacher had always been more akin to that of a facilitator than to anything else: one who "facilitates" the growth and empowerment of her students. This required making a *real* connection with my students, which I accomplished by encouraging them to reveal *where they were* intellectually, aesthetically, and humanly. It seemed that only then could we forge an intersection between what they as individuals needed and what I as a particular person had to give. But making this type of connection required the shedding of the traditional teacher role in favor of a more humanized interaction with the students.

It had always been extremely important to me that all of my students actively participate, be it by asking questions or engaging in discussion. In my earlier classes, I had noticed a tendency for some students (usually, but not always, the men) to dominate the classroom, while others (often, but not exclusively, the women) remained silent. To counteract this, I had developed a technique of going around the room, asking everyone to speak about the subject at hand (one fascinating result being my discovery that the quietest people were sometimes the most interesting). This was well before the days of consciousness-raising, with which this process has a lot in common, though with one important exception: Because I was the teacher, I could interrupt in order to make comments or suggestions that seemed appropriate.

This proved to be an effective way of combining education and empowerment—the most desirable goal for teaching, in my opinion.

One without the other seems to lead to only partial growth for students: the amassing of information without the ability to apply it in any meaningful way, or self-development at the expense of specific skills. One reason for my staunch and abiding commitment to feminism is that I believe its principles provide valuable tools for empowerment—and not only for women. In my view, feminist values are rooted in an alternative to the prevailing paradigm of power, which is *power over others*. By contrast, feminism promotes *personal empowerment,* something that, when connected to education, becomes a potent tool for change.

I brought these values and aims to my teaching, along with the patience to remain silent while students either summoned the courage to express themselves honestly or tested me to see if I would let them off the hook by resuming the teacher–student relationship to which they were accustomed. Too often this seemed to involve a level of passivity on the part of the students—particularly those of the female gender—that was unacceptable to me. When I first began to work exclusively with women, however (all my earlier classes had been mixed), I soon encountered an almost stubborn refusal on the part of the students to assert themselves in any real way.

Using the methods I have been describing, I gradually began to bring the students out, only to discover that many of them suffered from a significant lack of self-esteem, expressed most poignantly in their personal relationships, which went from bad to worse. Although I had never been as reticent or lacking in self-confidence as some of these young women, I could still relate to many of the problems they were facing, many of them resolvable (in my estimation) through personal empowerment. I had gone through this type of process myself in my studio: slowly struggling past my own limits and also learning to stand up to men's often misguided perceptions and expectations of me. I took my students through some of this same procedure, thereby helping them to build greater confidence.

But what about art, you might ask. Weren't you teaching art? My response is that the process I am describing might be best described as twofold: dealing with self-esteem issues while also doing what could be called a content search. Out of these discussions about what it was that the students were most concerned with—issues of independence, relationships, and sexual problems—I helped them to make art. I must point out that this is not at all the way in which art is customarily taught, certainly not at the college level.

I had managed to structure the Fresno program so that the students worked almost exclusively with me for a year. This allowed a kind of intensity of purpose that would be hard to achieve in traditional teaching, when people move from subject to subject and teacher to teacher, sometimes on an hourly basis. The resulting explosion of energy was probably a combination of this concentrated course of study and the fact that I gave my students permission to bring their real concerns to their artmaking. As a result, it felt almost as if I had lifted a lid off a kettle of boiling water—too quickly, in fact, because it frightened me. I was still a relatively young artist, not yet all that mature myself. Suddenly I found myself in the position of teacher, mentor, and surrogate parent all at once.

This was one reason I was so eager to make contact with the artist Miriam Schapiro when I met her during the school year. She and her husband, Paul Brach (also an artist), had moved to L.A. to work at the new Disney-sponsored California Institute of the Arts, where Paul was to be the chairman of the art department and Mimi a faculty member. The new campus was being constructed at the north end of the San Fernando Valley in a small, mostly residential suburb called Valencia. Meanwhile, classes were being held in a converted convent in Burbank, many miles to the east.

Mimi was a zaftig, middle-aged, dark-haired, attractive, though somewhat brooding woman, while Paul, who always seemed to be sucking on a large, aromatic cigar, was small, wiry, and intense. They were a lively couple and a dramatic study in contrasts, positively reeking of the New York art scene and full of juicy gossip about its complex political intrigues, which I knew little about. What I did know was that I felt an immediate identification with Mimi and thought that, in light of her own experiences as an artist, she might be sympathetic to my ideas and aims.

I had heard that she'd been one of the few women who had managed to become visible in New York during the heyday of abstract

JUDY CHICAGO Exhibition, Cal State Fullerton, Oct.
Preview 6 - 8 PM, Oct. 23, Faculty Club, Cal State
Manager, Jack Glenn Gallery, 2631 E. Coast Highway, Corona Del Mar

Exhibition announcement, Jack Glenn Gallery, 1971.

With Miriam Schapiro at *Womanhouse*, 1972, from the cover of the catalog designed by Sheila de Bretteville.

Menstruation Bathroom, from *Womanhouse,* 1972.

RIGHT: *Cock and Cunt* play, performed at *Womanhouse* by Faith Wilding (left) and Jan Lester (right).

With Arlene Raven (right) and Sheila de Bretteville (center) at the opening of the Woman's Building, 1973.

Lucy Lippard (right) visits Feminist Studio Workshop, Woman's Building, 1974.

Woman's Building, Los Angeles, 1973. Detail of brochure, designed by Sheila de Bretteville.

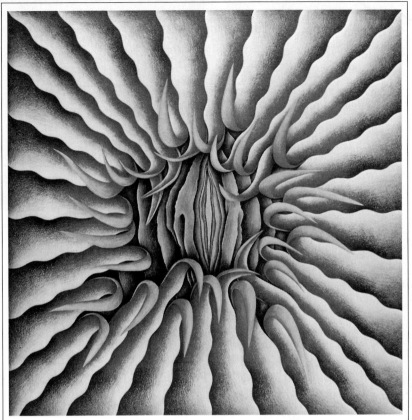

Detail, *Rejection Drawing #3*, from the *Rejection Quintet*, 1974; prismacolor on rag paper. Collection: San Francisco Museum of Modern Art.

FACING PAGE TOP: *Great Ladies,* installed at Grandview Gallery, Woman's Building, Los Angeles, 1973.

FACING PAGE BOTTOM: *Great Ladies Transforming Themselves into Butterflies,* 1973; sprayed acrylic on canvas, 40"x 40". Collection: Deborah Marrow, Santa Monica.

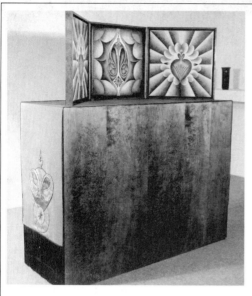

Did You Know Your Mother Had a Sacred Heart?, 1976; china-paint and pen work on porcelain, embroidery on fabric and wood, 60" x 60" x 12" (installed). Collection: Los Angeles County Museum of Art, Los Angeles.

FACING PAGE, TOP LEFT:
In the china-painting studio, Santa Monica, 1974.

FACING PAGE, TOP RIGHT:
With Diane Gelon in *The Dinner Party* studio, Santa Monica, 1976.

Center panel, *Did You Know Your Mother Had a Sacred Heart?*

LEFT: With Susan Hill in the needlework loft of *The Dinner Party* studio, 1977.

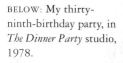

BELOW: My thirty-ninth-birthday party, in *The Dinner Party* studio, 1978.

The Dinner Party, 1979; multimedia, 48' x 43' x 36".

expressionism, which could be said to have personified macho attitudes, what with its emphasis on muscular "action" paintings, heavy
drinking, and late-night arguments at the then-popular Cedar Bar. I
admired her work, particularly a large canvas entitled *OX*, the abstract
form and open gesture of which seemed reminiscent of my own imagery, particularly that of *Pasadena Lifesavers*, a series I had painted
just before moving to Kingsburg. In these works I had been attempting to deal with issues of female identity and content, though their
form belied their real content. I sensed that, like me, Mimi might
also be forcing what was actually female subject matter into an overly
formal abstract visual structure. I thought that she might respond to
my desire to make my imagery clearer. (As it turned out, my intuition
about her proved correct.)

I arranged for Mimi to give a slide lecture about her career at
Fresno State University. The students and I held a party for her afterward at the studio we had rented so that the young women could be
assured of a "room of their own" (to quote Virginia Woolf) in which
to work. This was a large and run-down building where we had been
doing a lot of performance work. I had discovered this technique to
be an extremely effective tool for quickly reaching personal content,
which could then be transformed through a variety of more conven-
tional artmaking methods.

The students presented some of their performances to Mimi, as
well as their paintings and sculptures, much of which was somewhat
simplistic, for a variety of reasons. First, it was the work of young
people at the beginning of their development as artists. Second, there
was not a great deal of iconography to draw upon in terms of their
chosen subject matter, which largely had to do with their experiences
as women. Therefore, we had to *invent* it, which we did primarily by
turning around existing imagery of women, consciously presenting
women as subject rather than object, which is the way in which women
appear throughout most of art history. Finally, I had encouraged the
students toward rather direct work, because from the beginning, my
concept of Feminist Art was that it was not intended primarily for a
sophisticated art audience, one familiar with the sometimes arcane
visual language of contemporary art.

Instead, the aim of Feminist Art, as I then envisioned it, was empowerment and social change. This was to be accomplished by educating viewers about women's real feelings, experiences, and history *through* the art. From the beginning of the program, I shared my own discoveries about women's history with my students, believing that it would inspire them, as it had me. In fact, we read and looked at nothing but women's work throughout that year. As most of the students had gone through the usual form of education, I knew that most were probably already grounded in men's history; in my program, they would become educated about their own. It was incredibly exciting to watch the information the young women derived from this course of study empower them. But I am convinced that this only happened because I insisted that they translate their intellectual discoveries, along with their growing self-esteem, into action, which in this case was image-making.

To my mind, the study of women's art, literature, and ideas was important because it provided information that could be a foundation for personal and artistic growth. This growth would take place primarily through translating one's own empowerment into works of art that could facilitate the same process for others. This required that the art be accessible to many viewers, not so coded as to be intelligible only to the tiny, elitist art world. Moreover, Feminist Art would in no way be singular in style but, rather, pluralistic in both form and content in order to reflect the diversity of women's experience. The one unifying factor was that it would be openly woman-centered and geared toward a broad and diverse audience.

I imagined, at first, that the primary audience for Feminist Art would be women, in that they'd be the ones most able to relate to imagery that reflects their own experience and able, also, to evaluate its authenticity. Another seemingly important reason for addressing a female, rather than a male, audience was that I believed it would be liberating for women to direct their work to viewers of their own gender, instead of trying to please men or conform to male definitions of what constitutes worthwhile subject matter for art. But it never occurred to me that men might not be interested in art made by women that clearly addressed female concerns.

I cannot recall what Mimi said to me after seeing my students' work, although I know that she provided them with some really valuable feedback (she has a remarkable talent for critiquing art). But not too long after her lecture, Mimi proposed that I bring my program to Cal-Arts, where we would expand it into the Feminist Art Program, which we would team-teach. I was extremely excited about this idea, most of all because I was ecstatic about the prospect of having an ally in this somewhat frightening effort to give birth to Feminist Art. I looked to Mimi—as someone more mature—to provide me some level of support and understanding, such as I was giving to my students. I simply assumed that her goals were similar to mine, else why would she be inviting me to work with her?

Mimi had obtained the full backing of Paul, who assured us that the Feminist Art Program would have its own studio space, tools, equipment, and money for materials and projects. In addition, we were to have a trained art historian whose job would be to bring professional skills to bear on the rather ragtag slide library that I had begun, then expanded with my students as a first step in creating a Feminist Art history. After Mimi's visit, she also began searching for and collecting slides of art by women and sending them to us. Again, it seems important to emphasize the then almost total absence of knowledge about or interest in female artists, past and present. This might help explain why the idea of a major art school's being willing to provide a trained historian and devote so many resources to the needs of its women students was, to put it mildly, astounding, particularly in light of what I now understand to be the revolutionary nature of my program (something I have only recently realized).

I was also glad to be able to move back to L.A. because my yearlong separation from Lloyd had been difficult. By the time I left Kingsburg, he was also teaching at Cal-Arts, which was, from everything he said, an extremely stimulating place to be. Notable and talented people from all over the country were joining the faculty. In addition to being multidisciplinary (which was then unique in the arts), the school was hiring numerous husband-and-wife teams, which was quite unusual.

Early in the summer of 1971 I returned, followed shortly thereafter by quite a caravan down the highway: cars and trucks full of those students whom Mimi and I had helped get into the Cal-Arts program, along with a variety of husbands, boyfriends, significant others, pets, and furnishings. We were all so excited.

Lloyd and I were reunited in Pacoima, a nondescript town in the San Fernando Valley, right off the San Diego Freeway and not far from Cal-Arts. We rented a rather odd place that had once been the home and office of a chiropractor. The sprawling, one-story building had a long string of rooms that were easily turned into studios, offices, and living spaces. It was on a large, rather barren, fenced lot covered with gravel, where I took up running, circling the property numerous times each morning before doing my daily calisthenics.

We were to live there for several years, during which time I would do numerous sprayed acrylic paintings, this time on canvas, including *Through the Flower* and *Let It All Hang Out.* The latter, when finished, caused me to break into tears. The painting was forceful yet feminine, two attributes I had rarely seen wedded together. Moreover, its open sensuality frightened me, as I was still struggling to become comfortable with my creative and sexual power. But my imagery was gradually becoming clearer, though it would still be some time before my forms were entirely consistent with my intent.

When school started in the fall, the new buildings in Valencia were not yet ready and the temporary campus was full. Mimi and I decided to work on a special project focused on the designing of a house. After all, women had quilted, sewn, decorated, baked, and nested their creative energies into homes for centuries. What would happen, asked Paula Harper, the Stanford-trained art historian who had been hired for the Feminist Art Program, if these same activities were brought to bear on the process of creating art?

Our students broke up into teams and scoured Los Angeles for an appropriate space, finally finding an old, run-down mansion near downtown. On a bright November morning, Mimi and I and twenty-one students, along with a few interested local women artists, all arrived at Mariposa Street armed with mops, brooms, saws, ladders, hammers, and nails to begin transforming the dilapidated two-story building into the first openly feminist installation work to be seen in the United States.

Womanhouse, which was always conceived as a temporary exhibition, fused collaboration, individual artmaking, and feminist education to create a monumental work with openly female subject matter. When it was on display during January 1972, nearly ten thousand people swarmed through the house. They viewed the cascading egg breast forms in the pink *Nurturant Kitchen;* stared at the pile of tampons with what looked like blood through the white gauze covering the door to the *Menstruation Bathroom;* and gazed at the *Bridal Staircase,* where the hopeful-looking mannequin at the top of the stairway ended up colliding with a wall. Then everyone sat on the floor of the living room to watch the performance group (composed primarily of those former students who had relocated with me) present what we called "duration" performances, so called because they demonstrated the length of time it actually takes to do such "woman's work" as ironing a sheet or scrubbing a floor.

There were also more formal pieces, including one I had written in my meat locker/office in Kingsburg. Entitled "Cock and Cunt," it had scared me half to death when first I put pen to paper to compose this piece, which dealt with my rage at proscribed gender roles. I was nervous every time the students performed it, perhaps because at the time of *Womanhouse,* art that clearly exposed women's authentic feelings was absolutely unknown, which probably helps explain both the audience and media response, which was quite intense (thereby contributing to what I always knew would happen, which was that I was becoming famous).

The impact of *Womanhouse* reverberated for years, partly as a result of the marvelous documentary (which would be seen around the world) by a filmmaker named Johanna Demetrakas, whose appearance and decision to film the installation seemed perfectly timed. By the time the *Womanhouse* exhibition closed, the Valencia campus was ready and the Feminist Art Program could officially take up residence. Being in a high-tech, state-of-the-art building might have been stimulating to some, but from the first moment we arrived, I hated it. The sterile white corridors and multicolored though otherwise identical doors were in stark contrast to the homey feeling and independent situation of *Womanhouse* and the earlier Fresno studio.

My intense discomfort in such an institutional setting was complicated by problems that developed between Mimi and me, which were both philosophical and personal. As these have been neither discussed nor worked out between us, it would seem unfair for me to attempt to describe them in a public forum such as this manuscript. Suffice it to say that I do not think we had the same understanding of the nature of Feminist Art. Moreover, even though I believe—given my reputation for being confrontational ("direct" would be more accurate)—that what I am about to say might come as a surprise, I have always been somewhat shy of confrontation. Thus when Mimi would call me up early in the morning to castigate me about one thing or another that I had done to anger her, I would become intimidated. The consequence of these unresolved difficulties was that I ended up basically turning my program over to her, having decided to leave Cal-Arts as soon as my two-year contract was up.

I soon began making plans to start an independent art school with two other women, a designer named Sheila de Bretteville and Arlene Raven, an art historian who had moved west not long after we'd met at the Corcoran Conference for Women in the Arts, held in Washington, D.C., sometime in 1972, shortly after *Womanhouse* closed. By then there was a burgeoning movement of women in the arts all over the country, and the Corcoran museum had made the mistake of inviting all of us to get together in one space. Several hundred artists, curators, critics, and historians assembled, only to discover and become energized by the realization that most of us had been experiencing rather heinous forms of discrimination.

Sheila, a gifted graphics designer, had come to California with her architect husband, Peter, both of them to teach at the new Disney school. Stimulated in part by the Feminist Art Program, Sheila had instituted a somewhat comparable program in the Cal-Arts design school. Neither she nor Arlene (who had been hired there soon after she relocated to California) was unhappy at the Valencia campus, as I was, and both would continue to teach at Cal-Arts even after we had instituted the Feminist Studio Workshop. Though our plan was based upon the principles of my Fresno program, our intention was to expand beyond what I had done by fusing our three disciplines into an educational program whose aim was the expansion of the role of art and artist, in particular a broadening of the whole relationship between art and the wider community.

At first we met in Sheila's living room with an enthusiastic group of young women from around America who had been drawn to enroll in what was to be the first-ever independent (though unaccredited) Feminist Art institution. The Feminist Studio Workshop soon decided to join forces with a number of other women's organizations to create a common home, the Women's Building, in which, in addition to the FSW, there were to be several women's co-op galleries, a feminist bookstore, and other female-run businesses and organizations. Each of these was to be financially self-sufficient, with everyone pooling resources to cover the rent, utilities, and maintenance.

Based upon the model of the Women's Building in the Chicago Columbian Exposition of 1893 and run, like its predecessor, by a board of Lady Managers (in this case representing the various organizations), our Women's Building was set up in what had formerly been the Chouinard art school in the somewhat seedy McArthur Park area of Los Angeles, where Walt Disney and numerous prominent L.A. artists had gone to school. Disney later bought Chouinard, converting it into Cal-Arts, which he envisioned and endowed to be somewhat different from what it would eventually turn into. The old Chouinard building was abandoned, which is how we were able to rent it very cheaply. The oddity of leaving Cal-Arts only to take up residence in its ghostly predecessor was both evident and amusing to us.

In the fall of 1973, the Women's Building opened to an excited crowd of many thousands, apparently drawn by what was then a rapidly expanding and vibrant West Coast women's culture. That night and for many months to come, there were exhibitions, performances, music, and other events taking place all over the building. In conjunction with the opening, I held a show at Grandview Gallery, one of the co-ops that I had helped to organize. My exhibition featured a series of airbrushed paintings called the *Great Ladies*. My intention in these abstract portraits of women culled from my research was to communicate something about each of these figures and why they were so important, both historically and personally.

In some of these images, I inscribed phrases around the borders of the canvas indicating who the woman was and why I thought her especially significant. In others, I hand-wrote these descriptions directly on the wall (in the Palmer method, which I had learned in grammar school). I also wrote a personal statement explaining how crucial it was for women's art to be seen in a larger context such as that provided by the Women's Building.

Although I felt quite joyous about what proved to be an overwhelming response to the opening of the building and my own show, before the end of the year I had decided to resign, both from the school and from the institution I had helped to establish.

The explanation for this decision is complicated; it seems enough to say that by the end of 1973 I had begun to figure out how to make the kind of art I most wished to create. By the time the Women's Building had opened, I had identified the content in which I was most interested—specifically, women's history. I was increasingly determined to challenge the overriding presumption that women had no history to speak of, an attitude that had first been presented to me, when I was an undergraduate at UCLA, by no less an authority than one of the most respected members of the history department. I also wanted to call into question the assumption that there had never been any great women artists, an assessment that I had determined was simply prejudice elevated to the level of unquestioned belief.

In addition to having realized the subject matter with which I wished to deal, I had also been developing the technical means by which to accomplish this. One reason that I have worked in so many different media is that I firmly believe that various techniques are most appropriate to specific intentions. For example, during the late 1960s I began to work with fireworks, primarily because I wished to create ephemeral images. Plastics—my chosen medium for much of my work during that same decade—allowed for transparency, a layering of coloring and a fusion of color and surface, something that I had also achieved in my sprayed canvas paintings, including the *Great*

Ladies. I was dissatisfied with these, however, because the forms seemed too generalized. I wanted to effect a more precise rendering in terms of the images while still retaining the integration of color and surface that these works demonstrated.

In the early summer of 1971, shortly before I left Kingsburg, Lloyd and I had taken a long drive along the Northwest coast. In addition to doing a series of fireworks pieces in which I placed various smoke devices in one or another natural aperture (a series I called *Cuntholes*), I had also seen and become intrigued by a hand-painted porcelain plate that I stumbled upon in an antique store. I was fascinated by how its effects had been achieved, presumably through a technique called china-painting, which I knew absolutely nothing about. I would soon learn that this type of painting involves the applying of specific paints onto a glazed ceramic surface, then firing it until the colors meld with the glazed surface. In addition to providing the kind of visual fusion I liked, china-painting also seemed to offer exactly the precision of form I thought my sprayed acrylic paintings were lacking.

In 1972, while working out the second year of my Cal-Arts contract and making plans for the formation of the Feminist Studio Workshop (also working regularly in my studio), I had taken up the study of china-painting. After looking up "Porcelain" in the yellow pages, I had located a nearby class, in which I enrolled. I soon learned that, traditionally, one does not so much learn to china-paint as, for example, to paint a baby rose. The teacher was quite insistent that I spend my time mastering the "dots and dashes" essential to produce such a result, something I was not at all interested in doing. Rather, I was intent upon developing an understanding of the overall method of porcelain painting, which I was to discover was actually quite a difficult skill to master.

Finally I had found a teacher named Mim Silinsky, who was sympathetic to my desire to extract china-painting from its embedment in the world of craft, primarily by applying this seemingly extraordinary technique to my own imagery. (One could say that the main distinction between art and craft is that in art, techniques are customarily put in the service of personal subject matter, whereas in craft they are generally employed for other purposes, including the simple demonstration of skill.) Between 1972 and 1974, I basically apprenticed myself to Mim. Under her supervision, I analyzed and sampled the range of colors, their respective firing temperatures, and the potential variety of visual effects attainable. In addition to doing innumerable samples, I also worked on a series of test plates that demonstrated the basic components and techniques of china-painting.

Throughout this period, I was also continuing my research into women's history, one result of which was the *Great Ladies* paintings. After completing these, I decided that I wanted to undertake another series of abstract portraits of women, these to be painted on plates. Throughout the course of my apprenticeship, I had attended many china-painting exhibitions. In addition to being impressed by the large crowds (far more people than at most contemporary art galleries), I had also been struck by the array of domestic objects upon which many of the china-painters worked. I thought it would be interesting to present this next series of images of women in such a way as to imply that their various achievements had been "consumed" rather than honored by history, an implication I thought would be conveyed by the plate format. At the same time, I viewed the plate as a visually neutral surface, assuming that when these pieces were finished I would display them, like any other paintings, on a gallery wall.

By the time my course of study was complete, I had left Cal-Arts and was working at the Feminist Studio Workshop. Lloyd and I had moved out of the Pacoima place and into another 5,000-square-foot studio, this one in Santa Monica. Early in 1974, while finishing up my china-painting tutelage, I became deeply engrossed in trying to break through the overly formal visual structure I had been using in my work, something I finally did in a series entitled *Rejection Quintet,* five drawings done in one of my favorite media, prismacolor pencils. Step-by-step, in successive images, I "peeled back" the highly abstract forms I had been using to reveal a transformed vulval form.

At this point I realized that I had begun to forge an iconography that could provide me the basis for the next series of abstract portraits of women. The vulval image could act as a visual symbol for the physically defining characteristic of woman in an almost metaphysical sense; that is, as an entryway into an aesthetic exploration of what it has meant to be a woman—experientially, historically, and philosophically. Moreover, this form might also allow me to challenge prevailing definitions of the feminine as being inherently passive if only I could configure it into an energetic shape, one that could express an active female self.

In the final drawings, I was able to transmute this vulval image into myriad evocative organic associations to suggest the possibility that the female experience could be construed to be every bit as central to the larger human condition as is the male, which, historically, has been singularly identified with the universal. To put it another way, I was looking for a way of working from a female form base to remake the world in women's own image and likeness. In the final transmutation of this form, it turned into a winged butterfly, thereby providing me with the beginnings of an active female iconography. It was only later that I would learn that the butterfly was not only an ancient symbol of the Goddess but also of liberation, a seemingly fitting association for this moment in my aesthetic development.

The butterfly motif had been quite prominent in my early work, those paintings that I had felt compelled not only to repudiate but actually to abandon in an effort to put aside my female identity. In reclaiming this form, it was almost as if I were reconnecting with my younger, more authentic self and thereby finally achieving what I had set out to do when I first went to Fresno. It was at this moment that I recognized that I would have to stop teaching and also leave the Women's Building. I *had* to have uninterrupted studio time in order to concentrate on the bringing together of my chosen subject matter of women's history, my newly developed skills at china-painting, and now this potentially rich form language.

Arlene and Sheila were amazingly sympathetic to my announcement that I was going to resign, probably far more so than I would have been in their place. After I left, both the Feminist Studio Workshop and the Women's Building continued in operation until the early 1990s, though by that time at another location. Arlene taught until the start of the 1980s, then moved to New York, where she would become a prominent art critic. Sheila remained for some years longer, before going on to become the dean of design at Yale, where she continues to distinguish herself in her field. As for me, although I didn't realize it at the time, I was about to start down the long path that would eventually take me "beyond the flower."

Chapter Three

Dreaming Up
The Dinner Party

I loved my Santa Monica studio. It was some two miles from the Pacific Ocean, on the south side of what was then a small, mainly residential, and extremely pleasant community whose beach end has since become quite upscale. Lloyd and I were quartered in the rear of a large building that was part of a sprawling complex filled with assorted artists, designers, and craftspeople. In this area of town, offices, warehouses, and studios were interspersed with numerous hole-in-the-wall, family-style Mexican restaurants, whose spicy aromas wafted down the alley and into our studio.

Lloyd and I had large, side-by-side work spaces along with a modest living area in the back. Our studios were separated by a twenty-six-foot-high peaked wall, which I had painted using an extension roller that left my shoulder muscles sore for weeks. Nestled under my drawing loft (where I did the *Rejection Quintet*), there was a clean room that was to be my china-painting studio. As soon as I finished my apprenticeship with Mim, I proudly placed all my test plates on the wall.

Before long, I was hard at work on a series of porcelain miniatures entitled *Butterfly Goddesses and Other Specimens*. In these tiny pieces, I combined my developing vulval/butterfly iconography with various china-painting techniques to create an array of images that would serve as preliminary tests for the first abstract portraits of women on plates. Even now I can see myself at work in my new, pristine, white room with the exhaust fan carrying away the fumes from the exotic oils that are customarily used with china paints. Throughout the early months of 1974, I worked even longer hours than usual, often to the plaintive strains of Leonard Cohen, whose music has always struck a deep chord in me.

For much of this time Lloyd was away, doing an artist-in-residence stint at the University of Washington. He had been traveling quite a bit, teaching and doing site-specific installations like the one he was then working on in Bellingham. Although we spent a lot of time apart, I thought our relationship was in rather good shape. In fact, people often referred to us as an "ideal" couple in that we were both pursuing our own careers while also seemingly maintaining a close relationship.

I had arranged to join Lloyd for several weeks while he finished his sculpture. I intended to use the time in Washington to start the drawings for the first plates, which were to represent various ancient goddesses and historic personages. Because I wanted these to be more specific in both form and visual references than the *Great Ladies* had been, I had decided to infuse my evolving imagery with particular symbols related to the lives of each of these female figures. After many months of research and technical and aesthetic preparation, I finally felt ready to begin. Each plate was to be fourteen inches in diameter and painted in successive layers, then fired multiple times in order to achieve both a density and a luminosity of color. Because this was to be a complex process, I felt that I needed detailed studies.

At the end of June, as planned, I flew up to Seattle with some clothes, lots of drawing paper, and my colored pencils. I had been looking forward to seeing my husband, whom I missed. But almost from the moment I arrived, Lloyd acted quite strangely toward me, exhibiting considerable hostility. I couldn't figure out what was going on and couldn't get him to explain. Then things seemed to settle down, at least for a few days. We were living in a rented apartment, where I spent many hours alone drawing while Lloyd worked on finishing the installation. Toward the end of our stay, he came home one evening to announce that he had something to tell me, something that he felt horribly guilty about, adding that it was these unbearable guilt feelings that had caused him to act so angrily toward me.

With a sinking heart, I listened while Lloyd confessed that throughout the years of our relationship, including after we were married, he had engaged in a series of short affairs. Many of these interludes had been with his female students at the various schools where he had been teaching. Even now, I find it painful and humiliating to discuss this, primarily because his words hurt so much, especially his revelation that a number of these liaisons had gone on at the very time that I had been teaching young women. While I had been listening to their bitter complaints about how their male art professors seemed to be more interested in seducing than educating them, my own husband had been involved in such behavior. This realization absolutely horrified me because in addition to feeling betrayed, it made me seem like a total hypocrite.

Looking back, I recognize that I probably should have ended our marriage right then, because I never really recovered from this rather devastating experience. The reason I did not do so immediately can be explained by a number of factors. By this time Lloyd and I had known each other for almost twenty years, and in addition to being my husband, he was also my close colleague and good friend. Also, I was afraid to be so alone as I had been after Jerry's death, during which time I discovered that not all men were as sympathetic to my artistic ambitions or insistence upon sexual satisfaction as Tommy or Jerry had been or as Lloyd was. Finally, because so many relationships with people I loved had ended tragically, I found it almost totally impossible to *choose* to sever ties with someone I cared about. However, after Bellingham, it was never the same between Lloyd and me.

I now find myself wondering why we did not seek marital counseling when we returned to L.A., or at least try to talk things out instead of just glossing over these problems and attempting to go on, which is what we did. Perhaps I was still overly frightened of confrontation, and Lloyd too unwilling to examine the reasons for his infidelity and be honest about whatever unhappiness he felt in our relationship. Maybe I was too occupied with my work to pay sufficient attention to my marriage. All I know is that the minute we got home I went to see Anaïs, but certainly not to discuss my marital difficulties.

The drawings I had done in Bellingham emerged with so much force that I had become terrified. I could hardly wait to discuss this with her, saying that while I was working on them, I had felt "almost as though there was a malignant tumor growing in my womb." By then Anaïs was visibly ill with the cancer that would kill her within three years, and as soon as these words escaped my lips I felt altogether mortified. I still cannot imagine how she was able to discuss my fantasy concerning cancer when a real malignancy was consuming her body. But the grace with which she handled my utter thoughtlessness and the generosity with which she put aside her own problems to offer comfort to me is another reason I felt such reverence for her.

As I describe this situation I find myself becoming somewhat nervous because I realize that many people might find it difficult to accept that a woman can be so driven by her creative needs that she could be as oblivious as I was then. Anaïs believed women to be incapable of the same level of disconnection from emotional relationships and situations that men so often exhibited. The truth is that her assessment was incorrect, at least in regard to me. My artistic drive has always been so intense that I have often put aside personal concerns (as I did upon my return from Washington), guided mainly by what might be best described as an overriding artistic necessity. Whether such behavior is ultimately right or wrong, I have no idea. I only know that this is what I did then and it's how I have lived throughout most of my life.

At that time Anaïs told me that what I had experienced was not all that unusual for a woman artist and that she herself had felt such fears. She went on to explain that numerous women she had known had internalized the notion that our creative power was somehow frightening or destructive, even monstrous. It was probably no accident that such terror began to engulf me at precisely this time because I was on the brink of an extremely fertile creative period. Who knows?

Perhaps Lloyd's behavior was subconsciously intended to send a message that he, too, experienced my growing expressive freedom as threatening. If so, how sad for both of us that his actions would ultimately force me to choose between my own artistic growth and my feelings for him.

This and future conversations with Anaïs would help me to push through some of these irrational feelings, though in order to come completely into my own creatively, I would have to engage in an ongoing battle with the fear that by expressing my full power I was doing something terribly wrong. Although the anxieties I first experienced in Bellingham no longer plague me as they did then, even now, when I express myself too freely in the studio, at my typewriter, or in public, I sometimes become consumed with terror that I have suddenly become grotesque, that some great harm will immediately befall me or those I care about, or even that I will soon die.

This dread accompanied me almost continuously as I pushed on with my plans for the plates. The drawings I had done in the midst of my struggles with Lloyd in Bellingham became the basis for the first series of images, which, as I said, were intended to represent various goddesses or mythological figures and historical personages. The imagery was based upon the vulval/butterfly forms I described earlier, now fused with symbolic motifs. Another reason that I chose this vulval-form language was that I wished to suggest that the one thing these different female personages had in common was their gender. In fact, this was the main reason that their names and significance were so unknown to most people.

More and more, I was considering the idea of trying to teach women's history through art. First I conceived of a series of plates that would be entitled "Twenty-five Women Who Were Eaten Alive," a reference to the seemingly deliberate obscuring of women's achievements. Then I started thinking about doing one hundred abstract portraits of women, also on plates. Most of all, I was contemplating how to teach a society unversed in women's history something of the reality of our rich heritage. I began to cast about for a model by which I might reach a wide audience, at one point looking back to medieval art, which I had always admired. I found it instructive that the Church had taught Christian doctrine to an illiterate population through understandable visual symbols, and I thought to make my own iconography even clearer in order to accomplish a comparable goal.

I absolutely do not remember when I visited the china-painter who had spent three years executing complete place settings for sixteen. But my enduring memory is of exquisitely painted plates (including dinner, salad, and dessert); matching bowls (both soup and serving); similarly treated coffee cups and saucers; as well as a companion creamer and sugar bowl set. These were all arranged upon her dining-room table, where she kept them as a sort of permanent exhibition. While admiring the fine quality of the painting, I experienced an epiphany of sorts, realizing that plates are meant to be presented on a table.

This was probably the moment when *The Dinner Party* was born, because once I decided to present my abstract portraits of women within the context of a table setting, I immediately began to think about historical antecedents for such a tableau, notably the Last Supper. It seemed as though the female counterpart of this religious meal would have to be a dinner party, a title that seemed entirely appropriate to my desire to point out the way in which women's achievements—like the endless meals they had prepared throughout history—had been "consumed." In fact, when I thought about paintings of the Last Supper, I became amused by the notion of doing a sort of reinterpretation of that all-male event from the point of view of those who had traditionally been expected to prepare the food, then silently disappear from the picture or, in this case, the picture plane.

Before very long, I became focused upon creating a series of plates that could constitute a visual narrative of Western civilization as seen through women's accomplishments. Like most folks educated in Western history, I had been taught to view this record in a linear progression, which is how I approached my chronicle of women's history. Whether this is, in fact, an appropriate or accurate way to present history is definitely debatable. But at the time I was engaged in conceptualizing *The Dinner Party,* I chose to work within this traditional framework.

However, instead of representing various historical epochs in this chronology through the accomplishments or exploits of, say, Plato, Aristotle, Alexander the Great, or Richard the Lionhearted, my intention was that female heroines would stand for these same periods; Eleanor of Aquitaine, for example, would take the place of Richard as a symbol for the High Middle Ages. This substitution in the context of a "dinner party" was intended to commemorate the sundry unacknowledged contributions of women to Western civilization while simultaneously alluding to and protesting their oppression through the metaphor of plates set upon and thus "contained" by the table.

At some point I decided that I would like the plate images to physically rise up as a symbol of women's struggle for freedom from such containment. As I did not then have a high level of ceramics skills, I thought I had best look for an assistant who could help me figure out how to make such dimensional plates. In the fall of 1975 I met Leonard Skuro, a graduate student in ceramics at UCLA, who agreed to work with me. While I concentrated on researching and developing the next series of portraits (on purchased Japanese porcelain, much like the dinnerware the Grinsteins had sent many years before), he set up a ceramics area on the first floor of my studio, adjacent to my china-painting studio. His task was to devise a system for producing plates that could be reliefed, then painted as richly as the early plates. They would also have to possess a visual quality comparable to those first plates, while being strong enough to sustain the multiple firings that would be necessary to achieve a similar density of color and luminosity of surface. This undertaking would prove far more daunting than either Leonard or I ever imagined.

I cannot recall the precise moment that I decided to place the table on a floor made of porcelain tiles, although I do know what brought me to this idea. My ongoing studies into women's history, guided by my search for the women I wished to represent, were teaching me that there were far more women deserving of honor than I could possibly depict. Moreover, I had discovered that the then-popular notion that anyone could pull themselves up by their bootstraps simply did not hold up to intellectual scrutiny. In general, women seemed to have succeeded only when there was some context of support for their aspirations. I wished to signify this through what I called the *Heritage Floor*.

This porcelain floor would be inscribed with the names of hundreds of other women and the concept was, in part, intended to suggest that the achievements of such individual women as those presented on the table had to be seen against the background of this larger female history. At some point I decided to group the names around the plates to imply that each of the women on the table symbolized a far greater picture of female accomplishment. As to the criteria for each woman I chose for the table, they were multiple. First, her contribution or circumstances had to render her representative of a particular historical epoch. Second, her life needed to embody some type of significant achievement. Also, she had to have in some way worked toward the betterment of conditions for women. Ultimately there had to be enough information about her to provide the basis for a visually cogent image. In terms of the names on the floor, at this exact moment I had not yet arrived at definite criteria for their inclusion, but I was busily gathering material about dozens of women.

If any of my readers are wondering how I got the money for such an ambitious project, I must remind them of my earlier remarks concerning funding. By this time I had so internalized the understanding that every idea carries with it the obligation to find the necessary financing that, when asked, I find myself at a loss to remember how I solved this or that particular economic problem. Certainly, I never thought: I am going to need $250,000 (the approximate amount *The Dinner Party* would end up costing), or I would have been stopped before I even began. What I have always done is to try to figure out how to pay for this or that specific piece of equipment or type of material, and I've usually been able to accomplish this. But it seems important to point out that my ability to come up with money for my art was always tied up with my willingness to pour everything I earned into my work, with no thought of my personal financial security.

It was during this same period that I began to run into a young feminist activist and art history student named Diane Gelon (whom

I always called Gelon). She seemed to turn up unexpectedly at some of my lectures or openings around the country. Whenever I asked her what she was doing there, she would answer blithely that she was a "Judy Chicago groupie," a reply I did not take seriously. One day late in the fall of 1975, when she again appeared at some public event, I asked her a different question: What was she doing with herself? When she responded, "Not much," I inquired as to whether she might like to volunteer some time for a project I had started on women's history.

Soon afterward she came to the studio, having demonstrated considerable enthusiasm about the prospect of working with me. I showed her the card file I was assembling for the *Heritage Floor*, which at this time contained information on some three hundred women. I asked her how long she estimated it would take her to triple this amount of information. "That should take about six weeks," she announced, a statement that would prove to fall into the category of famous last words. Gelon sat down at the table, put on her glasses, and commenced work. Within short order, she was not only doing a considerable amount of research but also providing me with a level of personal support I had never before enjoyed.

Even now, I do not know why she made the decision to offer this type of valuable assistance. Perhaps it was because she had realized that one of the primary reasons that women artists have had such difficulty achieving at the same level of accomplishment as some of their male peers is that they have not had access to a comparable level of support. Maybe, as she had told me, she just admired my work and also liked the idea of doing something to challenge the (still prevalent) idea that women have no significant history, which was one of my primary aims. Of course, the social and political climate might also have had something to do with her decision. It was the height of the Women's Movement, a time when women all over the country were coming together, joining consciousness-raising groups, organizing and agitating and generally making trouble in an effort to effect some level of change.

Even to this day, Gelon is not the most forthcoming of people, especially regarding herself and her motives. Add to this my own rather trusting nature, and it should come as no surprise that I simply accepted her assistance at face value. At any rate, she changed my life, primarily by freeing me to entirely concentrate on artmaking, especially as the project grew, a consequence of which were numerous administrative and organizational responsibilities.

Around this same time, it had occurred to me that the table on which the plates were to be presented should be covered with a tablecloth. I had also been puzzling over how to identify each of the women to be represented, and I decided that their names could be embroidered on the tablecloth. At first I thought to stitch identifying phrases about the woman in circles around each plate. I purchased a Bernina embroidery machine (again, I have no memory of how I paid for it) and began experimenting to see if I could use the different cams to achieve the supposedly dazzling array of stitches promised by the manufacturer. Almost simultaneously with initiating this effort, I received a letter from a woman named Susan Hill. She had read and been inspired by *Through the Flower* and was writing to inquire if I ever accepted assistants, as she wished to volunteer her services. I invited her to the studio and introduced her to Gelon, with the suggestion that she might be able to help with the research.

I am often asked how I felt about the 1975 publication of *Through the Flower*, which was put out in hardcover by Doubleday. To tell the truth, I do not recall having any reaction at all, except that I was glad to see so much of my art reproduced in the accompanying illustrations. I perceived writing as merely a sideline activity to my artmaking life. Writing the book had been motivated entirely by my confusion about what was happening to me as an artist, and it had served to help get me back on track, which was all that was important to me. I had always taken it for granted that I was destined to become famous and the attention the book received seemed like just one more step toward that goal. In short, I did not pay all that much attention to its publication, although I did appreciate the fact that the book produced an expanded audience for my art and numerous offers of assistance, Susan's being the first.

It turned out that research was not Susan's forte. Many years later, she told me that she was so determined to work with me that she

somewhat jokingly suggested that she could "always cook or sew." I
have no idea if she even knew that I was then thinking about incorporating embroidery, which is why I immediately responded by in-
quiring whether she might have needlework skills. She confessed that
even though hers weren't all that good, many of the women in her
family had been extremely skilled. This instantly made her seem far
more qualified than I, who can barely sew a button on a shirt, which
prompted me to appoint her "head of needlework." I set her to work
on the Bernina embroidery machine, and she soon enrolled herself in
an embroidery class in order to expand her admittedly limited skills.
Then she invited me to an exhibition of some of the other students'
work, and off we went to something called the Episcopalian Embroidery Guild.

I can still remember entering the dim, slightly claustrophobic
exhibition hall filled with displays of vestments and church furnishings. Although I had absolutely no idea what most of these ecclesiastical objects were used for, I could see that the embroidery
embellishing them was altogether superb. Many of the needlewomen
were proudly standing by or demonstrating the techniques by which
they had rendered these objects so exquisite, seemingly oblivious to
the fact that their talents were being spent upon a religious system
that was essentially oppressive to the female sex. Even more unsettling
was the fact that the women received absolutely no credit for their
work; they were not even allowed to stitch their names on the pieces
they had spent months and sometimes years creating. As I commented
to Susan, it was almost as if we were seeing women's overall historical
and social circumstances being displayed right along with their splen-
did array of needle skills.

Some time after visiting this exhibition—which prompted me to
start researching the history of needlework—Susan informed me that
it would be entirely out of the question to embroider the names directly onto the tablecloth in the manner I had envisioned, as it would
have involved the near-impossible manipulation of what would be a
long piece of fabric through the sewing machine. Instead, she suggested the idea of placing individual cloths or runners under each plate
and on top of the tablecloth. I thought about the elaborately embel-

lished altarcloths that we had seen at the ecclesiastical embroidery show and realized that adopting this approach would certainly solve some of the logistical problems. But even more, I recognized that this might actually open up whole new expressive avenues, particularly in light of my needlework research, which was demonstrating that the vicissitudes of women's condition through history were rather clearly reflected in the needle and textile arts.

Runners connoting altarcloths might lend a sacramental quality to the table, which I found appealing in that I might thereby be able to suggest the table as a dual metaphor, encompassing both the domestic and the sacred spheres. Also, the runners could be designed to drop over the front and back of the table, thereby allowing the women's names to be embroidered on the front while leaving an area that could be stitched in order to provide a visual environment for the plate. This seemed a good idea for several reasons. I was already worrying about what to do with the large expanse of white that would be established by the tablecloth; embroidering the runners might provide an aesthetically satisfying break. Then it dawned on me that if the plate was each woman's symbolic portrait, the runner could be thought of as the context providing a space that could be used to convey something about her life and particular historical circumstance.

I started out by taking those plates that I'd already completed and placing them on the white-hemmed cloths that Susan had prepared, just extending the plate imagery onto the cloth. At first my ideas were fairly simple, but even so, it soon became apparent to Susan and me that we would need a team of skilled stitchers to produce these designs. This seemed to present no problem, as we quickly found many interested volunteers. In fact, throughout the course of work on *The Dinner Party*, people seemed to come forward at precisely the moment they were needed.

Before long, numerous stitchers were vying with one another to see who could best achieve the types of color blends that typify my work and characterize the designs that I had painted somewhat crudely on the cloths to create what we described as mockups. As these became transformed into brilliantly hued and subtly stitched fades, I discovered that, despite my ineptitude with a needle, I seemed to have an unaccountable talent for designing for the needle arts. I also learned that thread could be thought of almost as a brushstroke. Soon thereafter, I became interested in knowing more about ecclesiastical embroidery, whose opulent quality had definitely appealed to me.

At one point I had the opportunity to try on an elaborately stitched bishop's glove. As I drew the jeweled and gold-encrusted object onto my hand, I could literally *feel* the hours of human labor that had gone into creating it, which seemed to me one reason that ecclesiastical objects appeared to bestow so much importance upon their wearer. It suddenly occurred to me that it might be fascinating to take the same needle techniques that had been lavished upon such vestments and bring them to bear on the honoring of women and our own history. What I am discussing here, of course, is the same type of transformational impulse I described in relation to the Fresno program, one that began to increasingly infuse the way in which I approached *The Dinner Party*.

I soon decided that, in addition to turning around needle techniques on behalf of women, I would also raid art history—as male artists constantly do—by adapting various art-historical motifs from the period in which each of the women lived, not only for the plate imagery but also for the runner designs. In the case of the runners, I would combine these with needlework styles or techniques that had been employed during, or associated with, the same period. My aim was to imply that history should be seen as belonging just as much to women as to men, while also paying homage to needlework, which, like china-painting, was primarily a female craft. In addition, I very much liked the idea of telling "herstory" through these particular "womanly" techniques.

Before too long my studio was quite crowded, and my assistants —Leonard, Gelon, and Susan—each had his or her own assistant. People kept popping up, apparently drawn by my passion for communicating women's history through art. The only real problem was that the plates were going at an agonizingly slow pace. Somehow we couldn't seem to get any of the reliefed plates (which required endless hours of carving) out of the kiln. Toward the end of the summer of 1976, Leonard began to bring a friend, Ken Gilliam, to the studio.

Kenny was an industrial designer and quite technically clever, so Leonard thought he might be able to help solve the plate problems.

Throughout much of 1976, Lloyd was away, teaching and doing sculptural installations here and there. Certainly, my side of our shared space was becoming considerably different from the quiet tandem studios we had originally set up. As I think about this period, I am astounded that Lloyd and I seem never even to have discussed this rather dramatic change. But he acted supportive of all that was happening, and since I was so deeply engrossed in *The Dinner Party*, I let it go at that.

As Kenny had a full-time job, he had been coming to the studio at night, where we were frequently alone. From the start there had been a strong attraction between us, and before very long Ken had begun to actively court me. In retrospect, I guess that it was probably inevitable that something like this would happen. Lloyd's confession in Bellingham about his infidelities had dealt a severe blow to our relationship. He was away so much, and even when he was there, there seemed to be a growing distance between us.

Then there was the fact that Kenny had a capacity for intimacy that I had never before experienced with a man, possibly a consequence of his being of a younger generation (there were almost twelve years between us). I found myself responding to it with an eagerness that suggested I was terribly parched for such a connection. *The Dinner Party* was also very much the toughest work I had ever undertaken, and perhaps I needed a romance in order to take the edge off of what was an increasingly arduous task. But I do not wish to qualify my relationship with Kenny in any way, because during the period it went on (well into 1978) I would find most of our time together quite wonderful.

Moreover, Kenny made a rather substantial contribution to the project, bringing an array of skills to bear on problems that hadn't even been identified until he arrived. Having an industrial designer involved provided the opportunity to develop specific systems to meet various needs, such as his devising special runner frames that allowed the needleworkers to see the overall designs stretched out like paintings, rather than rolled up on small frames and worked in their laps.

This helped to bring the rigor of a fine-art approach to what can sometimes be the rather wonky craft of embroidery. At this point I feel compelled to say that, even though much would be made of my homage to such crafts, if truth be known, it was the intersection of what have been called male and female techniques that would contribute to *The Dinner Party*'s technical excellence. In fact, by combining these, my intention was to suggest that the often arbitrary gendering of specific art or craft methods generally serves only to hobble the imagination.

In November 1976 I told Lloyd about my relationship with Kenny, to which he responded by saying that he already knew about it. Given his own behavior, I imagine that he didn't feel he had any real right to become irate. Nonetheless, there were scenes and arguments, culminating in our decision to separate, though we agreed that we would view this as temporary and leave the door open for a reconciliation. As it turned out, it was not all that easy to make the break. We had known each other for a long time, and even though our marriage had ceased to be all that satisfying, at least to me, ending it was like ripping up the fabric of much of my adult life. By New Year's Day, however, Lloyd had moved out; Kenny moved in with me, and shortly thereafter, *The Dinner Party* expanded to fill the entire 5,000-square-foot space.

My mother was very upset about our breakup, so much so that she did something that enraged me. Without asking me anything about the circumstances of our separation, she invited Lloyd over to find out what had happened. Exactly what transpired during their conversation is unknown to me, though I made it clear that I felt betrayed by her having done this. My relationship with my mom had become somewhat improved, though just under the surface lurked the same unresolved issues. Nevertheless, I tried to make a practice of seeing her regularly, sometimes flying her to one or another of my openings, which she loved.

Around this time my mother retired from her full-time job, and she started coming to the studio two afternoons a week to type research cards for the steadily expanding file of names for the *Heritage Floor*. Even her sister, my Aunt Do (with whom I had lived when I first went to California), became involved in *The Dinner Party*, bringing both her embroidery skills and an extremely shy temperament to the needlework loft (formerly my drawing studio). There she had an experience that she said changed her life, because she felt appreciated by the other studio members in a way that had never happened to her before. This same life-changing experience was reported by many other volunteers, some of whom were even relocating from other parts of the country in order to work in the studio.

The studio environment is somewhat difficult to describe, particularly the sense of excitement that was steadily building behind the doors at 1651B Eighteenth Street, our address. As more and more people came to work on the project, they often went through the same experience as I described having had in my Kingsburg studio: first an incredible sense of revelation that women had such a rich history, followed by rage that it was still so unknown. Perhaps it was the almost indescribable excitement of participating in uncovering this heritage that caused the studio to be so compelling. Or maybe it was the chance to help translate this information into art. Whatever the reason, the energy that developed there became so high that it would sustain me even when I was so tired that I could barely force myself to take up my paintbrush or my carving tools.

I have sometimes described this period as a process of discovery for all of us (the research was ongoing and ever expanding) almost akin to the opening of King—or, one could say, Queen—Tut's tomb. I was beginning to realize that there was too much material for one work of art to convey, even one so large as *The Dinner Party* was to become. *Through the Flower* had been put out in paperback by Anchor Books, which was run by a woman named Loretta Barrett. At the time of its issuance, sometime in 1976, she had informed me that she was interested in a long-term relationship with her authors. She came to visit me at the studio, and when she saw what I was working on she urged me to think about doing a companion book in order to deal with the emerging historical information, some of which seemed more suitable to a literary than a visual presentation.

Loretta sometimes chastises me for never having adequately conveyed what *The Dinner Party* studio was actually like. Maybe it was because I was so involved that I found it difficult to step back and comment upon the apparently unusual nature of the environment. But I have to admit that I myself didn't find it all that unique, although she insists that it was unlike anything else anywhere in the country. To me, the studio environment felt entirely natural. In fact, it was a lot like the boisterous family environment of my childhood, which I had lost so abruptly and had probably always continued to crave.

If I were to make a stab at a description, it might go like this. By early 1977, there were anywhere from twenty to thirty people working at any given time, generally in teams focused on particular tasks. Each team had a leader, selected on the basis of talent, commitment, and the ability to take responsibility. Most of the workers were women, but there were usually a few men in the studio, not just Leonard and Kenny but others who worked in research and even needlework. By this time Johanna Demetrakas, who had made the *Womanhouse* film, had decided that what I was doing should be documented, and she had assembled a crew—which included several men—and was filming on a regular basis, particularly on Thursday nights, when we had group potlucks.

Early on, Gelon and I had instituted these weekly sessions, primarily so that any problems could be openly aired and resolved. These discussions were an important part of the studio process, which was set up according to the same principles by which I had run my Feminist Art programs, with one fundamental difference. The education that took place was primarily the result of everyone's working on an artmaking project that brought many of the participants to enter into my own sense of being in the service of a larger vision, something that has motivated me throughout most of my life. It was this mutual commitment to the higher purpose of conveying the crucial importance of women's history that probably most shaped the studio environment. This shared perspective allowed us to leapfrog over our individual egos in order to support whatever idea would seem to most benefit the project, no matter who suggested it.

I am often asked whether the process of creating *The Dinner Party* was even more important than the final work of art, and my answer has always been no. It is not that I considered this process unimportant. On the contrary, I tried to structure the studio so that the people involved could become empowered. But this growth happened through work, and it was around work that the studio was organized. Except for Thursday nights, people were discouraged from engaging in personal conversations or emotional exchanges because these distracted from focusing on the tasks at hand. The studio was set up this way because I believe that the empowerment process—facilitated by both the studio environment and the nature of the project itself—had to be translated into a concrete result, which in this instance was *The Dinner Party*.

If people had difficulty working, we made an effort to help them, but if what they wanted was the opportunity for endless dialogue or seemingly fruitless arguments, Gelon would politely ask them to leave and not come back. Sometimes the person would denounce the studio structure as hierarchical and authoritarian, usually during the Thursday-night sessions that Johanna and her crew so liked to film. She seemed to intuit when there was going to be an intense session (and some of them got pretty hairy) and would often arrive unannounced. After a while, everyone seemed to become quite accustomed to being filmed, though I have no way of knowing if the film crew's presence acted as a stimulus for the expression of anger or frustration.

It is true that the studio was a hierarchy, but not in the way this accusation implied. From the beginning, people came to work within the framework of my concept. Moreover, they depended upon me for aesthetic guidance. Within the parameters of my vision, there was plenty of room for both active participation and some degree of collaboration. But the authorship of the concept and the images, along with final visual approval of the work, were mine. Some confusion about this was probably inevitable, given the fact that this was the 1970s, when many women's collectives were operating. From the beginning, however, *The Dinner Party* was my piece, though it embodied information that presumably belongs to everyone and seemed particularly meaningful to women. Additionally, working on it cooperatively would forge bonds among the participants that connect us even now.

The intensity of the studio environment and the demands of the work were such that I would spend most of 1977 and 1978 within the white walls of my space, except for running, which became increasingly important to me. Leonard and Kenny were both distance runners, and the miles they covered seemed staggering to me. But as the project continued, I found myself craving the glow of the afternoon light and the adrenaline rush that results from pushing one's body over long runs. The first time I ran six miles—three in the morning and another three in the late afternoon—I was ecstatic.

I rarely ran with the guys, as they were too fast for me. Instead, I would run with some of the women from the studio. We would pace and push each other along a path that parallels the beach in Santa Monica, enjoying the shared rhythm of our matched steps. But as my work hours began to increasingly stretch through the day and late into the night, my running became more solitary. This provided some sense of escape from the pressures of the project and my ever-more-crowded studio space. Even more important, the running path gave me a place to deal with the fear of my own power.

Each time I descended from the slope of the park onto the beach, I would first experience a sense of freedom that was both exhilarating and addictive. Reveling in the pleasure that can come from challenging one's body, I soon began to do longer and longer runs. Inevitably, at a certain point, often just as I reached full stride, I would clutch up with terror as the sense of running freely and strongly somehow triggered the anxiety that there was something wrong with a woman being so vigorous. It was on the running path that I began to accustom myself to these still-frightening feelings, a process that took many months.

I was slowly able to translate that which I was accomplishing on the running path into my studio life, a process that allowed me to reach an increasing level of aesthetic freedom. The studio environment aided this process greatly, because within it I felt accurately perceived and completely supported. This only reinforces my earlier point about the crucial connection between support and achievement, because most of the studio members had a similar experience. We were all able to transcend our creative limits, one result of which was that we were able to successfully complete *The Dinner Party*. But in addition, some of us became attached to each other and the work in a way that is inexplicable to anyone who wasn't there.

In terms of the piece itself, let me briefly state that I eventually decided on thirty-nine plates, to be presented in place settings that would include not only a runner but a ceramic chalice and flatware, along with a napkin edged with gold. A corresponding gold edging embellished the tablecloth as a way of extending the sacramental associations of the table settings. These thirty-nine place settings were configured on an open, triangular table resting on the *Heritage Floor*. Nine hundred and ninety-nine names were selected from a larger assemblage of nearly three thousand, culled by a team of twenty researchers under the leadership of Gelon and an artist named Anne Isolde. These names, chosen according to agreed-upon criteria, were hand-inscribed in gold china-paint onto the 2,300 porcelain tiles that comprised the triangular floor, then lustered to create a luminous foundation for the table.

For more information about *The Dinner Party,* I must refer readers to the many art books in which it is now featured, including my own, and also to Johanna Demetrakas's film, *Right Out of History: The Making of Judy Chicago's The Dinner Party,* which may be rented from many libraries or obtained from film distributors. Unless I move on to the events surrounding the completion and exhibition of what became a monumental work of art, I will never be able to finish the story of the ensuing twenty years.

The Dinner Party was scheduled for exhibition at the San Francisco Museum of Modern Art thanks to Henry Hopkins, the museum director, who had followed my work for many years. About midway through the project, he had come to the studio and offered to premiere and tour the work if I finished it (which he apparently considered a dubious prospect, given how much financial and volunteer support I would have to muster). He offered to set up a fund at the museum so that we could accept donations to cover the costs of materials, which were becoming ever more expensive as the concept of the piece expanded. By this time Gelon had taken over much of the fund-raising, supplementing what I brought in from lectures, sales, and book royalties with private contributions and a few grants. But we were always on the verge of running out of money, and the project account that Henry had set up was extremely helpful, as it allowed people to make tax-deductible donations.

Sometime in 1978, Henry came to Gelon and me to say that the museum comptroller was tearing out his hair. Instead of receiving the large contributions to which they were accustomed, they were getting a seemingly endless stream of small checks from the various grass-roots efforts that had sprung up around the country in support of *The Dinner Party*. Much of this activity was a result of Gelon's constant lectures about the piece, which were building considerable interest. "What should we do?" Gelon and I asked rather plaintively, to which Henry responded by advising us to start our own nonprofit organization.

I didn't even know what a "nonprofit" was, nor was I at all patient with the many hours Gelon and I had to spend with a newly established lawyer named Susan Grode, who had offered to charter such a structure for us. She explained that the educational mission of *The Dinner Party,* along with its participatory nature, qualified us for the 501-C3 status, which would allow the ongoing tax-deductible contributions upon which we were increasingly dependent. Needless to say, at that point I would have done anything in order to complete the piece, even sit in a lawyer's office or take out a loan, which Gelon and I were forced to do in 1978, the last year of the project. As we had no collateral, this was only made possible through the generosity of a woman named Joan Palevsky, who basically co-signed for us at the bank.

We decided to call the corporation Through the Flower, after the title of my book, thinking that this reflected some of our joint goals. I and a number of the studio people had begun discussing the idea that if *The Dinner Party* proved successful, we might be able to build an ongoing organization that could support other projects whose values and aims were consistent with both the piece and the principles of Feminist Art. The existence of the corporation also suggested a way of accomplishing what I began to dream about once the concept of *The Dinner Party* was finalized and we were in the last stages of production on the piece: that is, its future. In order to understand how

I could have imagined the kind of far-reaching project that I am about to describe, it is important to keep in mind my ideals, my seeming naiveté, and the incredible level of support that surrounded the studio during the last year.

Not only were dozens of people working day and night, but there was a steady stream of visitors, including such august personages as Joan Mondale, the wife of then Vice President Walter Mondale. She toured the studio, guarded by a phalanx of Secret Service men, and particularly liked the plates, probably because she herself is a ceramicist. At this time I thought that if *The Dinner Party* proved to be the kind of success the growing enthusiasm for it suggested, I might have many opportunities to realize what became my most cherished dream: the creation of a porcelain room whose imagery extended that of the plates into an environmental installation of monumental proportions.

As a way of earning money, I had continued to deliver lectures about my work around the country throughout these years, and I knew, therefore, that there was an overriding hunger among women for images that affirmed our experience. If this audience was greatly moved by *The Dinner Party,* perhaps there would be support for both our ongoing institution and the permanent housing for which I began to plan. So convinced was I of the possibility that this dream might come true that I decided to set up a ceramics studio in Northern California to begin tests on such a room as soon as possible after the exhibition opened, a date that had been postponed several times and was finally set for March 1979.

Sometime in late 1978, I was sitting in one of those charming espresso shops that can be found in so many San Francisco neighborhoods. I was there to supervise the production of a series of woven banners that were to grace the entryway to *The Dinner Party,* which I had designed earlier. Looking around at the clear blue sky and lovely pots full of bright flowers that adorned the sweet Victorian houses in the area called Nob Hill, I suddenly thought I'd like to relocate to the Bay Area.

My rather impulsive decision was probably motivated by a number of factors. I had been confined inside my studio space for an awfully long time and found myself craving a natural environment. I found myself extremely attracted to the verdant atmosphere of Northern California. My relationship with Kenny was over, and I felt that L.A. was filled with too many memories; I wanted to start over. I had seen a small town outside San Francisco that appealed to me: Benicia, where a number of artists lived. I found a small studio space there and began to make plans with Judye Keyes, one of the women who had come to assist Leonard with ceramics, then ended up heading the ceramics team of seven or eight people after Leonard had left the project. She expressed great interest in starting to work with me on plans for my envisioned porcelain room.

Although I imagined working and even living in Benicia, I intended to help set up Through the Flower in the Santa Monica studio as a self-sufficient entity that could support ongoing projects and also provide fiscal and administrative support for the permanent housing effort. I in no way perceived my planned move to the Bay Area as an abandonment of either the studio or what was a potentially permanent staff, to be made up of the most dedicated *Dinner Party* workers.

But all these hopes had to be put on hold while we struggled to finish what seemed to be unending last-minute exhibition details. Early in 1979, a number of the studio members went to San Francisco to start installing the piece, as we had absolutely no idea how long it would take. I stayed in Los Angeles in order to complete the hand-coloring of the large photo murals that explicated the names of the women on the *Heritage Floor*. Everyone on the installation team insisted upon this, probably to keep an extremely nervous artist out of their hair. But by the end of February, I was commuting to the Bay Area and Henry was smoking too much while pacing the floor of the large rotunda of the museum, where the piece was being installed.

None of us had ever seen *The Dinner Party* entirely assembled, and therefore we had no idea if all the systems would work. As March 14, the date of the opening, drew near, both our anxiety and our excitement mounted. For many of the studio members, this opening would be their first exposure to the hubbub attendant on a major museum opening. Despite the fact that by then we were no longer lovers, Kenny and I did the lighting together in a mood almost reminiscent of our earlier days, becoming absolutely elated as we discovered that the lights he'd selected provided a wonderful surprise. The framing projectors that spotlighted each place setting spilled light onto the porcelain tiles, which bounced onto the runner backs, dappling them with reflections from the rainbow luster that covered the surface of the floor. The magical effect that this created was entirely unanticipated, but it added immeasurably to the spiritual aura of the piece.

It was the physical presence of *The Dinner Party* that was most overwhelming. It seemed to float in the rotunda of the museum, almost entirely filling the huge room, the diameter of which was well over sixty feet. As I stood alone in the space with this work that I had struggled so long to create, I was flooded with emotion and, at the same time, an enormous sense of relief. I had carried its image in my mind for so many years, and to finally see its tangible realization was difficult to take in. By the time the studio members greeted each other on opening night, all decked out in fancy party clothes, the long years of effort began to take on an air of almost total unreality.

Chapter Four

Controversy?
What Controversy?

The Dinner Party premiered at the San Francisco Museum of Modern Art on March 14, 1979. The evening, one of the most glorious in my life, was marred only by Henry's absence. He was ill with a virus so severe that this was the only time in his long and illustrious career that he ever missed one of his own openings. Cousins Howard and Arleen flew in from Chicago, having rented a plush suite where the three of us had a private, pre-opening party, complete with champagne. Peter Schauseil, my hairdresser, paid his own way from Los Angeles, joining us for a drink and to do my hair. For years, Peter had visited the studio on a regular basis to provide haircuts at a discount. That night, we giggled as he placed flowers in my hair, for we could not help but think about the contrast between this glamorous evening and the many times he'd done shampoos in the grungy fiberglass sink that had been used for ceramics debris.

Five thousand people turned out for the opening, patiently waiting in line to view the piece. All night long, press photographers' cameras flashed, television crews filmed, and I was presented with gifts, covered with flowers, and congratulated on my "stunning accomplishment."

There was so much media coverage in the Bay Area that the museum's publicist commented that one would have had to be living in a cave not to have heard of *The Dinner Party*. All the local papers carried feature articles, there was a glowing piece in *Mother Jones,* and *Life* magazine sent a photographer to do a two-page color spread showing *The Dinner Party* from overhead.

As part of the opening celebrations, performance artist Suzanne Lacy (my former student) organized the International Dinner Party. People from all over the world—including my brother, Ben, and his new Japanese wife, Reiko, in Kyoto—held dinner parties in their communities. Everyone sent telegrams extending congratulations, which Suzanne posted on a giant map of the world that was mounted in one of the museum corridors.

During the three months it was on view, one hundred thousand people came to see *The Dinner Party*; the museum brought in substantial revenues; and their bookstore made so much money that they purchased a new, computerized cash register that they affectionately named "Judy." There were events, classes, tours, and parodies. Everywhere I went, I was recognized, greeted warmly, told that seeing *The Dinner Party* had changed the person's life, or was thanked for having created the work.

Sometime after the opening, I was interviewed by Susan Stamberg for National Public Radio's "All Things Considered." I excitedly described the opening, the enthusiastic crowds, and the thrill of seeing the overwhelming reaction to *The Dinner Party*. I concluded my remarks by stating that I believed this to be an indication that women could now openly express themselves and their own perspective. I was utterly shocked when Susan asked, "But Judy, what will you do when the controversy starts?" Without missing a beat, I replied, "Controversy? *What* controversy?" I honestly did not know what she was talking about, probably because I was so completely caught up in the popular fervor that surrounded the exhibition.

The opening took place on a weeknight, and there were public activities throughout the ensuing weekend that were mobbed. On Friday night I lectured to a capacity crowd, and on Saturday and Sunday, Through the Flower, in cooperation with the museum, sponsored panels, workshops, and poetry readings. The entire weekend was like a dream come true: a mainstream museum playing host to a major work of Feminist Art while also providing a framework for women of all persuasions to come together to demonstrate the larger intellectual and aesthetic context from which this work emerged. The only negative note was sounded during the question-and-answer period after my lecture. I can remember being altogether stunned when a couple of women in the audience made comments implying that the people with whom I had worked on *The Dinner Party* had been *exploited*.

As there were a number of studio members present, they immediately jumped up to counter these charges, stating that their experiences had been altogether empowering and growth-producing. None of us took this accusation seriously, for a number of reasons. First, we all assumed that the testimony of those who had actually worked on *The Dinner Party* would weigh more heavily than the attitudes of people who had not been there. Second, none of us could ever have imagined how distorted were some of the perceptions of the studio environment, myself, and the art. Third and most important, I for one had absolutely no idea how unusual the studio environment actually was.

One of the truly unique aspects of *The Dinner Party* studio was that it provided continuous reinforcement for a feminist perspective and feminist values. I defined these as being woman-centered and supportive of honesty and the open expression of one's vulnerability. Outside this environment, not only were honesty and openness often eschewed, but women and women's concerns were almost always marginalized, which is possibly why so many of the studio members used to comment, upon going home at night, that they were returning to their "real lives." For me, the studio *was* my real life in that it reflected my values and aspirations. Moreover, there was an incredible sense of freedom and hope—a result of experiencing the thrill of having the power to shape our own history and to define both the nature of art and what constitutes aesthetic quality. Also, within the walls of the studio environment, a woman-centered point of view was not only possible but seemed entirely natural.

When the accusation about exploitation first came up, I should have confronted it head-on, but I didn't, not then and not later, when it was reiterated both in print and in public forums. I always felt so hurt by this unjust charge that I could not muster a response. I now recognize that those who issued this accusation were ignorant about the real nature and very egalitarian quality of the studio. True, *The Dinner Party* was my piece, but that did not mean that those who helped me complete it were exploited. On the contrary, they were enriched by the experience, not only by the artmaking but by my treating them and their ideas with a level of respect that most of them had never enjoyed before.

When *The Dinner Party* was exhibited, some people might have misinterpreted the fact that, despite my efforts to acknowledge everyone who had worked on the piece—in both credit panels in the exhibition and in *The Dinner Party* books—most of the attention was on me. But this is not unusual in the art world, where everyone focuses on the so-called star. And even though a few studio members might have felt resentful, I believe that most understood that ultimately *The Dinner Party* was my conception and were glad that my long and arduous years of work were being recognized.

In addition, some of the people who came up with this notion of exploitation must not have had any idea how unusual it was then for an artist to give *any* credit to collaborators, artisans, or assistants. Although a good deal of art is not created solely by an individual artist, it is not at all customary in the art world to acknowledge those who, for example, do the bronze casting for a Picasso or Henry Moore sculpture. Nor does one generally see panels in museums listing the team of printers who produced a suite of Rauschenberg lithographs (which are generally more a collaborative effort).

It is true that these people are usually paid in wages, but in the case of most artists' assistants, the sums are often exceedingly small. Even so, there was no way I could have paid everyone who worked with me. Furthermore, who is to say that money is the only adequate payment for such work? Instead of money, I provided something that women in particular have had little access to: the opportunity to participate in work of both personal and historic meaning, as well as the chance to learn from another woman artist in an environment conducive to growth.

But considering the fact that no *Dinner Party* worker has ever told me that he or she felt exploited (nor has anyone else with whom I've worked over the years), why should anyone feel compelled to come to their defense? In addition to being entirely unfair, this accusation is extremely insulting. It characterizes me as unscrupulous, when in fact I should have been praised for attempting to credit everyone, even those who worked for the briefest of time. Also, by suggesting that the people who worked with me were exploited, the speaker implies that they were so stupid as to be unable to recognize their own exploitation. The truth is that some people traveled many miles, gave up paying jobs, and chose to make considerable sacrifices in order to have the opportunity to work in the studio. I guess this whole misunderstanding just demonstrates the degree to which I have been unintelligible to some observers, who, in this and other instances, have utterly misperceived both me and my motives.

As to *The Dinner Party,* there were probably warning signs of what was in store for it, but I really paid them no heed. I remember being altogether flabbergasted when Manuel Neri, one of my artist friends, told me about an argument that he had had with another male artist, who insisted that *The Dinner Party* was "politics rather than art." We laughingly agreed that, had I wished to "do politics," I would have been better off running for office. Considering the number of years I had spent drawing, painting, sculpting, and designing, I could hardly believe that anyone would attempt to argue that *The Dinner Party* was not art. But there were some people in the art community who were doing just that. However, with the exception of this one conversation with Manuel, I had no inkling at first that this was taking place. To me, the long lines and enthusiastic crowds at the museum seemed to attest to exactly the conclusion I had drawn and communicated to Susan Stamberg on NPR: that "women's time had finally come."

To fully appreciate how I could have assumed this, it seems essential to point out the flood of enthusiastic response that greeted me whenever I appeared in public, which I did quite often that spring.

In fact, it seemed as if I were constantly lecturing to large crowds, giving interviews, or signing piles of books. And then there was the crucial fact that my upbringing had taught me to treat people equally, regardless of their supposed position in the world. As a result, I did not take into account any differences between "important" and "unimportant" people. Thus it never crossed my mind that because many of the museum visitors were women or from outside the art community, their opinions might not mean much to the art world.

As I have already described my rather casual attitude toward art reviews (which, throughout my career, have more often than not been negative), it will come as no surprise that I paid little attention to a nasty article by Suzanne Munchnick, the art critic for the *Los Angeles Times,* which appeared some weeks after the opening. Hers seemed like a small and unimportant voice, especially as it was vociferously protested by numerous irate viewers who had seen and loved the work. From my perspective, the atmosphere surrounding *The Dinner Party* seemed so encouraging that I had no reason to doubt that my plans for its permanent housing could be realized.

In June, Judye Keyes and Juliet Myers, another *Dinner Party* worker, drove a huge rental truck from Santa Monica and joined me in Benicia, a small town on the Carguinez Straits, at the outskirts of the Bay Area, east of Berkeley. At that time there were only sixteen thousand residents there, the foliage was lush, and the town's rolling hills were still bare of development. As I went to help Keyes and Julie unload the van, I noticed a couple standing by the truck holding a bouquet of homegrown flowers.

Although I had never met them before, I knew that the artist Sandy Shannonhouse and her sculptor husband, Bob Arneson (now deceased), lived in Benicia, as did my friend Manuel Neri, which is how I had happened to discover this out-of-the-way little town. The cordial welcome of Sandy and Bob seemed to augur well for my change in domicile. I had settled in a small apartment, and for the first time in my life I had a separate studio. It was about a mile from my apartment, in a sprawling industrial complex of funky buildings filled with assorted artists and artisans. Although both my living and work quarters were humble, I viewed them as a first step toward establishing something more substantial.

About this same time, I ran into Paula Harper, who had returned to Stanford after her tenure as art historian for the Feminist Art Program at Cal-Arts. She reported that she had been hearing many negative comments about *The Dinner Party* from her colleagues. But my own experience at this point was so affirming that I found it almost impossible to believe that there was such an undercurrent of negativity in the art community. I can still hear her saying sympathetically, "Well, Judy, my dear, the prejudice [against women] in the art world is obviously much deeper than we had ever imagined."

Given the passionate reaction of the general audience, one might ask why I cared so much about the art community. The answer is that it is within this community that art is ultimately validated. I had contrived something of an alternative support structure in order to accomplish *The Dinner Party,* but I believed that it was essential to earn acceptance and recognition within the art world. With hindsight, I can see that I must have been unrealistic in my expectations. I firmly believed that the size and ardor of the audience—along with the financial benefit from admissions and sales—would convince museums to show the piece, thinking that the planned museum tour would soon include more than the two other venues that Henry had secured.

However, even though I believed the overwhelming viewer response to be an indication of the power and allure of the work, I certainly did not assume that its financial success could be considered any indicator of its aesthetic achievement. I fully understood that the determining factor in the evaluation of art has traditionally been its importance *as art;* one can earn six figures and not be thought of as a serious artist, or be impoverished but considered significant. Art is, at best, about ideas and values, and art objects both reveal and help to shape our concept of what is important and—more significant—what constitutes the universal.

Historically, women have either been excluded from the process of creating the definitions of what is considered art or allowed to participate only if we accept and work within existing mainstream designations. If women have no real role *as women* in the process of defining art, then we are essentially prevented from helping to shape the cultural symbols.

In part, *The Dinner Party* was intended to test whether a woman artist, working in monumental scale and with a level of ambition usually reserved for men, could count on the art system to accept art with female content. The response of visitors to the studio, the support of Henry Hopkins and the San Francisco Museum of Modern Art, and the unbelievable audience reaction suggested that I had every reason to be hopeful, despite some negative press and a few disgruntled art historians. After all, one could hardly hope for unanimous accord.

However, a very pressing reason to have been more concerned about some of the hostile art world attitudes was that they would greatly affect the exhibition tour. First and inexplicably, the two other institutions scheduled to exhibit the piece canceled. When I spoke to Henry, he said, with distress in his voice, that he just couldn't understand it. If there weren't some museum people eager to show *The Dinner Party,* he stated, then his profession wasn't "worth shit." But despite the huge audience, the ongoing press interest, and the profit shown by the museum, no other venues appeared. On June 17 *The Dinner Party* closed, was dismantled, packed in crates, and placed in storage. I was in a state of shock, and the staff in Santa Monica was not much better. As Julie Myers put it, "I can't even bear to think about it."

The remaining loyal members of *The Dinner Party* core group slowly began packing up and closing down the once-humming studio. It seemed obvious that without an exhibition tour, our hopeful plans for an ongoing arts institution were ludicrous. Both I and Through the Flower were broke. I was still digging out from the financial burden of finishing the work, having poured all my resources into keeping the studio going. Gelon and I were trying to figure out how to repay the $30,000 bank loan we had taken out at the end of the project. On top of this, there was now a monthly storage bill.

It may surprise some readers to learn that, when an artist has a museum exhibition, he or she is not paid, nor was Through the Flower then able to receive any revenues from the show; all monies went to the museum. Even though we had been able to elicit numerous contributions for the artmaking, it is difficult, if not impossible, to interest most donors in the unglamorous project of paying storage bills. I had hoped to make some money from a commercial gallery show that was held in Los Angeles during the spring, featuring *Dinner Party* test plates, but nothing was sold. I was only barely scraping by through lectures and monies from book advances and royalties.

And then there were the constant phone calls. Before the Santa Monica studio was shut down, people were calling from all over the country asking when *The Dinner Party* would be coming to their city, finding it impossible to believe that there was no tour. In Benicia, reporters doing articles were phoning to ask why there were no other bookings, which I found difficult to explain, not only because I was so distraught but because the art world couches its decisions and rejections in polite phrases like "too expensive," "too big," "doesn't fit into our schedule," and other such euphemisms. I may have quipped then that *The Dinner Party* seemed to be a work that everybody wanted to see but nobody wanted to show, though I was not in much of a joking mood.

Before *The Dinner Party* people went their separate ways, they seemed to wander around the Santa Monica space in a state of stunned disbelief at its hollow emptiness, which must have been amplified by my increasing absence, though for a while I went back and forth between Santa Monica and Benicia. At one point, the photographer Annie Leibovitz came to photograph me for a Canadian magazine. She arrived in Santa Monica, took one look around, and left, stating that my "spirit wasn't there anymore."

She was right: My spirit *had* left, not only the Santa Monica studio but also, to some extent, my own body. As it seemed entirely futile to start doing tests for a porcelain room when *The Dinner Party* was packed away in crates, I encouraged Keyes to pursue other work and soon sent my kiln and most of my supplies to my brother. By then Ben had apprenticed himself to a famous Japanese potter, having discovered that he had a talent for pottery. Luckily the studio I had rented was quite inexpensive, as it was to sit empty for many months while I tried to come to terms with what had happened to *The Dinner Party,* not to mention all my dreams.

When Annie Leibovitz tracked me down in Benicia, she was probably surprised to see me holed up in such a humble apartment. To most people, it appeared that I had just enjoyed a major success. Though cleaner, this apartment was very much like the railroad flat I had in New York during the early 1960s. I was sleeping on a mattress on the floor of the bedroom and had set up a drawing studio and an office in two small end rooms. The only other rooms were a tiny kitchen and a bathroom, and for almost a year, that cramped place was my refuge.

About a mile and a half from the apartment was a state park, where every day I would seek out the solace of the running path, the comforting beauty of the hills, and the silence. For months, I woke up every morning with an overwhelming sense of futility. What's the point? I asked myself. Forcing myself out of bed and into my running clothes, I needed two or three hours of exercise to help pull me out of my depression so that I could face the day.

This was the summer I turned forty. I had been a professional artist for almost two decades, and I felt as though I had absolutely nothing to show for it. Had it not been for a horrible experience with Lloyd early in the summer, I might have even begun to regret the breakup of our marriage, as I found myself missing him. We'd continued to see each other on and off after he moved out of the Santa Monica studio, and even discussed the possibility of a reconciliation. But this desire on my part had been definitively ended by our conversation about *The Dinner Party*. He had refused my invitation to the opening and gone to see the piece on his own. We saw each other shortly thereafter on one of my visits to Santa Monica. Walking down the Venice boardwalk together while discussing his reaction to the work remains an unforgettable and exceedingly painful memory.

Lloyd mentioned the floor-level lighting system that Kenny had designed to illuminate the fronts of the runners (which, as it turned out, we hadn't needed, as there was sufficient light from the overhead projectors). This lighting grid doubled as a guardrail, and Kenny had decided to soften its appearance by rounding the edges and covering the outside surfaces with carpet. All Lloyd could say about the piece was that he guessed I had finally achieved what I always desired. "What do you mean?" I asked. "Now everyone can kneel down and genuflect in front of you," he replied.

Since that day we have run into each other only once or twice. I don't even know what has become of Lloyd, although I heard that he had gotten married again, to a woman twenty years his junior. From time to time, I feel sorry that we were never able to discuss what happened between us, never mind what could have made him say something so unkind. Perhaps he felt threatened or jealous; I really don't know. Whatever the explanation, it seems unfortunate that an important relationship (to me) disintegrated into what might be described as just another marriage that did not survive the 1970s Women's Movement.

After this horrible encounter I returned to Benicia and to one of the most difficult periods of my life. *The Dinner Party* seemed to have no future. I had no marriage; no money; no staff; no support system for my work; no shows, sales, or commissions; and for the first time in my adult life, no male companionship. Although I tried to meet men, I had one unsatisfying encounter after another. It seemed that not only were the male-dominated institutions disdainful and rejecting of my art, but men were altogether uninterested in me personally. Throughout that summer of 1979 I was almost entirely alone, and I was achingly, desperately lonely. I felt as though what I had learned as a child through my experiences with my father and what I had carried in my heart as a longing and an expectation—that I could be loved for being and expressing myself honestly—was being entirely contradicted by what I was experiencing in both my career and my intimate life.

Family and friends from around the country called constantly to ask how I was and to urge me to "hang in there." I could tell from the concern in their voices that there was some worry that I might commit suicide. Certainly there is no doubt that their love and constancy helped to pull me through. I was also aided by the countless letters I kept receiving, mainly from women, telling me how much

seeing *The Dinner Party* had meant to them. These many writers probably had no idea what their words meant to me, but they helped me
maintain my hold on sanity. The contrast between my own experience
of *The Dinner Party* and the art world's rejection of it was so stark
that it threatened to undo me, and I am fortunate to have had so
much help from both close friends and total strangers.

For some reason, I cannot remember any conversations that summer with Gelon, although I am sure she called me. She probably knew
me well enough to know that nothing anyone could say could compensate for the absence of an exhibition tour. To this day, all she will
ruefully admit is: "When you went into shock, I went on the road,
as there was no way that I was going to let all those years of work go
down the tubes." She was spending all her time traversing the country,
meeting with countless interested individuals and community groups
in an effort to secure venues for the show.

From my journal entries, it is clear that Gelon and I had had a
few discussions about what we would do if museums refused to exhibit
The Dinner Party. In fact, I can recall overhearing a few phone conversations in the Santa Monica studio in which Gelon was discussing
someone's idea of showing the piece in a railroad station or some other
unlikely venue. One such call came from a woman who was going to
become an important person in my life. Mary Ross Taylor had retained
the mellow-toned voice of her Arkansas upbringing when she moved
to Houston in the 1970s, though, as I was later to discover, she was
anything but mellow. Her rapid-fire delivery was somewhat hard to
follow, but I finally understood that she was asking how she could
bring *The Dinner Party* to Houston. I turned her over to Gelon and
promptly forgot about the phone call.

I generally paid no attention to these types of inquiries because I
was so convinced that the art system would eventually come through.
In retrospect, I realize that Gelon was probably not so surprised by
the negative stance of the institutions; she certainly wasn't as devastated. Because she had been visiting museums and consulting with art
world people while I was at work in the studio, she might already
have heard some of the attitudes and comments that were to come as
such a blow to me; but as was her wont, she had chosen to protect

me. Even now I have no idea what she actually did during that summer of 1979, nor am I clear on how she managed to put together what would eventually become a worldwide exhibition tour.

It was a good thing I had a contract with Doubleday to do the second *Dinner Party* book. Although I had been afraid that they might cancel the contract, Loretta assured me that she would get the book into print. The first volume was doing quite well in sales but, more important, she had been radicalized by what had happened with the first book at the publishing house: She had been accused of promoting pornography. This utterly flabbergasted her—and me—since the plates seemed anything but pornographic. True, they employed a vulval metaphor, but that was just one way of demonstrating that the oppression experienced by the women represented at the table was a result of their gender.

One thing that was interesting about this misperception was that it was not put forward only by men. Some of the women at Doubleday were the most vociferous in attacking Loretta, whereas she was entirely supported by the male head of the publishing house. All I could make of this distortion was that many people, including women, have internalized the idea that women's sexuality is negative, destructive, and, even worse, obscene. Moreover, there appeared to be a strange analogue between the accusation that I had exploited the people with whom I had worked and the misrepresentation of the plate images as being pornographic. In both cases, the message being sent seemed to be that there was something wrong with female power, in whatever manner it was expressed, whether visually or through women giving their support to another woman rather than, I suppose, to the patriarchal home, church, or institution.

In the fall of 1979, I forced myself to do what I had done so many times before in painful circumstances—that is, go back to work. Kate Amend, sometimes with Susan Hill, made numerous trips to Benicia to assist me with *Embroidering Our Heritage,* the second volume of *The Dinner Party*. Katie had come to work on *The Dinner Party* some years earlier, when she gave up her teaching job and moved to L.A. from San Francisco in order to work on the research for the *Heritage Floor*. She had helped me with the first book and we had become extremely close, particularly during a period toward the end of the project when we were holed up in a loaned house in the funky town of Bolinas, frantically trying to get the manuscript ready for publication.

My plan for this second book was to create a modern-day illuminated manuscript, which would involve illustrating the text with black-and-white line drawings based upon the runner designs. My goal was to demonstrate how the needle and textile arts could be seen as reflecting the same changes in women's circumstances throughout history as were chronicled by *The Dinner Party*. I also wanted to show how I had incorporated this information into the runner designs.

I worked steadily on this project until early in 1980. Except for the periods when Kate and/or Susan was there, I spent most of the time by myself, working long hours in my small apartment studio, running daily in the state park, eating, sleeping, and occasionally visiting Marleen Deane, a local woman who had befriended me. Although this quiet type of life can be conducive to creativity, those months were some of the most cheerless of my life. Perhaps my depressed state helps to explain how vague my memories are of the time between the fall of 1979 and March 1980, when *The Dinner Party* came out of storage, thanks to the efforts of Gelon, Mary Ross Taylor, and a community group in Houston.

Mary Ross Taylor (whom I usually call MR) owned a feminist bookstore, where she often held cultural events aimed at raising consciousness and promoting the arts. It was from Evelyn Hubbard, her Doubleday representative, that she first heard about *The Dinner Party*. Even before the work premiered, Evelyn had walked into her shop carrying a copy of the first book, saying "Mary Ross, we need to get this piece here."

It was extremely fortuitous that *The Dinner Party* was structured so that the information it embodied was able to enter the culture in several forms. Consequently, when the work of art was blocked by the art system, the book brought the concept of the piece to what turned out to be an extremely receptive audience. The level of national media coverage certainly worked in our favor, stimulating people to come together to bypass the museums' negative stance. Later, Johanna Demetrakas's film *Right Out of History* also helped to bring word of the piece and its plight to what turned out to be millions of people.

MR had followed the events surrounding *The Dinner Party* and soon discovered that the museums in her area were not willing to show the piece. Fortunately, she found numerous people both in and out of the art community who were interested in trying to exhibit the piece alternatively. A volunteer site committee found a black-box the-ater space at the University of Houston, Clearlake City, where NASA is located. Calvin Cannon, one of the deans, had proposed the space, forged bonds between the university and the community group, and also taken on responsibility for making sure the space was ready and organizing an installation crew.

Although I was extremely relieved that *The Dinner Party* was to come out of its crates, I was not at all enthusiastic about the Houston venue. The University of Houston at Clearlake City was a far cry from the prestigious galleries of the San Francisco Museum of Modern Art. Sometime before the exhibition, I went to see the space and, according to Gelon, "went numb" when she showed me the site. The theater itself was all right, but the unattractive university building that housed it had a bland, institutional appearance. The corridors intended for the banners and documentation panels were illuminated with fluorescent lighting and not at all suitable for hanging art. All in all, the campus seemed more geared toward training astronauts than exhibiting contemporary art.

But when I returned to Benicia, I decided that, despite my am-bivalence about the Houston setting, given the obdurate museum stance, it was a triumph that *The Dinner Party* was to be exhibited again. In celebration of its reemergence, I decided to initiate some-thing I named the International Quilting Bee. People would be invited to submit triangular quilts—two feet on a side—honoring women of their own determination. By doing this, I intended to provide an opportunity for community participation and also to counter another criticism that had emerged, this time about my choices of women. I wished to suggest that my selections needed to be viewed *symboli-cally*—that is, intended to imply a larger historical picture.

I also hoped that if *The Dinner Party* continued to travel, more quilts could be added and exhibited in an ever-expanding ancillary show that would demonstrate my commitment to inclusivity. For it seemed that Gelon was succeeding in finding ways to exhibit *The Dinner Party* alternatively. She reported that the piece would probably go directly from Houston to Boston, where a community group had also organized and was searching for a space. Despite my ambivalence about non-museum venues, I desperately wanted the work on view.

However, installing *The Dinner Party* involves weeks of work and preferably an experienced crew. The prospect of setting up the piece in nonart spaces with volunteers totally unfamiliar with art installation, exhibition standards, or the handling of textiles was frightening, which was one reason for my misgivings. It was fortunate for both me and *The Dinner Party* that all of the organizational, administrative, and installation logistics were handled by Gelon, along with Susan Hill and Peter Bunzick, for without their dedication there might have been considerable damage to the art. Peter had come to work at the end of the project, taking over Kenny's position as installation supervisor after the San Francisco show. My role was limited to approving the site, installation plans, and graphics, then working on the lighting and participating in opening events, including the press preview and media interviews.

The Houston site needed considerable preparation even before the installation could begin, and the school had either underestimated the scope of the installation or lacked the resources to handle it adequately. When I arrived about a week before the scheduled opening, I was confronted with a chaotic scene. Peter, Diane, and Susan were exhausted, and there was still an overwhelming amount of work to be done. At what seemed like the last minute, MR managed to round up a group of people to help finish the complex installation. I shall always remember the humorous sight of one of her male friends sweeping in, wearing a floor-length fur coat that barely missed being splattered with paint by someone entirely inexperienced at wielding an extension roller.

As in San Francisco, over the opening weekend in Houston there were conjoint events, including panels and lectures, along with an exhibition of local women artists' work. There were some wonderful moments, most memorably when the late Eleanor Tufts, an art historian, presented a hilarious spoof on art history featuring only women artists. Her presentation culminated with a manipulated photo of me as "Woman of the Year" on the cover of *Time* magazine. At some point during the weekend, I apparently alienated some of the women by being somewhat critical of the aesthetic and intellectual dialogue, which seemed considerably less developed than what I was accustomed to on the West Coast. Although I thought they might be interested in my feedback, they just took it as criticism.

I should probably have been more sensitive, but tact has never been my middle name. Perhaps my direct manner collided with the gentility of the Southern temperament, but, as is not unusual for me, I was oblivious to the effect my remarks had. I remember being totally taken aback by someone saying I was "trampling on people's feelings" when I thought I was only being my usual honest self. I now wish that I had done a better job of communicating with the women in the Houston community, as it was certainly not my intention to make anyone feel bad.

One charge that was leveled against me in Houston was to come up again later on: I was not sufficiently appreciative of all that had been done *for me*. It was as if people there thought that by helping to exhibit *The Dinner Party,* they were somehow doing something for me personally. Other women have also felt this way, it seems, for I was recently told that some of the women who helped to bring *The Dinner Party* to Chicago in 1982 were still angry at me for "alienating people who were only trying to help me." But it never occurred to me that anyone was operating out of such an assumption. Had I realized this, I would have made every effort to correct what to my mind was an inappropriate reason for supporting *The Dinner Party*.

I thought that people were coming together to exhibit the work because they understood its critical symbolic importance in that it represents and celebrates women's rich heritage. It was the task of communicating something of this still largely unknown body of knowledge about women that motivated me and everyone who worked with me to devote so many years to what we viewed as almost a historical imperative. It is for this same reason that I have found it so difficult to separate from the work or to destroy it in order to be free of the responsibility it involves.

One reason I was so impervious to the expectation that I should be appreciative is that I had almost always exhibited within the framework of the art world. When an art institution shows an artist's work, it does not usually view this as a favor to the artist but, rather, as a benefit to the larger community. Although I was pleased that so many people were organizing to see that *The Dinner Party* was shown, I perceived their efforts as a direct response to the importance of the *art*, not as any personal kindness to me. I wanted the piece on view because that was where it belonged, particularly given how much interest there was in the work, an attitude I thought everyone shared.

Despite all of the problems I've been describing, the Houston show drew sixty thousand people, another round of media attention (generally positive though, as usual, I didn't pay that much attention), and was considered a huge success by most people there. I had not actually encountered MR until shortly before the opening for, as she confided to me, she preferred to remain behind the scenes. When we finally met, we hit it off immediately, perhaps sensing in each other some commonality of interests.

After the Houston opening, and using monies from the advance for *Embroidering Our Heritage,* I went on a much-needed vacation to the Yucatán with Katie and Marleen Deane. We drove around visiting ruins and lounged in jungle hideaways for ten glorious days. Perhaps it was the relief of having *The Dinner Party* on display again or the benefits of the long, hot afternoons of rest that allowed me to finally begin turning my attention to ideas I had been considering before *The Dinner Party* was even finished.

My interest in the subject of birth and creation had first been piqued when I had designed the runner back for the Mary Wollstonecraft place setting. The image depicts the tragic death from "childbed fever" of this great eighteenth-century feminist writer and theorist several weeks after giving birth to her daughter, Mary (who, as Mary Shelley, would write *Frankenstein*). My black-and-white drawing was so raw and graphic that it unnerved me, but when it was translated into stump work, petit point, needlepoint, and delicate embroidery, it became entirely transformed. I had decided then that if I was interested in creating images of birth and creation, the needle and textile arts might be a perfect—and softening—medium for this particular subject matter. But for all the reasons I've been discussing, I had not yet been able to begin work on these ideas.

After my vacation, I returned to Houston before going back to California, considerably more relaxed and in better spirits. Mary Ross and I spent a long evening together discussing the possibility of working together. I had been quite impressed by the way she'd organized the Houston community, and I asked whether she would consider applying her organizational skills to the project that I was already formulating. While on vacation, I had thought about the many letters I'd received from women who had seen or read about *The Dinner Party*. In addition to expressing their appreciation, many of them had stated their desire to volunteer should I decide to do another participatory work. Among these writers were numerous needleworkers who stated that their only requirement was that "they wouldn't have to move to Santa Monica"—or to Benicia, I presumed.

While lying in a hammock in Palenque, a tropical paradise in the south of the Yucatán, I had ruminated about the various community efforts that were bringing *The Dinner Party* out of storage. Although I did not yet have a clear plan for my next project, I did know that I wished to build upon this outpouring of support from around the country, and I wondered if I would hear from people in other communities after they had seen *The Dinner Party*. Perhaps I could do another participatory project on the subject of birth in which people worked on my images in their own homes. Recognizing that I would need someone to act as administrator, I hoped that MR would be interested in playing this role. She promised to pay me a visit before too long in order to continue our discussion about joining forces.

Sometime earlier I had spoken to Audrey Cowan, a weaver who had worked on *The Dinner Party*. Toward the end of the project, Audrey had indicated that she would like to work with me again, an offer that I had not yet had the opportunity to pursue. But the completion of the needlework book and my renewed energy allowed me to think about contacting her, which I did shortly before the Houston opening.

In our phone conversation, Audrey and I discussed the idea of my designing a tapestry cartoon (the drawing or painting from which the weaver works). In addition to admiring Audrey's weaving skills—she uses a modified form of the traditional Aubusson method typical of the great Renaissance tapestries—I very much liked the idea of using this technique for the subject of birth and creation, which I was now ready to take up. It seemed both amusing and ironic to choose this method, as women had not been allowed to work on the huge looms that produced the Renaissance tapestries, often on the pretext that if they were pregnant they might fall and miscarry. I promised Audrey that I would begin working on the cartoon as soon as I returned from Houston.

However, no sooner had I returned to Benicia and the ceramics studio that Peter Bunzick had rebuilt for me while I was away than I spoke to my mother, who told me she had been diagnosed with cancer of the liver. I called Ben in Japan, and he made arrangements to meet me in L.A., where I immediately took my mom to my long-time internist. The doctor did some tests and concluded that the diagnosis was wrong. Unbelievably relieved, Ben and I took the opportunity of being in L.A. together to help our mother move into a retirement community, something she had wanted to do for some time. Ben stayed to help her pack and move, and I went home.

Within a few days I was at work in my new studio, with its unfamiliar sounds and atmosphere. My quarters were a somewhat cramped space in the back of a large metal building, the remainder of the building being occupied by two other artists. Although it was not the most comfortable of structures, before very long I was completely absorbed in the problem of trying to depict the creation of the universe from a female point of view. I planned that this creation tapestry would be based upon a myth that I had written while working on *The Dinner Party,* a kind of recasting of Genesis.

My rewriting of this story had been intended to challenge the notion of a male god creating a male human being with no reference to women's participation in this process, except as an adjunct figure to Adam. I wanted to see what other creation myths existed, so I went to the library to do some research.

It was fascinating to discover that there was a variety of myths, some of which seemed to demonstrate the same historical chronology represented by *The Dinner Party*—that is, the changeover from matriarchal to patriarchal societies, in this case reflected in a gradual transmutation from female to male deities. Eventually, creation came to be represented as the act of a single male god, notably in Genesis. Interestingly, when I rewrote this myth—long before this focused study —I intuitively went back to the earlier concept of the creation of life as an entirely female act, an idea that not only seemed closer to the truth but also celebrated women.

Once in the studio, I felt like I was all thumbs at first. But after a few days I found my rhythm, and that part of me that had always directed my creative life seemed to be doing it once again. My first sketches were rough, but the imagery was already all there. I then set out to translate these drawings into a full-scale painted cartoon. I did not know whether to work abstractly or more representationally, as my imagery had changed so much over the years of working on *The Dinner Party*. In 1974, when I began the first plate drawings in Bellingham, I was an abstract artist, still trying to bend my forms to the specific content of women's history. But over the years and particularly while designing the runner backs—which were often narrative in nature—I had gradually begun incorporating more representation. I soon began to fuse abstraction with representation in the tapestry design, and later I would bring this same fusion to the other birth and creation works I designed.

After several months, I had to interrupt my studio work to go east, stopping in New York before going on to *The Dinner Party* opening in Boston. But I stayed there longer than I had planned because the Boston installation was behind schedule due to a leak in the roof of the building where the piece was to be exhibited. I was concerned about the state of the building, the shabby condition of which seemed not to bode well for the safety of the piece. But Gelon, Peter, and

Susan convinced me that all would be well. They urged me to stay in New York and concentrate on the final details for *Embroidering Our Heritage,* which was to be published in the fall.

The publication date was set to coincide with the October opening of *The Dinner Party* at the Brooklyn Museum. Needless to say, I was ecstatic that the piece was to be back in a museum, particularly one in New York. Michael Botwinick, the museum director, had been approached about showing the work by a group of prominent New Yorkers. They had been working with Gelon and Loretta Barrett, my Doubleday editor, to find a suitable venue for the exhibition, with Gelon operating out of an office provided by Loretta. Even before seeing *The Dinner Party* in Houston, Michael had agreed to its being shown at the museum, and when we met in Texas he was quite encouraging about the response I might anticipate on the East Coast.

New York had never been particularly friendly toward my work, but then I had never had a show there. Michael said I might be surprised by what might happen, especially because it was during that spring that Lucy Lippard's cover story about *The Dinner Party* appeared in *Art in America.* To this day, her piece remains the most insightful and substantive writing about the piece. I had known Lucy since about 1960, when I was living in New York with Jerry, my first husband. She worked at the library of the Museum of Modern Art, and she used to let Jerry in for free, which is how I first happened to meet her. Like me, she was living in the East Village then. She and I forged a friendship, and we often met during the 1970s to develop strategies by which the Feminist Art movement could be helped to grow. Frequently, when I would lecture in some city, I would answer a question only to be told that several months earlier, Lucy had been there and had said practically the same thing.

I really hoped that Michael would be proved right—that as a result of the Brooklyn Museum show and Lucy's article, there might be a change in New York's previous indifference toward my work. If *The Dinner Party* was successful there, I imagined, I might finally get a significant gallery to represent me, which could mean a stipend, sales, and, most important, the placement of my art in major collections around the world and support for future projects. Perhaps it was because I was focused on this happy prospect that the Boston opening on the weekend of July 4 remains so unclear in my mind. I mostly remember feeling altogether taken aback when I walked in and saw a huge portrait of myself advertising the audiotour of *The Dinner Party* that Michael had convinced me to record.

I realize that it might sound odd when I say that I was made unbelievably uncomfortable by this sign, as I was by the sight of my name in large letters on the sides of the buses that were shuttling the boisterous crowds to the opening. The months following the closing of the show in San Francisco had been terribly difficult for me, and I had spent much of that time hidden away. Even the success of the Houston show and all the hoopla involved had not made me realize that I was becoming so well known. Although I had always known that I would be famous, I was finding out that the idea of it and the reality were not necessarily the same.

I ended up sitting outside all alone, feeling quite alienated. I had suffered what I believed to be a psychosomatic outbreak of hives all over my face, or maybe it was an allergic reaction to a new hypoallergenic makeup that I had decided to try. Whatever the explanation, I scrubbed my face raw in the bathroom trying to get the makeup off, after which I didn't much feel like the belle of the ball.

Actually, I was getting kind of sick of *The Dinner Party*. Despite its success in Boston—it would attract forty thousand people and a lot of good press—I wanted to get on with new work. I returned to Benicia to focus on the tapestry cartoon, with the idea of further developing my ideas about the subject of birth, soon becoming engrossed in this process. Certainly, I had no notion whatsoever about all that was in store for either me or *The Dinner Party* in the Big Apple, when, in the fall of 1980, Susan Stamberg's prediction would finally come true.

Chapter Five

Giving Birth to the
Birth Project

*T*he Boston opening marked the end of my first year in Benicia. Although this period had been incredibly lonely, I had gradually widened my circle of acquaintances in the Bay Area. I had continued to spend most of my time alone, but I slowly began to see more people, while also speaking regularly by phone with my longtime friends. I began to get to know Stephen Hamilton, a San Francisco–based designer whom I had first encountered when he was working on a Chevron-sponsored traveling exhibition on creativity in which I was included. Through him I met Brian Klimkowsky, a friend and former lover of Stephen's who, though basically gay, sometimes had affairs with women.

Before too long we began seeing each other regularly. Brian was young, darling, and not to be taken seriously, but he was great in bed. Around this same time I also became involved with a man named Dusty, whom I came to care about. In contrast to Brian, Dusty was my age and intellectual equal, but he was full of sexual hangups (like many men of my generation, which was one reason I found myself drawn to younger men).

Although it was good to have male companionship again, I was determined to avoid some of the frustrations I had experienced in previous relationships. Over the years, I (and many other women, I would imagine) have had sex with men who seemed focused only on their own satisfaction. Needless to say, this always left me furious. I decided that I would try to discover how to get what I needed in bed, no matter the circumstances of the exchange. I wanted to leave each and every encounter having wrested satisfaction from even the most recalcitrant man.

I learned how to guarantee my own sexual gratification, in part by clearly stating my desires. For some men this was pleasurable and even a relief, as they confessed that they had always wanted to satisfy their partners but hadn't been told how. But for others it was threatening, although I really didn't care. I had always envied men's seeming ability to achieve orgasm in almost any situation, and I no longer felt jealous or angry once I could ensure this for myself.

My mood was further improved during the summer of 1980 because *The Dinner Party* was back on view and the needlework book was finished and going into production. I was working on the tapestry cartoon and also doing research on the subject of birth. I had thought that I would easily find a wealth of information, as one would have thought birth to be a significant subject. Strangely, there was almost no material.

There were some photographs, but these were scarce. And when I scrutinized the art-historical record, I was shocked to discover that there were almost no images of birth in Western art, at least not from a female point of view. I certainly understood what this iconographic void signified: that the birth experience (with the exception of the birth of the male Christ) was not considered important subject matter, not even to women. Despite the significant number of major female artists in the twentieth century, none had seen fit to address this subject—or if they had, their work had not entered the cultural iconography. (At this time Frida Kahlo's work was still relatively unknown in the United States, so I was not to become familiar with her treatment of this theme until much later.)

Because it is problematic to tackle a subject about which there is little or no historical image bank, I decided that I would have to turn to direct experience for knowledge about the birth process. While continuing to work in the studio daily, I began seeking out private photographs and descriptions from people who'd either given birth, witnessed and/or participated in the birth process, or studied and documented it. It was an advantage to be in the Bay Area, where there was an active natural-childbirth movement. As a result, many people seemed eager to share their birth stories and pictures with me.

In July, shortly after I returned from the Boston opening, my old friend Janice Johnson came to visit me. Since she had had four children, I thought I would ask her about her birth experiences, having realized with some chagrin that this was something we had never talked about. Somewhat sadly, we admitted to each other that it had never occurred to either of us for me to be invited to the births, even though they had all occurred while I was still living in L.A. Although Janice could recall many details of her birth experiences, she told me that they would recede in her memory until the next time, when, in the throes of labor, she would angrily ask herself, How could I have done this to myself again?

Listening to her made me wonder whether the absence of images depicting the birth experience might actually reinforce such lapses of memory. If women saw numerous images presenting the actuality of birth and were thus reminded of both the pain and the responsibility for another life ushered in by this process, would they still give in so often to what Janice and many others have described as an overpowering urge for a child?

Perhaps if I had felt the powerful desire for a child that I heard described by so many women, I might have felt similarly compelled. But I never did. Moreover, I have never regretted my decision not to have a child, because I always knew that motherhood would interfere with my creative life. I wanted my days to myself so that I could work in my studio. Moreover, while I was in my thirties, when many women reportedly feel their biological clocks ticking, I was steeped in research into women's history. Discovering that most successful women artists had been childless, I consciously chose to pattern my life upon theirs.

Over the years and particularly while I was engaged in my work on birth, I was questioned endlessly whether never having given birth made it impossible for me to deal authentically with this subject. I tried to point out that personal experience is not always an adequate criterion for creativity, else we would have no great paintings of, for example, crucifixions. Also, it seemed obvious that having a child did not necessarily qualify one as an expert on this subject, as a woman who had given birth in an anesthetized state could hardly be assumed to be more knowledgeable than I was to become after all my years of study.

Soon after my conversation with Janice, my Benicia friend Marleen Deane invited a group of local women to her house to talk about their birth experiences. When I arrived, all of them excitedly told me how much this meeting meant to them, as none of them had ever had the opportunity to publicly discuss what most of them described as a pivotal moment in their lives. Some of the younger women had benefited from the alternative birthing movement, characterizing their natural childbirth, at home or in a cozy birthing room, as altogether joyful. The older women (like my own mother) had given birth under anesthesia while their husbands paced in waiting rooms. As a result, they remembered little but the excitement of holding their babies in their arms.

This session was to be the first of many in which I would hear stories about the nature of the birth experience. Nothing I heard ever caused me to lament my childless state, particularly after listening to considerable testimony by artist mothers who expressed a seemingly irreconcilable conflict between their lives as artists and the demands of motherhood. And then there were the horror stories: of extended labors, breech births, excruciating pain, and descriptions of some of the terrible and rarely discussed consequences of childbirth, including fistula, incontinence, and, most of all, unremitting exhaustion.

However, the moment of birth seemed a momentous one—an existential event, if you will—one in which a female is faced with one of life's great challenges: the bringing into being of another human life with all its attendant agony, triumph, and bliss. The actual process of rearing a child was secondary to my focus, although many women were to tell me that it was the satisfaction of doing so that made all the discomfort associated with birth worthwhile.

The more I learned, the more outraged I became that such a universal topic was so shrouded in mystery and, more, taboo. Over that summer of 1980, it became obvious that, given the lack of iconography about this subject, I would have to basically start from scratch to invent forms and symbols that could represent what was so obviously a primal human experience. The fact that I had been classically trained in art would prove crucial as I attempted to create what might best be described as an original, woman-centered iconography about the birth experience.

The most overwhelming event of those months was the witnessing of my first birth, an experience that I believe everyone should have. Thanks to some friends, Karin Hibma and Michael Cronan, I had the opportunity to see a well-prepared natural childbirth in a hospital with a cozy birthing room, attended by a doctor and a resident who were not only women but feminists and, hence, sensitive to a birthing mother's needs. I can only imagine my reaction to less empowering birth experiences, like those suffered by too many women in the world.

My journal entry for July 25, 1980, best conveys the vividness of my original impressions:

It was incredible. . . . Lots of vivid visual images that sunk into my mind, the expression on her face, the glazed look that came over her eyes during the height of the contractions, the darkening of the cunt and pelvis as she pushed. Her husband was a real ally in the struggle—but what a lot of pain. At one point, I really understood why some women choose and so many doctors want to administer painkillers. It requires a lot of courage to go through a natural birth, especially one as long as Karin's. She was in labor for almost eighteen hours. . . . I was there for the last three and a half, the most intense part.

She had to have an episiotomy and there was an enormous amount of blood. . . . But once the baby was in her arms, it was as if she totally disconnected from her body. There she was with her legs spread, the center of her body covered with

The *Dinner Party* in storage.

In my Benicia apartment, summer, 1979.

Runner back for *Mary Wollstonecraft* place setting, from *The Dinner Party,* 1979; needlepoint, petitpoint, embroidery, crochet, and china-painted porcelain.

Birth Tear/Tear, EU 4, from the *Birth Project,* 1982; embroidery by Jane Thompson, cotton floss on silk, 21"x 24". Collection: Through the Flower, Santa Fe, New Mexico.

With Mary Ross Taylor (above, second from right) in the Houston *Birth Project* space and (right) in the Benicia office, 1981.

Building 57, Through the Flower headquarters, Benicia, CA, 1981–90.

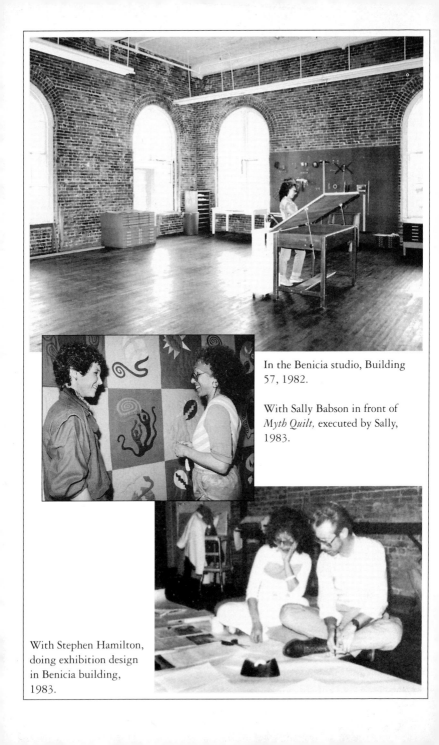

In the Benicia studio, Building 57, 1982.

With Sally Babson in front of *Myth Quilt,* executed by Sally, 1983.

With Stephen Hamilton, doing exhibition design in Benicia building, 1983.

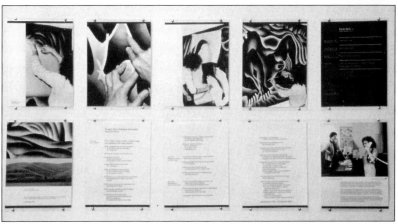

Earth Birth, EU 62, from the *Birth Project,* 1983. TOP: overall installation,
65" x 20'. MIDDLE: *Earth Birth,* quilting by Jacqueline Moore, sprayed acrylic and
quilting on fabric, 65" x 12'. Collection: Through the Flower, Santa Fe, New Mexico.
BOTTOM: documentation panels.

Birth Trinity, EU 58, from the *Birth Project,* 1984; executed by Martha Waterman, filet crochet, 42" x 118". Collection: Rose Art Museum, Brandeis University, Waltham, MA.

Birth Trinity, 1981; prismacolor on rag paper, 16" x 42". Collection unknown.

FACING PAGE, BOTTOM: *Holding onto the Shadow,* 1983;
prismacolor on rag paper, 23" x 29". Collection of the artist.

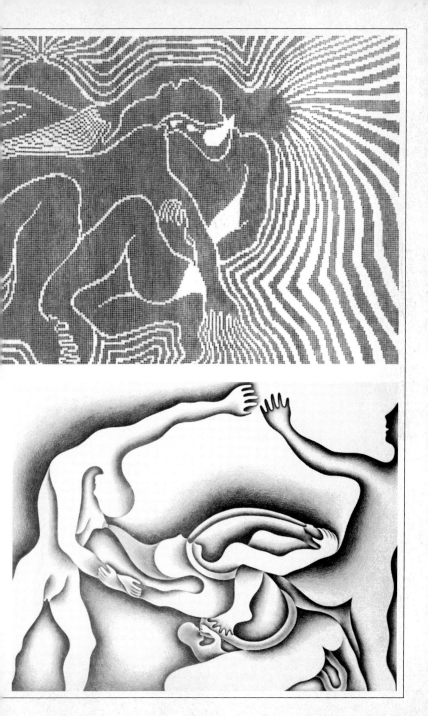

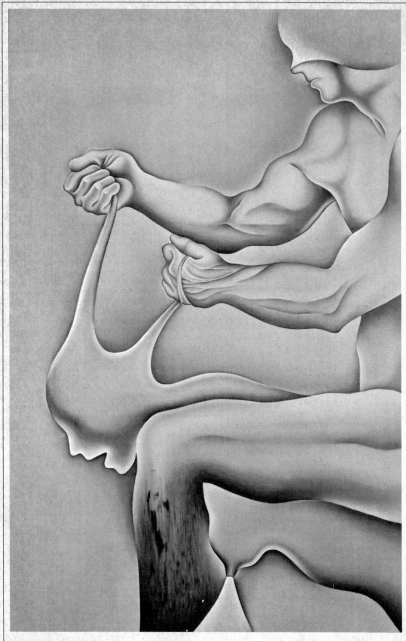

Crippled by the Need to Control, 1983; sprayed acrylic and oil on Belgian linen, 9' x 6'. Collection of the artist.

sheets. She and Michael were holding the baby while the doctor cut and groped and stitched. . . . A halo of satisfied maternity seemed to suffuse her upper body, along with an almost unearthly glow, while the lower part of her body was cut and bleeding. . . .

Looking at that dripping, engorged cunt with the lifeless umbilical cord hanging out afterwards was really something —a view of the cunt I've certainly never seen before nor, I would imagine, have many other people.

I was shaking by the time I left.

I was particularly struck by the strength of the vulva as it expanded and contracted in childbirth; its power was overwhelming, having little to do with sex (although it is always referred to as a sex organ) and everything to do with the life force. I thought then that if everyone were brought up with a familiarity with the birthing vulva, it would be difficult for anyone to imagine the female gender as passive. Moreover, to my mind, the childbirth experience surely qualified as a heroic struggle, which caused me to wonder again at the absence of images and the mystery surrounding this subject. When I went home and thought about what I had just witnessed, I realized that I was gathering information and materials with the idea of becoming an expressive vehicle, putting my talents in the service of breaking the silence that surrounded the subject of birth in order to honor women and to demonstrate that when one gave birth, one could be thought of as participating in a universal life experience.

It seemed to me that another consequence of the absence of images was that women are not provided a way of seeing the birth experience in its larger, more universal dimension. It was striking that no woman I interviewed ever discussed her birth experience from anything but a personal perspective. If a man were to go to war without ever having been exposed to any paintings, plays, or movies valorizing the soldier's life, he would see only the dirt and grime, the bad rations, and the peril. He'd be unable to understand these in the larger context of the national importance of his task, the opportunity to transcend his limits and to achieve heroism through his courage. Why should a woman not have the possibility for this same experience when facing the comparably strenuous, often dangerous, and altogether challenging act of giving birth?

These insights helped shape my determination to make myself into a conduit for the unexpressed realities of the birth process, a goal that evolved out of my ideas, born in Fresno, of redefining the role of the artist so that my images might give voice to some of the unarticulated emotions of a larger community, thereby making an aesthetic contribution, while also helping to reconnect art to the fabric of human life. I also wanted to do something about the fact that, while men publicly celebrated almost everything they did, women seemed to deal with what were some of their most important experiences only in the privacy of the home. "If men had babies," I used to joke at the time, "there would be thousands of images of the crowning."

During that summer of 1980, my workdays again extended into the evenings as I continued my research while trying to complete the tapestry cartoon. As a result of having witnessed the birth of Karin and Michael's child, the imagery underwent some changes, specifically the tearing of the Earth/body in the center of the design. While still immersed in the struggle to finish the cartoon, I paid a visit to Sally Babson, a local dressmaker and quilter. She had made me a top for *The Dinner Party* opening in Boston, and at that time I had commissioned a small, quilted book as a present for Brian.

Because her quilting skills had impressed me, I wondered if she might be interested in doing other work with me. I was thinking about adapting the tapestry cartoon into a more simplified design, one that could be translated into different needle techniques. While engaged in *The Dinner Party,* I had had many occasions to visit needlework shops, which is where I first came into contact with the needlework kits that are used by thousands of stitchers. I had always found it maddening that even some of the educated and sophisticated needlewomen with whom I had worked would use these kits, whose trite sayings and overly cute drawings were, at least to my mind, insulting to their intelligence and demeaning to them as women. I can recall thinking that it might be interesting to infiltrate this sea of trivia with some better images. As I was completing the tapestry cartoon, I began thinking about how this one creation image might be made into a series of patterns or "kits" for different needle techniques.

Sally responded quite eagerly to my suggestion about doing more work together, and we arranged to meet at my studio so that she could see the cartoon. Once there, we began making plans to buy fabrics together for a quilt that would be smaller and simpler than the fourteen-foot tapestry but based upon a similar conceptual design. I was also interested in trying to create some images based upon some of the birth testimony I'd heard. At this point I was thinking of making a series of patterns that could be adapted for quilting and also embroidery. I planned to look for other stitchers who, like Sally, might like to participate in what I spontaneously dubbed the *Birth Project* in response to Sally's query about the title of this new work. I thought that I might even contact some of the many women who had written to me about their impassioned responses to *The Dinner Party*.

By the end of the summer, Sally had fabrics spread all over her living room in preparation for appliqueing, then starting to work on a creation quilt. Audrey was busily warping the loom in her Los Angeles studio, the first step in weaving a tapestry. I was feverishly trying to finish a series of drawings of birthing women in a variety of positions in order to reproduce them in different sizes, much as kits are done. I was hoping to initiate at least a few more projects before I left for New York at the end of September.

In the middle of the month there was to be a publication party for *Embroidering Our Heritage* at the San Francisco Museum of Modern Art, which would also be a sort of farewell party before I left. I had arranged to sublet Paula Harper's New York apartment for several months, as she had taken a teaching job elsewhere for the semester. Her place was only a few blocks away from where Jerry and I had lived twenty years earlier, though since then the East Village had become considerably more fashionable. I even thought that if things went well in New York, I might relocate there. As my plan for the *Birth Project* already involved the idea of people working in their own homes, there seemed no reason that I myself could not live anywhere. For even though I liked Benicia, the Bay Area art scene seemed somewhat provincial.

I had asked Sally to set up her quilting frame at the publication party as a kind of advertisement for interested stitchers; we were planning a meeting at the museum a few days after the book signing. To announce this upcoming gathering, Sally and I copied flyers to be given out at the publication party. We also made another of what were to be regular trips to Britex, a fabulous dry-goods store in San Francisco, buying more fabrics that could be used in the translation of my designs.

Shortly before the book signing, I was interviewed by Mildred Hamilton, a reporter for the *San Francisco Chronicle* who had previously written several sympathetic pieces about my work. This article was supposed to be about the needlework book, but she became so fascinated by the patterns and images she saw in the studio that she ended up focusing on the fact that I was starting another participatory project. Almost immediately after her article appeared, I began to receive letters from people interested in volunteering for the *Birth Project,* and when the publication party took place it was mobbed.

A few days later, thirty people came to the scheduled needleworkers' meeting, all of whom seemed quite enthused about the prospect of working with me. Fortunately, Mary Ross and Katie, both of whom had come for the publication party, had agreed to stay long enough to assist with what turned into a rather chaotic afternoon.

We began by going around the table, with each person introducing herself, sharing her background and interests, then showing examples of her needlework. I discussed my concept for the *Birth Project* and my plan to apply the same collaborative principles that had produced *The Dinner Party*—that is, people working on my images under my supervision, but in their own homes. There was some discussion about my insistence about retaining aesthetic control, until Sally pointed out that the reason she—and, she assumed other people— were drawn to work with me was the quality of the art that had resulted from precisely this process.

We talked about my patterns, which Sally and I had put up on the wall. I was extremely gratified by the response of the women present, most of whom had children. They all said that I had expressed many of the complex feelings they had had about their own birth experiences. The meeting went fairly smoothly until Sally and I started passing out the pieces, trying to match up each project with a woman's specific interest and set of skills. For some reason, suddenly, there was an uproar, with everyone yelling and grabbing patterns and materials.

Meanwhile MR and Katie were getting everyone to sign the contracts that I had prepared. These were relatively simple, vesting joint ownership of the finished works in each needleworker and me. At the same time, they were trying to record everyone's name and address and take individual Polaroid pictures to be put into a notebook with the information about each stitcher and the pattern she had chosen.

Then, abruptly, the room emptied. Even though the afternoon had been productive and exciting, it was also somewhat disconcerting to realize that I had just turned over numerous images and more than seven hundred dollars to total strangers, who had been provided with all the materials they would need to do a piece except the needles and thread. At this point MR turned to Sally and me and said, somewhat wryly, "I guess you-all are going to need some sort of help." For it was obvious that there would have to be some kind of organizational structure to handle these multiple projects, something that Sally and I had not really talked about. This was precisely the reason that when I was in Houston I had asked MR to consider working with me. I had hoped that she would think this project was right up her alley.

Later that day, after we'd had a chance to catch our breath, MR suggested that I do a presentation in Houston in early 1981 after *The Dinner Party* closed in New York. She said that it might give a sense of whether a comparable level of interest existed outside of California. She asked if I thought she could coordinate the *Birth Project* from Texas, traveling west whenever we deemed it necessary. As I was envisioning a decentralized project, I could not see why this would not be possible.

MR went back to Houston with the idea that she would return to Benicia in November, when I intended to come back for a few days in order to meet with the needleworkers and review their work. When

I took her to the airport, she announced that she planned to attend the New York opening. Even though I didn't know her all that well, I was pleased because I very much liked the idea of being surrounded by family and friends at this momentous occasion. Howard and Arleen were coming, as were Katie and Susan Grode. After chartering Through the Flower, Susan became my pro bono lawyer, adviser, and friend. She once told me that she would always be there for me, a promise that she has upheld for over twenty years.

Sally agreed to communicate with the needleworkers, answer any technical questions, and oversee their progress while I was away. She also offered to handle letters of inquiry, though she had no idea what she was letting herself in for. Over the next few weeks we were to receive over three hundred pieces of mail from eager volunteers. Sally sent polite refusals to those women she deemed unqualified in their needle skills, invited promising stitchers to the November review, and forwarded the most interesting letters to me. Some of these were from people who did needlepoint, a technique with which I had little experience.

The reason I mention all this is that I was then giving out only black-and-white reproductions of my original designs, whereas needlepoint is often done on top of hand-painted canvases. One woman wrote offering her skilled services in the preparation of a series of such canvases. It was one thing to give out blueprinted multiples of an image, however, and quite another to hand out original paintings to strangers. But the prospect of transforming this technique—usually associated with throw pillows or homely wall hangings—was irresistible, so I said I would work with her after I had returned from New York.

I left Benicia at the end of September, thinking about the long months since The Dinner Party had closed in San Francisco. At that time it had appeared that the work had no future. But thanks to the outpouring of support from around the country and Gelon's dedication and hard work, the piece was being exhibited in a New York museum.

Because Embroidering Our Heritage was being published in conjunction with the opening, the Brooklyn Museum was working with Doubleday Anchor to obtain media coverage. Perhaps one reason my work had attracted so much press attention over the years is that the books I have written about my projects have been put out by mainstream publishers. The public-relations resources of such a publisher combined with those of a major art institution can produce more media coverage than is normally accorded art exhibitions, which are usually dealt with only in the art press.

In New York, for example, this joint venture resulted in a beautiful television piece on CBS network news, a *People* magazine spread, an appearance on the *Bill Moyers Show,* and, later that fall, a six-minute interview on the *Today* show with then-host Jane Pauley. Although such media attention has helped bring my art to a large audience—which has always been one of my goals—it has also produced some negative consequences in the art world, where I have sometimes been accused of being a "media phenomenon" rather than a real artist.

The *Dinner Party* opening was spectacular. Loretta arranged for an elegant pre-opening cocktail party at the Fifth Avenue Doubleday suite, and Howard, Arleen, and I greatly enjoyed being chauffeured to Brooklyn in the limousine that Michael Botwinick provided. We were overjoyed by the sight that greeted us, for there were thousands of people at the opening. The only unpleasantness was a fistfight that broke out among visitors who were less than sanguine about having to wait in a long line in order to see the show.

The next few weeks were full of interviews and lectures, in New York and elsewhere on the East Coast. Katie and MR took turns with Loretta to accompany me, MR having announced that she was appointing herself my protector and adviser. Everywhere I went, there were enthusiastic crowds, standing ovations, and considerable hoopla. The highlight was a packed lecture at the Harvard Institute for Policy Studies, where I presented a talk on the relationship between art and politics, in which I questioned some of the traditional categories and evaluative standards for art.

Like most of the groups I addressed at this time, the Harvard audience only wanted to talk about *The Dinner Party,* despite my desire to expand the discussion. In retrospect, it seems reasonable that this would be the case; after all, the piece had just opened in New York, the center of the art world. But I can recall becoming frustrated, and

also a little trapped, by people calling *The Dinner Party* the "culmination" of my career. I knew that it was just the beginning of my
mature work, and I wanted it to be seen as such.

Also, I was considerably more sensitive and vulnerable than I appeared in public, and I actually found all the attention somewhat
frightening. Most of my friends knew that I was nowhere near as tough
as I was thought to be, which was the reason they took care of me. I
often broke down or developed a variety of physical manifestations of
my feelings. For example, I would come down with laryngitis when
I couldn't stand talking about *The Dinner Party* anymore, or I'd develop a bladder infection because I got "pissed off" having to answer
the same questions again and again. Finally, I could not bear the
unreal way in which people were beginning to treat me because of my
seeming celebrity status.

When I came back after several weeks of travel, Michael Botwinick
reported that the Brooklyn Museum was mobbed consistently, with
people waiting in line as long as five hours to see the show (in fact,
The Dinner Party turned out to be the museum's most successful exhibition). There were positive pieces in *Ms.* and the *Village Voice,* while
New York magazine declared that "*The Dinner Party* had caused more
furor than any other contemporary sculpture." John Perrault wrote a
glowing review for the now-defunct *SoHo News* that praised *The Dinner
Party* as the "most magnificent and moving work of art" he had ever
seen.

Only someone as utterly naive as I was at the time could have
imagined that all this positive press could counterbalance the article
that appeared on the front page of the "Friday Arts and Leisure"
section of *The New York Times.* Written by Hilton Kramer, then regarded as the most important art critic in America, the review described *The Dinner Party* as "grotesque kitsch" and little more than
vaginas on plates. Then a few weeks later, in a kind of double
whammy, Robert Hughes, the major art writer for *Time* magazine,
went after the piece with equal venom. In his piece, which was laced
with nasty references to pudenda, Hughes singled out the needleworked runners for the only faint hint of praise. But he went on to
say that "regrettably," these had been designed by me—that if only

the stitchers had been able to fashion their own designs they might have attained great visual heights.

Perhaps I was exhausted from so many uninterrupted weeks of public activity by the time the Hughes piece came out, or maybe it was its particular mixture of ignorance and misogyny, but it really got to me. I bought the magazine as I was on my way to meet film-maker Claudia Weill for dinner in the Village, and I read it walking down the street. When I arrived at the restaurant Claudia was sitting at the bar. I walked up to her clutching the magazine, sat down on a stool, put my head down on the bartop, and sobbed.

But I think it is important to emphasize that I was *personally* hurt and embarrassed by the Hughes article, as I thought about how millions of people were going to read his low opinion of my work: Because there had been such extensive national coverage in the general press, most of it with such a positive tone, I did not at all realize what the Hughes and Kramer pieces might mean in terms of my career. I still assumed that their hostility toward my work was nothing more than their particular opinions. The degree to which I did not *"get it"* amazes even me; but to tell the truth, it would be many years before I was able to comprehend the degree to which art world attitudes are controlled by the assessments of the very few. And once these folks publicly render their verdicts, they are rarely inclined to change their minds.

During this same period, a writer for the *New York Review of Books* discussed going to the Brooklyn Museum three times, only to see long lines of people waiting to see *The Dinner Party*. He was quite convinced that all those people were wrong in their positive assessment of the work; in his opinion, it was entirely worthless. I chose not to read this article because by this time, I was beginning to feel like a punching bag.

Although I had no real understanding of all the ramifications of this critical assault, I did come to realize that I was not going to secure any of the professional opportunities for which I had hoped. In sharp contrast to what happens to many male artists, who are usually besieged with offers from the major dealers after an important museum show, I received no phone calls of interest or invitations to lunch, followed by polite inquiries about my future "career plans." And it wasn't just the dealers who were uninterested: No other American museum would exhibit *The Dinner Party* after its New York showing, no matter how much community pressure was brought to bear. And since that time, people sympathetic to my work have told me stories about how, when they mentioned my name to influential art world figures, they were met with a wall of resistance.

One more result of the New York critics' negative assessments was that the discourse about *The Dinner Party* seemed to become peculiarly skewed, not only in the art world but also among numerous feminist theorists. After the Brooklyn Museum showing, the phrase about vaginas on plates began to be repeated, mantra-like, even in feminist circles. As I was far away from the universities, where feminist theory was then being hotly debated, I had no idea that a number of academic feminists were apparently accepting this description of the piece and, as a result, describing me as an "essentialist" (whatever that means), supposedly degrading women through my use of vulval imagery. When I became aware of this charge years later, I could not figure out how seemingly erudite women could completely miss the point— understood by so many less sophisticated viewers—that *The Dinner Party* entirely *celebrates* women's sexuality, history, and crafts.

Before leaving New York, I stood in the museum gallery one last time. As I watched the hundreds of viewers silently walking around *The Dinner Party* table—seemingly engrossed in and enthralled by the art and the history it conveys—I thought that, ultimately, the evaluation of the work boiled down to the question: Who decides? I recognized that once again, I would have to make a choice as to whether to stand by my own experience of the piece—its beauty and importance—or to accept other people's opinions. It would be glib to say that I just picked myself up, dusted off my bruises, and went on with my artmaking life—but this would be untrue, as the New York experience really hurt. It also denied me what I most desired: support for my art.

In due time, I would realize that one does not die from bad reviews or negative criticism, no matter how excruciating they might be to read. I would also come to understand that controversy usually accompanies any attempt to introduce new ideas or achieve even a degree of change. In fact, it might be said that one measure of my accomplishment was the degree to which *The Dinner Party* continues to stimulate dialogue—even now, years after its exhibition tour.

Given the virulence of the New York critical assault, I suppose that some artists would have stopped making art altogether or at least retreated from public view. But these were not options for me, probably because of how I was raised. I was always encouraged to believe in myself and trust my own experience, a trait that has been tested many times. Whenever this happens, I remind myself of something my cousin Howard says: "In the face of life's adversities, one either gives up or gets up and in our family, *we get up*."

It was probably a blessing that I was still so naive about the far-reaching powers of the New York art critics. Moreover, I was not alone in choosing to disregard their opinions. No matter what they wrote, it only served to make community groups more determined to get *The Dinner Party* shown. More and more people were forming committees, raising money, and pressuring institutions—and when they encountered disinterest or resistance, they found alternative spaces and installed and staffed the show with volunteers.

Eventually *The Dinner Party* would travel to several more sites in America, then Canada, England, Scotland, Germany, and Australia. It would be shown in a total of fourteen venues in six countries and seen by nearly one million viewers. This tour was the result of what became a worldwide grass-roots effort, which, as far as I know, is altogether unprecedented in the art world. Much of the credit for this victory lies with Gelon, who continued to work with the various community groups and act as administrator even after she went to law school in New York, then moved to London (where she now practices art and entertainment law).

Although it was absolutely amazing that *The Dinner Party* was able to be exhibited so widely—given the ongoing art world opposition—I kept wishing that it could always be safely exhibited in museums (which it was about half the time in countries other than the United States, most often as a result of intense community organizing), so that I would never have to worry about leaky roofs, faulty wiring, or untrained installation crews. The piece was imperiled in at least several of its venues, kept from irreversible harm only through the devoted attentions of Gelon, Peter, and Susan.

This dedicated crew handled most of the logistics of the installation, their modest salaries and expenses paid for by exhibition rental fees paid to Through the Flower. *The Dinner Party* tour, which continued until 1988, inevitably shaped the structure of the corporation, which became the touring agency and sometimes the fiscal receiver for the monies raised by the various community groups.

It was extremely fortunate that we had established the corporation. Certainly, at the time we did so, none of us could ever have predicted the degree to which Through the Flower would become essential to my career as an artist. Slowly, the board would expand as various women around the country came forward—many of them, like MR, after seeing the impact of *The Dinner Party* in their community—to gradually assume most of the fiduciary and governing authority for the organization. Without their support, I do not know how I would have been able to continue working as an artist, at least not on the scale that the framework of the corporation has afforded me.

By the time I finally left New York, I was exhausted and run down and, therefore, extremely grateful that MR offered to take me to Santa Fe for the Christmas holidays. She owned an old adobe house on the historic Canyon Road which she promised would provide a restorative retreat. She and I flew separately to New Mexico, meeting at the Albuquerque airport, where we were greeted by a ferocious thunderstorm. The rain slowly subsided as we drove north. When we reached the La Bajada hill and began our descent into Santa Fe, the storm suddenly stopped, leaving in its place the perfectly clear, crisp air that has drawn so many artists to New Mexico, along with a spectacular double rainbow arching over the mesas. MR told me that this was an especially good omen, one that meant my life circumstances would soon improve.

Chapter Six

Is There an Alternative
to the Art World?

*I*n November, as planned, I had returned to California for a few days to see what had happened with the *Birth Project* and whether any work was being done on the pieces we had started in September. I had spoken to Sally several times, always with the same question: Were people stitching? I was relieved to discover that work seemed to be going forward, though at a slower pace than I had hoped. Looking at the in-progress pieces, I noticed that when the needleworkers transferred my patterns to the fabrics in preparation for stitching the images, the line quality of their drawings was far from precise. Moreover, the thread-color choices they had made were not to my liking. As visual rigor is important to me and color one of my strong suits, I decided that I had best transfer the images myself and also establish their tonal ranges.

By then there were already a number of people waiting for projects. As I had limited time, I worked frantically, trying to get some more pieces ready. Sally informed me that several women had complained that the fabrics we had given them were puckering, so we decided that batting, or backing fabrics, should be placed behind the cloth so it would stay flat. While transferring more images to newly purchased fabric for the waiting stitchers, I suddenly became anxious about whether this whole project was such a good idea. But then Sally backed the designs I had prepared and she put them on the wall, and the moment I saw them I felt reassured that I was conceptualizing this work appropriately. The softening that took place, even before any needlework was added, helped transform the raw and somewhat graphic nature of the images, which is precisely what I had hoped would happen.

When I got home in January, it was to discover that the *Birth Project* was exploding. Information about my new undertaking had apparently been spreading, through the media as well as word of mouth. We were receiving ten letters of inquiry a day; women seemed to be coming out of the woodwork. People were calling with suggestions that would not only give me the opportunity to design for needlepoint but for other techniques that I had never tried. Others proposed various methods of generating multiples. For example, one person offered to silk-screen some of my designs onto fabric, while another put forth the idea of applying her tie-dye and batik skills to a series of pieces. It seemed obvious that without such help, there would be no way for me to create enough work to provide for what seemed an enormous amount of interest. Another reason these suggestions were so appealing to me was that these proposed methods would allow stitchers to create an array of translations of one pattern while also allowing me considerable visual control of the base image.

My first weeks back in Benicia were extremely busy, which was probably a good thing, as it gave me little time to think about how devastating the New York experience had been. Before long I was meeting with various people, arranging for images to be silk-screened and patterns to be batiked and tie-dyed; then I started painting needlepoint canvases. Toward the end of January, Sally and I held another review. MR, with whom I had been in constant contact, flew in to provide organizational support.

The first review in November had been limited to dealing with the most immediate technical problems. For this second meeting, Sally and I wanted to work with each needleworker in greater depth, so we'd planned to set aside an entire weekend. By this point there were already almost twenty projects under way, with still more qualified stitchers waiting. We invited everyone to attend, scheduling appointments on the half-hour to look at works in progress and give out new pieces. By noon of the first day we were already running behind, so Sally, MR, and I worked exceedingly long hours. Because my studio was unheated and Benicia quite cold and damp at that time of the year, everyone spent a lot of time huddling under blankets and sharing sweaters or jackets.

This review process, when work would be submitted to me for approval, was fundamental to the *Birth Project.* Also, these reviews were a time for needleworkers to have the opportunity for some interaction with each other and to see other pieces that were under way. At the initial meeting in September, I had requested that everyone do something called "translation samples" before they started on the actual pieces and that they bring them to the January review. These were intended to give each stitcher a chance to think about how best to "translate" my design or embellish it with thread and also how to bring her particular technical expertise into the framework of the image.

Needleworkers often have a way of stitching that is unique to them, but the problem is that these special methods generally have no relationship to subject matter. As an example, one woman specialized in bullion knots, which have a distinct texture and look. She used this stitch quite indiscriminately in her own needlework, whereas I thought it might be better applied for specific visual effects, like simulating hair or to make it seem that flesh was crawling.

I had anticipated that this January review would consist almost entirely of these types of aesthetic issues. But we ended up spending considerably more time dealing with the needleworkers' personal difficulties than with creative problems. For it seemed that once the women had brought their pieces home, most of them had been faced with numerous obstacles, ranging from a lack of confidence in their own abilities to resistance from their mates. Over the weekend we listened to an endless list of reasons why nearly every woman had been unable to stitch regularly, which helped to explain the slow pace of the work that I had observed in November. To my dismay, I discovered that many of the women had always found it difficult to make time for the things they wanted to do, whether it was their own needlework or the *Birth Project* images, to which they had so eagerly committed themselves just a short while ago.

As I am accustomed to working a minimum of ten hours a day, I found it startling to realize that for many of these women, devoting even a few hours a week to stitching was a significant problem. For one thing, few had disciplined work habits, which I tried to address by suggesting that they commit themselves to a regular schedule, putting in at least ten hours of stitching weekly. When they objected, I explained that I could see from their work when they put down their needles, that the stitching appeared disrupted. In my opinion, the rhythm of the needle establishes an energy that is essential to the quality of the stitching; sustaining this rhythm is an important ability. The idea that the interruptions in their stitching were evident shocked most of the women, as they seemed to think it made no difference whatsoever if they worked for only moments at a time.

And then there were the guilt feelings; that no matter what they did, they would be letting someone down. If they stitched, they felt guilty for neglecting their families, particularly their children; if they didn't stitch, they felt as if they were failing me. Add to this the demands of jobs, housework, and sometimes even school, and it was easy to see why so many of the women described themselves as constantly stressed out and conflicted. Moreover, most of them confessed to myriad unrealized ambitions. Though some had studied art in college and even dreamed that they might become artists, after marriage and giving birth to children, they found themselves mired in domestic life, often taking up needlework in order to find some kind of creative outlet. Others declared themselves ardent feminists who wanted to feel that they were making a contribution to enlarged opportunities for women, particularly their daughters. Still others were devoted needleworkers, angry that needlework was not considered art. What they all had in common was a belief that by working with me they would be able to accomplish something important to them—something, all admitted, that they felt they could never hope to achieve on their own.

However one wishes to interpret these self-evaluations—as low self-esteem, the result of bad childhoods, oppression, or whatever—I have always believed in accepting people wherever they were in terms of their development. This approach was basic to my teaching methods and to the principles by which *The Dinner Party* studio was organized. I was convinced of the importance of encouraging people to grow from a base of self-acceptance, for in my opinion, real empowerment begins by honestly confronting oneself. Though few would admit it, it is probable that most of the *Birth Project* participants hoped that by working with me, everything that had previously prevented them from achievement would magically disappear.

Another significant hindrance seemed to be that most of the women were encountering the presumptions of their families, friends, and community that they should put their own needs last. We heard about angry husbands, who expressed considerable resentment that their wives wanted to stitch rather than spend time with them; about family members who came to town and simply assumed that the women would drop everything and squire them around; about calls from school-board members and PTA officials insisting that the women help with one or another seemingly pressing crisis. They also seemed to be hearing the accusation that they were being exploited because they were working on my images without pay.

The needleworkers all stated that they felt quite baffled by the way this issue of exploitation kept coming up, no matter how many times they insisted that they did not feel exploited, that they had chosen to work with me, and that they *would* profit from any sales. I was then forced to admit that my original idea about joint ownership of the finished needlework had proven entirely unworkable for several reasons. The first was my decision to paint needlepoint canvases, including some of so large a scale that they could only be accomplished by groups of stitchers.

The previous fall, some people had asked about the possibility of doing group projects, something that, before I decided to take up needlepoint design, I had no plans to offer. However, I had begun to reconsider this idea, not only because of the tantalizing prospect of designing for needlepoint but also because I realized that such group efforts would allow more people to participate. But as MR and I pointed out at this January review, we could not figure out how to deal with multiple ownership of these pieces if they were ever sold. Given that people move, change names (upon marriage), even die, how would we keep track of everyone, much less their heirs?

Even more of a problem was that the *Birth Project* was taking off so quickly. At that time we were financing the pieces one at a time. I was putting up all the money for patterns and fabrics, which was becoming a rather expensive proposition. If the project kept expanding, how would we be able to fund and also coordinate so many works? MR and I had been thinking about putting the *Birth Project* under the sponsorship of Through the Flower, which would allow for the establishment of some formal organizational framework and also the possibility of accepting donations and applying for grants.

Everyone thought this a good idea, even though no profit-sharing would be possible in the event that any of the pieces were sold (this would be illegal when operating out of a nonprofit structure). After some discussion, with everyone insisting that profit was not their motive in working with me, we all agreed to discard the original contract in favor of turning over all finished works to Through the Flower. In exchange, the corporation would furnish all materials and provide administrative support.

In addition to solving some of the practical problems that I have been describing, I hoped that by giving all the work to Through the Flower, the accusation of exploitation that seemed to be starting up again would be forever defused. Like all the needleworkers, I would be working as a volunteer. This meant that throughout the five years of the project, I would not receive any direct financial benefit, not even a salary. I would support myself as I always had: independently. Moreover, any money that I earned above what I needed to live on was funneled back into the project, which prompted me to sometimes laughingly tell the needleworkers that at least they didn't have to pay to work.

However, even this did not stop the misperception that the stitchers were being exploited while I was laughing all the way to the bank. As to grants, I must have been my usual naive self in anticipating such support. Despite dozens of grant proposals written by MR and a volunteer fund-raising team, we would receive just one, which was only for $6,000. Fortunately, we would be sustained by numerous private donations, provided by people who believed in my work generally and the *Birth Project* in particular.

At the end of the January review, I felt both exhausted and conflicted. On the one hand, I desperately wanted to do another big project. The subject of birth was so large and virtually unexplored that it seemed to lend itself to monumental scale. Moreover, one of the things that I had learned about myself in *The Dinner Party* studio was that I am at my best creatively when involved in a large-scale, complex project that is challenging on multiple levels.

I now feel forced to ask my reader's indulgence while I take a short detour. Recently I have come to understand that numerous feminists have been arguing that aspiring to the monumental is inherently a male trait. Why does this make me livid with rage? Perhaps it is because, after so many centuries of effort, women are finally throwing off the many constraints that have prevented us from reaching toward the highest levels of achievement, a struggle that, in my opinion, carries with it a profound sense of satisfaction.

The Dinner Party taught me two important lessons about achievement: first, that there have been many women who have aspired to high levels of accomplishment; and second, that real achievement is impossible without substantive support. For centuries, talented women were thwarted by so many obstacles, yet some few managed to sufficiently overcome these so that their voices could be heard by us centuries later. I am so grateful that they were able to manage this and am entirely unwilling to allow such aspiration to be considered the province of men. Why shouldn't we make monuments of all kinds? I would love to see them everywhere, and in fact, I feel altogether deprived by the presence of so many memorials to and by men and so few devoted to members of my own sex.

As to support, what I had realized from my study of women's

history was that when women *were* able to achieve in their chosen occupation, it was because they enjoyed some significant degree of support, be it from royalty, church, state, family, or friends. As an example, *The Dinner Party* could have only been accomplished because I had a team that stood behind me and around me.

Previously, I had been able to find some modicum of support for my work, but only to a certain level; then I would hit a brick wall. Unlike the artist Christo or the environmental sculptor James Turrell, an old friend, I have never been able to garner millions of dollars for my work, although, like them, I have also had big ideas. A good example of this was my "Atmospheres," executed in the late 1960s and early 1970s, when few artists were doing such process pieces and none that I knew of were working in fireworks. For several years I did smoke pieces that cost only a few hundred dollars, aided by friends who traveled with me around California to help stage these events. After a while, I was able to get some galleries and museums to finance a few works that cost a little more. Finally, in 1974, the Oakland Museum commissioned me to do "A Butterfly for Oakland" as part of their Sculpture in the City show. This piece, which required $2,500 and a large crew, was performed on the banks of Lake Merritt at sundown. Over a period of seventeen minutes, an enormous butterfly with a wingspan of two hundred feet came into being, erupted with color, then died in a Life/Death/Transfiguration image.

Although I knew that I was capable of going much further with these "Atmospheres"—envisioning multicolored plumes of smoke billowing up from the Grand Canyon or cascading down huge mountainsides—I was unable to obtain the commissions or financial backing that makes such ventures possible. Instead, frustrated at not being able to follow my ideas to fruition, I stopped doing "Atmospheres" and, as had happened numerous times before, started on another path. Eventually this led me to *The Dinner Party,* which again was conceived in monumental terms. For once I had been able to realize my vision, and seeing its impact made it seem ridiculous to go back to solitary artmaking and small-scale work.

All of this contributed to my conflicted emotions following the January review. On the one hand, I wanted to do another large-scale project for the reasons that I've already outlined. And although it was hardly my primary motivation, I also wanted to demonstrate that *The Dinner Party* had not been a fluke; that I could accomplish another such undertaking if that was what I chose to do. But I had no real support base to build on—no large studio, no staff, no funds. All I really had—in addition to MR's willingness to help and Sally's skills—was this enormous outpouring of interest from people wishing to work with me. The problem was, as had become quite apparent from this review, these offers came with a caveat: I would have to make a commitment to support these women as they struggled to overcome all the obstacles they faced and also help them to wrest some semblance of order from what appeared to be terribly fragmented lives. Creative endeavors require at least some degree of uninterrupted time, and from the evidence thus far, this seemed to be one thing most of these women didn't have.

I felt caught: I wanted to move ahead as an artist but realized that making this commitment to the needleworkers would mean that, in addition to making art, I would have to provide a level of emotional support that promised to be nothing short of exhausting. On the other hand, I felt as if I had no choice. The male-dominated art world had evidenced its disdain for my work by depriving me of the opportunities and support that I believed I had proven myself as deserving of.

My troubled state of mind was reflected in a recurrent nightmare that I began having at this time. I would dream that a man was pursuing me, intent upon destroying me. I kept running and running but couldn't get away, waking up just as he was about to catch me. My anguish also manifested itself in an increasing obsession about my weight. Although I had never been fat, I had tended to be somewhat stocky, until I started running long distances. Even though my many hours of exercise had whittled down my body and changed my shape, for the first time I became overly concerned with even minor fluctuations on the scale, castigating myself for eating when I was probably feeling uncomfortable about the high price I was paying for having evidenced my creative power.

Making the level of commitment to the needleworkers that seemed necessary was frightening to me for many reasons. I knew that I would be confronted with everything that I had run away from when I left Chicago many years before. I had never wanted to be like my mother or her friends, rejecting an "ordinary" woman's life in order to pattern mine upon men's. Moreover, given my life history and my feeling that my mother had entirely failed me when I needed her most, becoming so embroiled with women terrified me. But perhaps my reader is wondering how I could say this after spending so many years in the worlds of the china-painter and embroiderer, not to mention *The Dinner Party* studio.

To tell the truth, I was a visitor in the world of women's crafts, intent upon taking these out of their existing context and transforming them into fine art. As for *The Dinner Party,* when I started it I was part of the Los Angeles art community, and support came from both the art establishment and the many volunteers. And even though people worked in my studio, I had managed to stay aloof; in fact, doing so had probably been essential in order to get any work done. I can still remember one woman becoming furious with me because I wouldn't let her tell me about her marital problems in the middle of a workday. Thursday nights were the only time I made myself available for such conversation, which was one reason I found our potlucks so tiring.

When I began work on the *Birth Project,* I had planned that people would work in their own homes—not only because this is what they preferred, but because I did not want so many people in my studio again. In order to preserve my psychic privacy during *The Dinner Party* days, I had closed myself off from many of the interactions that went on in the studio, which is probably why I had so often felt as if I were separate from the group even while I was its essential core. In structuring the *Birth Project,* I had not anticipated that, because the participants would be taking my images into their houses, whatever was happening in their lives would impact so heavily upon the art. The January review made it all too clear that I would have to be willing to deal with all that this might mean.

After all, I am not a therapist, nor did I want to be; rather, I wanted to make art. How to accomplish this while also providing the necessary support to those who were offering to support me was the challenge. It was a trade-off, and in my opinion, once I made the commitment I gave as good as I got. I brought to bear my years of work with women—my time in Fresno, Cal-Arts, the Women's Building, and *The Dinner Party* studio—along with my intuition, facilitating skills, and, more, my feminism. This last shaped my notion that I have a personal obligation to other women that involves extending my hand.

However, throughout the *Birth Project,* I would feel torn, except when I was in the studio, when the long hours of creating would make this personal effort worthwhile. But one consequence of my decision to make this commitment was that I had little time for any sort of personal life. When I wasn't making images, doing reviews, or counseling troubled needleworkers, all I wanted was to be by myself: to exercise, rest, or find a way to get my energy back. Not only was I emotionally exhausted most of the time, but I was living almost entirely within the framework of a women's community.

This put me in a place that made relationships with men seem out of the question, though my longing for male companionship would not subside. But the gap between me and most men appeared too large; I couldn't traverse it. And I kept wondering whether, at that moment in history, it was even possible to live a life such as mine, which was so totally devoted to women's issues and the expression of women's experience, while being involved with a man.

Over the course of the next few years I would be almost totally involved in what might best be described as hand-to-hand combat with all the obstacles the women were facing. With Sally as my ally, I pushed, supported, taught, and guided them as they struggled to transcend the limits of their lives. Sally occupied a singular place in that she was a lot like the other needleworkers, facing many of the same external hindrances and internal blocks. But as she was to realize, she was far more capable, and stronger, than she had ever dreamed. As she took on more and more responsibility in the *Birth Project,* soon becoming its official needlework supervisor, she discovered the range of her talents, which were remarkable, to say the least.

In addition to Sally, Mary Ross generously decided to bring her many resources to bear on the organization of the *Birth Project.* Without her support, neither the artist nor the art project would have stood a chance. First, she helped me rent the apartment next door to mine, which she set up as a *Birth Project* office, instituting procedures that allowed us to find out more about prospective needleworkers than just their needle skills. We began sending out a "tell us more" letter, in which interested applicants were asked a series of questions intended to help Sally and me evaluate which women seemed the most prepared for all that working on a *Birth Project* piece had actually turned out to entail.

Sometime after the January review in Benicia, I presented a slide lecture about the *Birth Project* in Houston, showing some of the initial images and discussing my ideas for extending the participatory nature of the project to people in Houston and other parts of the country. At the end of my talk, when I asked how many folks would be interested in working with me, a hundred and fifty hands went up. MR offered to set up a space in a building next to her bookstore (whose operation she was slowly turning over to the staff) where the *Birth Project* could have an office and where everyone could meet with me for regular reviews. We thought that we might set up other such regional offices as the project grew.

By the time of this lecture, I had decided that it would be important to establish an archive containing information about worldwide historical and contemporary birth practices, a resource I could draw upon for image-making. (This turned out to be more difficult than I had anticipated, as many countries keep no maternal mortality statistics.) I also began to develop a questionnaire that would elicit information about women's birth experiences in other parts of the United States. Several women in Houston volunteered to begin compiling such an archive and to help organize the mailing and collating of information from this survey. Thus began the research wing of the *Birth Project,* which was soon being coordinated out of both Houston and Benicia.

Before too long, both offices were beehives of activity, with their own volunteer administrators. MR was flying back and forth between Texas and California, trying to keep track of all that was going on.

By late spring there were almost fifty projects under way and many dozens of people involved. Some were stitching alone, others in groups, many were doing research, and a few were helping in each office. Two needlepoint groups had formed, one in Houston and the other in Benicia. No one had room in her house for the large, specially built frames on which the large canvases were to be rolled and worked. Instead, the groups set them up, one to each space, and before we knew it there was a steady stream of visitors to both offices. It seemed that people just couldn't get enough of watching the stitchers select, strip apart, then insert and blend the brilliantly colored threads into the tiny holes that characterize eighteen-mesh needlepoint canvas.

Imagine just one project. A letter of inquiry arrives and must be answered with a request for more information about the person and her skills. Then, when this query is satisfied, a decision has to be made whether to accept the stitcher and, if so, which project to assign. Moreover, for every application that is endorsed, ten have to be turned away with polite letters of rejection or reassuring phone calls. The new needleworker has to be scheduled to pick up the piece and meet with Sally and me, or the work has to be packed and shipped to her along with extensive instructions. Materials have to be ordered and sent regularly and reviews—either in person or through the mail—scheduled and recorded. Multiply the number of projects by fifty, double or triple the number of people involved, and add to all this the continuous questions to be fielded, and one can see how intensely busy MR, Sally, and I became.

I don't know how MR was able to handle all the administrative work, which for some time she did almost single-handedly. As the project expanded, she was aided by a small staff, a few paid but most volunteers, who brought with them many of the same anxieties, insecurities, and problems that so many of the stitchers had. Eventually we established what might be best described as a national creative network whose interactions were facilitated by the U.S. Postal Service, Federal Express, UPS, and AT&T. I shall always be thankful to MR because, like Gelon before her, she made it possible for me to bring all my focus to the array of artmaking problems associated with a major project, along with the particular challenges of the *Birth Project*.

In addition to creating images and supporting the needleworkers while they brought their skills to bear on the work, I began to grapple with three issues that I believed were crucial to the organization of the *Birth Project*: that is, the problems of audience, context, and distribution (exhibition). In terms of audience, many artists are fond of saying that they work for nobody but themselves, but in my opinion, this is a conceit. Consciously or unconsciously, I believe that everyone shapes art for an intended audience and that most serious artists envision their finished works presented in pristine galleries or airy white museum spaces.

For example, *The Dinner Party* was conceived to be exhibited in major museums, and I had wrongly assumed that its broad audience success would appeal to such institutions. But despite the negative art world response, I liked that my work was being seen and appreciated by so many people. One thing that was very striking about *The Dinner Party* audience was its diversity. Not only were there individuals from the art, feminist, and gay communities, but also traditional families with children, elderly folks, students, china-painters, and needleworkers. In fact, over the years, many people have told me that they still remember the conversations they had while waiting in line to see the piece, probably because they talked to people with whom they might never have interacted otherwise.

As long ago as the early 1970s, I had begun to think about the problem of audience when I tried to figure out how to bridge the gap between the art and feminist communities, both of whom were then seeing my work. Art world viewers brought with them a sophisticated aesthetic knowledge, along with a general ignorance about women's issues. Conversely, most feminists were often less aware of how to decipher contemporary art but far more understanding of women's circumstances and history. My efforts to create art that was intelligible to both audiences influenced the way that I had shaped *The Dinner Party,* whose popular success brought me new and interesting challenges about how to continue reaching such a heterogeneous audience.

After New York, I concluded that the reason I had come up against so much resistance in the art world was that there was no place for art that so openly expressed a female perspective as did *The Dinner Party.* However, since then there has been a good deal of art being made and shown that clearly features a female point of view. As a result, I have come to believe that the more important reason for the hostile response to my work from many members of the art community is that I entirely rejected the coded language forms of contemporary art.

In *The Dinner Party,* as in all my subsequent art, I *deliberately* discarded the visual posture and markings that typify most contemporary art. To my mind, it was desirable to break out of the limits imposed by the overly abstract or self-referential nature of the prevailing art language because only by so doing could art communicate to a broad audience. Since the end of World War II, art has increasingly become the province of the "cognoscenti," those few who are versed in the history of modern art. To people outside this world, most contemporary art is baffling even when the subject matter might actually be something they care about. But because the form in which it is presented more often than not renders the content obscure, the potential communication between artist and most viewers is blocked.

At this time I did not really understand the possibility that one explanation for the art world's fury at *The Dinner Party* was this issue of "decoding" art. When I went to Fresno in the early 1970s, I did so not only to create the Feminist Art program but to see if I could figure out how to reverse the process I had gone through in becoming a professional artist, which basically involved learning how to code my content—or, as I like to say, to talk in tongues. Although I had to do this in order to be taken seriously in the L.A. art community, I later came to the conclusion that this coded art language is actually the symbol face for a set of values and attitudes that are *encoded into* these forms and that serve white men. My experiences with *The Dinner Party* made me realize that, although it vociferously protests otherwise, the art world is actually a mirror of the larger society, in that it exists primarily to support the creation and distribution of art by and about men. There are individuals who dissent from this position, and some of them have supported my work and/or that of other artists whose art evidences a dissenting point of view. But they cannot single-handedly overturn a larger system which promotes an art language that is in and of itself exclusive.

Within this system, those in power are the "experts," adept at decoding this rather incomprehensible art language; and because the system is so undemocratic, their power is almost complete. Women participate but only marginally. As dealers, critics, historians, and curators, they are deluded into thinking they have real power, when in fact their positions depend upon being willing to support what men do and define as important. As to women artists, although many more are now exhibiting, in order to fit in and be accepted, they still have to work within these coded language forms. The irony of this situation is that even when their work evidences female subject matter, as much of it now does, the use of these forms often renders the work unintelligible to most women, thereby depriving these artists of a broader base of potential support. This problem seems particularly pertinent at the moment, when arts funding is shrinking while grad-uate schools continue to pump out hundreds (if not thousands) of students who desire to be artists. It seems quite obvious that the art system, which has always been quite small, cannot accommodate all of the work being done by male artists, much less add to its already strained resources the amount of art being made by their female peers.

Moreover, many artists seem to have forgotten the larger purpose of art, which in my opinion is to communicate. I for one am glad for the recent collapse of the art market, which so many other members of the art community bemoan. For the first time in many years, artists will have an opportunity to rethink their role, the function of art, and how to help the larger society understand the importance of what we do. This should be particularly helpful to women artists, who, if you ask me, have nothing much to lose in reevaluating their careers, as most still face considerable discrimination, particularly in the upper reaches of the art world.

However, artists generally suffer from an incredible lack of con-sciousness in that, like women before the advent of the Women's Movement, they fail to see that they are oppressed. One result of this is that because there are far too many of us for the tiny art system, dealers enjoy a buyer's market in which they seem to feel that they can be as rude to us as they choose and we rarely protest. A particularly egregious example of the arrogance with which artists are treated is the Art Dealers Association's continued opposition to something that artists of all persuasions other than the visual enjoy; that is, royalties.

As I am both an artist and a writer, the contrast between the art and literary worlds is quite apparent (and shocking) to me. All writers receive royalties on their published works, but when artists attempted to establish the Resale Royalty Act—which would grant us a meager 5 percent of the profit on any work resold for more than $1,000—dealers prevented it from becoming part of the accepted procedure in the art world. But it is not just dealers who oppose artists' rights, for when a well-known artist attempted to make this contract part of her sales agreements, one major museum immediately threatened to cancel her scheduled exhibition, believing, I am sure, that the curator could easily find dozens of artists so desirous of exposure that they would be far more compliant.

One could say that with *The Dinner Party* in particular, I had openly broken the "code" of contemporary art. But long before that, I had begun to reject the traditional artist's role, which might be best described as quietly working in your studio and waiting for one of the "experts" to discover you, bring your work to the marketplace (in this case, the art world), and decode it (at least partially) while extolling its merits. In retrospect, it seems clear that I had never felt comfortable with the prescribed role of the artist, nor could I accept the narrow confines of art's place in contemporary society. After New York, I started to rethink everything, asking myself: Who is the audience for my art and how can I best reach it while remaining true to myself, my ideas, and my aesthetic intentions? How can I exhibit (distribute) my work so that the varied audience I have built will be able to see it? And how can I ensure that my work will be presented so that its larger context will be clear?

This last was extremely important to me because I believed that another explanation for *The Dinner Party*'s impact was that viewers entered an installation that extended a woman-centered perspective into an environmental space. This allowed women to experience their own bodies, their everyday work, their crafts, and their history in a public arena, sharing this space with others and thereby seeing themselves and their lives validated in ways that were entirely new. For men, the viewing experience was every bit as unusual, albeit in other ways. For probably the first time in their lives, they were not at the center of the viewing experience; for some, this was altogether unpleasant, for others, fascinating. However, both women and men experienced something quite unusual, which was seeing female subject matter in a female context rather than in relation to male art history.

This issue of context is one reason that I understand the importance of the National Museum for Women in the Arts in Washington, D.C. Even though I confess to preferring the idea of integrated institutions, still, it is crucial to be able to see women's art in relation to women's own aesthetic history. Too often, women's work, if exhibited at all, is presented in a way that is entirely decontextualized, leaving viewers with no understanding of where this work fits in the history of women's struggle for full humanhood or women's efforts to arrive at an openly female perspective.

Place one or two paintings of women by men like Renoir, De Kooning, or David Salle in a room full of images of women by such painters as Artemisia Gentileschi, Berthe Morisot, Mary Cassatt, Suzanne Valadon, Käthe Kollwitz, and Frida Kahlo, and see how they fare. I would suggest that at least to this viewer—in contrast to the full human beings presented by the women artists—the men's work would look more like the projection of male fantasies, desires, or fears than the great icons they are touted to be. Again, this raises the issue: Who decides what is art and according to what criteria is its quality to be measured?

And when some women argue that museums devoted only to the achievements of women ghettoize us, I always wonder why they don't say this about all the museums that feature only, or primarily, work by men. To be kind, I might suggest that they have not counted the paltry number of women artists included in most museum collections, but for those who have observed the reality of our exclusion and still put forth this argument, all I can say is that they qualify for the "I like their ghetto better than my own" award (though I, of course, long for the end of ghettos of any sort).

As I pondered these questions, it seemed to me that one of the reasons for the art world's continued power was that there were—and still are—so many artists and such a restricted number of outlets for serious art. I am speaking now exclusively about those artists whose intention it is to participate in the world of serious contemporary art, for among the hundreds of thousands of working artists, only a small percentage are concerned with this particular goal. But even this number is too large for the art world's distribution system, which involves a limited number of galleries connected to a small number of art magazines and a tight structure of critics, curators, and collectors.

The more I thought about it, the more it appeared that at its base, the art world is actually a distribution system—the only such system, in fact, for the exhibition of serious art. The question was: Could I develop an alternative strategy for the creation and exhibition of my work that would allow me to operate independently of this system, one that had proved itself so resistant—or, worse, hostile—to my art, while still having my work remain visible? For, as I've already pointed out, for better or worse, it is within this system that art is ultimately validated.

During this period I was convinced that the eager response to *The Dinner Party* was indicative of a widespread hunger for affirming and empowering images of women. Thinking that I might be able to use my growing fame to bring attention to the work of other feminist artists, MR and I came up with something called JC/WIN (Judy Chicago Word and Image Network). This was to be a mail-order business featuring feminist books, posters, postcards, slides, and other visual materials. MR set up a space on her Houston property (next to the bookstore and *Birth Project* space) for inventory storage, and we arranged for Sheila de Bretteville to design a catalog describing the goods we planned to sell.

Our intention was to offer numerous already published products with an eye to also producing some new materials. We were particularly interested in pairing artists and writers in a series of illuminated poems, and with this in mind, I contacted a number of women, among them Ntozake Shange. I had first met Zake at a panel at Hunter College organized by its then-president Donna Shalala, at which time I had been extremely impressed by her. She and the other writers were quite enthusiastic about this project (which came to fruition), but I encountered antagonism where I least expected it: from some women artists.

Given the competitive nature of the art world, I can now see that they might have been put off by the fact that the business carried my name. I had sincerely thought that this would be an effective way to attract audiences who might not otherwise be interested. As I am not by nature a competitive person, it never occurred to me that these other women artists might not have understood my intent, which was to create a larger context for Feminist Art, theirs as well as my own. Profit was never the motive; MR and I were both guided by this rather idealistic goal. Before too long, MR was expending a lot of time and money trying to get our business off the ground.

At this point we had not yet discovered how difficult it would be to establish an economically viable distribution system, one that at least broke even. Our major obstacle would be women's lack of understanding that they must financially support the work that speaks to them. It was disheartening to both of us to see how few women were willing to put their money where their mouths were, a problem to which I shall return when I take up why *The Dinner Party* is not yet permanently housed. MR eventually gave up on JC/WIN and the idea of an alternative distribution system, but I have not. To this day I remain convinced that women have to create such systems, be they mail-order networks or museums.

Neither MR nor I remember exactly when we made the decision to rent one of the large buildings in Benicia's old industrial park for the national headquarters of the *Birth Project*. I know that the small apartment that housed the West Coast office was overflowing, and we had realized that it would be too expensive to operate multiple regional centers (partly because of how much the Houston space was costing, I think). Instead, we decided to consolidate the organization in California. But we planned to keep the Texas space open as long as projects were going on there and to show some of the work as it was finished both there and in our new quarters, which were renovated over the summer of 1981 under the direction of my friend Marleen Deane.

Building 57 was a spacious, two-story, 11,000-square-foot structure that had originally been part of an old army installation. The military had vacated the whole area in the 1950s, and the vast, cavernous structures they had occupied had gradually been taken over by a variety of light-manufacturing industries. Then, slowly, artists began to move in, attracted by the large spaces and cheap rents. Our building's light-filled upper floor was to provide me with a huge, gorgeous studio, a tiny living loft, and an attractive drawing studio. The second floor would also afford a large workroom for Sally, who would have gigantic tables and floor-to-ceiling storage cabinets. It was here that she would prepare the pieces to be sent to the needleworkers and where we would hold reviews. On one wall, all my thread palettes would be hung in preparation for color-coding the various works.

The downstairs space was to house the office, work and meeting areas for group projects, my library of books by and about women, and a large gallery. In addition to a changing exhibition program, MR and I intended to offer lectures, workshops, and public events, hoping to attract many visitors to Benicia and to thereby interest them in supporting Through the Flower with donations or by buying products from the retail shop we planned to set up in front of the building, to be operated under the aegis of JC/WIN.

In October 1981 the building was ready, and we held a public opening. Hanging on the entrance wall was my large painting *Through the Flower,* graced by a hand-written phrase welcoming everyone to the corporation's official new space. We had organized ongoing slide shows about the *Birth Project,* offered by various needleworkers, researchers, and office volunteers. The first finished works were hanging on the walls of our brand-new exhibition space. The JC/WIN shop was filled with colorful posters and an array of books and published materials. Hundreds of people streamed into the building to watch slides, examine the needleworks, rummage through the materials for sale, and check out books from the library. As I watched the crowds milling around, I thought about the time since *The Dinner Party* had closed in San Francisco more than two years prior to this day; what a dismal time that had been and how much effort it had required to rebuild my support structure. I was definitely lucky to have MR at my side, for throughout the years of the *Birth Project,* she was my partner, my patron, and my best friend.

Chapter Seven

Beyond the
Female Experience

Shortly before the public premiere of Building 57, I left Benicia for Chicago because *The Dinner Party* was scheduled to open in my hometown. It was being brought there by a grass-roots effort spearheaded by the Roslyn Group for Arts and Letters. Gelon had been working with them for many months while they raised money and searched for a site. In this case, the Chicago Museum of Contemporary Art (MCA) was actually supportive of the piece but didn't have the space to show it. I had met with the organizers once or twice before the opening, having made several trips there in what turned out to be a vain effort to arrange cosponsorship between the community group and the museum. Unfortunately, negotiations between them broke down and the group was left to mount the exhibition on its own, without the help of the trained installation crew it might have had or the prestige of the museum behind it, which upset me.

The exhibition was held at the old Franklin Building in the South Dearborn area, and both the site and the neighborhood were quite run down. The piece was presented on the top floor of the building, with the documentation show, banners, and International Quilting Bee in a ground-floor space, next door to which a shop was set up to sell arts and crafts items by local women artists. The upstairs space, which was totally raw, had a huge glass ceiling and no floor to speak of. The developer who owned the building was willing to use his own construction crews to renovate the space, which was quite a formidable task.

Although I found this developer incredibly attractive, going so far as to indulge in a brief fling, I soon got into trouble with him. *The Dinner Party* requires a darkened space, and the guy was less than enthusiastic about blacking out the gigantic skylight, because he hoped to turn the upper floor into a restaurant after the show was over. (Later, when this plan didn't work out, he put the building up for sale with the enticement that people might enjoy living in apartments where there had once been a famous work of art exhibited.)

The Roslyn Group was not at all happy that I would not back down from my insistence about covering the skylight; in fact, I bumped heads with them more than once, particularly with the group's leader, whom I did not like. And though the exhibition proved to be a tremendous success, this did not prevent many of the organizers from (reportedly) retaining very negative feelings about me.

As I mentioned, I wasn't all that fond of some of them either, but I tend to have a short memory and until recently—when I was reminded of their antipathy—had forgotten all about what troubles had transpired between us. My more important recollections of the Chicago show have to do with what happened with my family.

A few hours before the show premiered, my cousin Howard called. He wanted to hire a limousine to ferry close family members to the opening and was wondering if this would seem pretentious. He reminded me how much fun it was being chauffeured to the Brooklyn Museum opening in a stretch limousine, adding that the only time our family rode in limos was on the way to funerals. His one proviso was that the car had to be white, as "black would be too reminiscent of all the deaths our family suffered over the years."

I was touched by his suggestion and thought that my mother, whom I'd flown in for the opening, would really get a kick out of this, as she always said she loved "to be treated like a queen." I had hoped that Ben would come for the opening, but he had declined on the grounds that he couldn't afford the airfare and that he was so busy with his pottery that he couldn't spare the time. My mother, Howard and Arleen, Aunt Enid, Cousin Corinne and her husband, Gene, and I squeezed into the stretch limo, which went speeding down the Outer Drive so fast that the driver got stopped by the police. Then the cop took so long writing the ticket that we were late for the opening.

Although my mother had attended the original premiere of *The Dinner Party* in San Francisco, I thought that she would probably enjoy the Chicago event far more because I had invited so many of her longtime friends, along with all the remaining members of my father's family. Throughout the evening I could see her beaming as they all crowded around her with congratulations. Afterward Howard hosted a banquet at a Chinese restaurant for everyone near and dear. He and his sister Corinne told me how proud they were of me, saying that I was the "pearl" of the oyster that was our family in that some of its best traits seemed to have come together in me.

In addition to the joy their words brought me, I was also deeply gratified by another event: touring the show arm in arm with my old art teacher Manny Jacobson. By then he had retired from teaching at the Art Institute's Junior School, where he had trained not just me but numerous other well-known artists, though he would never admit how many or who. I can still hear him confiding, in his soft and distinctive voice, that he had always known that I was destined to do something important.

Shortly before the opening I appeared on Irv Kupcinet's TV show. He was a well-known celebrity figure when I was growing up, beloved like another famous Chicagoan, Studs Turkel. In what still strikes me as an extremely ironic twist of fate, I arrived at the TV station to discover that one of the other guests was Roy Cohn, the lawyer best known for his association with McCarthy during the worst days of Red-baiting.

An old-time liberal, Kup knew nothing of my background and probably thought that I was just a hometown artist with an interesting show. As is wont to happen, the men talked to each other almost as if I weren't there and were taken aback when I interrupted what was a discussion of the Rosenberg trial. I don't even remember what I said, but before long Cohn and I were shrieking at each other, while Kup's wife was standing in the wings offstage, yelling, "Give it to him, girl, give it to him!" At any rate, I believe I did a good job defending the Rosenbergs and liberal causes in general, because for the next few days, people stopped me on the street and thanked me for what I had said. But flattering as their comments were, what meant more to me was the praise of my family, who told me that I had vindicated my father in standing up to this loathsome man.

A few days after the opening, I did something I had long wanted to do. Before going to Chicago, I had asked Howard if he would take me to my father's grave, which neither Ben nor I had ever seen. My relationship with my brother had remained quite strained, and the fact that he lived so far away didn't help. He came to Los Angeles to see our mother about once a year, and I would always try to meet him there in hopes of establishing some better communication. But he would become quite defensive whenever I started to discuss our childhood and how we had come to be so alienated. I always ended up feeling frustrated because he seemed unwilling to make any effort to resolve what was still considerable tension between us. But he would always ask me to visit him in Japan. However, I never wanted to go, as it seemed so distant and foreign. In retrospect, I wish that I had agreed to see him in his Japanese life, since it was obviously important to him and it might have helped our relationship.

My mother was not at all happy about the cemetery visit. When I asked her to come with us, she reluctantly agreed, saying that she had "no need to do this." When we arrived, I became upset that the grave was entirely overgrown, and I decided then and there to start paying for in-perpetuity care. My mother walked away while I knelt down in front of the simple marker and spoke to my father, then cried and cried. I told my father everything that had been going on with me—all that had happened with *The Dinner Party* and my confrontation with Roy Cohn—and how I wished he were alive to see how I had turned out. But I also told him how angry I was that he had made me believe I could be loved for being who and what I was, which didn't seem to be true.

Even though I knew full well that he couldn't hear me, saying all this out loud at his grave helped me no end, as did being able to finally release my long-held grief. And despite my mother's refusal to fully share this experience with me, I found myself able to forgive her for what she didn't—or couldn't—do for me at the time my father died and during the terrible years afterward when I felt so utterly confused.

I returned to Chicago several times, the last time toward the end of the show. It was in the dead of winter, but despite a windchill factor of well below zero, the exhibit was mobbed. In fact, viewers were packed three deep, many carrying large handbags and wearing bulky backpacks. I complained to the guards that this was potentially dangerous to the art but was told that, when people were asked to check their belongings, they refused on the grounds that "this wasn't a museum." As glad as I was of *The Dinner Party*'s popularity, I was also concerned that such mass viewing—in addition to the possible dangers it posed to the work itself—did not seem to allow the kind of one-on-one relationship with art that, in my opinion, yields the greatest rewards. With this in mind, I returned to Benicia and to long months of work in the studio, preparing *Birth Project* images while pondering the best way to achieve both a broad audience and a more intimate viewing experience.

As I thought about my goals for the *Birth Project,* I realized that I definitely wished to avoid another head-on collision with the art world and was therefore determined to find a way to distribute the work so that it would not encounter the kind of institutional resistance that had met *The Dinner Party*. At the same time, I wanted the art to be seen by a wide range of viewers because I was intent upon trying to extend the process of democratization exemplified by both the creation and (although I had not planned this) the distribution of *The Dinner Party*. In terms of the *Birth Project,* I was accomplishing this goal in that the images were being executed through a national network of participants. As to exhibition, even though *The Dinner Party* was being successfully shown through community efforts, it was complex to install and expensive to display. I wondered whether I could figure out a way for the *Birth Project* to be easier to set up and at the

same time structured so as to allow the type of viewing I deemed
more desirable.

My initial ideas about exhibition were based upon the way I had
seen quilts displayed many years before. During our 1972 stay in New
Mexico, Lloyd and I had taken many weekend jaunts, including one
to the small village of Hatch in the southern part of the state. In
addition to being known for its fiery hot chili, Hatch also featured a
restaurant serving luscious—and unusual—raisin pie. While drinking
coffee and enjoying this delicious treat, I perused the local paper and
noticed a quilt show, which we stopped to see on our way out of town.
I became quite intrigued by the fact that the quilts were being displayed on clotheslines. When I began thinking about how to exhibit
the *Birth Project,* I thought how wonderful it would be to see images
of birth and creation cropping up on clotheslines all over America—
and I realized how unstoppable this method of exhibition would be.
Moreover, I loved the idea of art (or craft, as in the case of the quilts
in Hatch) hanging in the middle of communities where the work
could be viewed by just about anyone.

I wish to remind my readers that the *Birth Project* was originally
conceived to be translated from a series of basic patterns into fairly
straightforward needleworks that were intended to be quite sturdy
and, hence, could have been presented rather informally, if not literally
on clotheslines. The problem was that my original idea of creating
multiples had rapidly given way to ever more unique works of art.
This had occurred for several reasons. First, I began receiving appli-
cations from exceedingly skilled stitchers, some of whom offered expertise in techniques I had never explored. Pursuing these provided
fascinating aesthetic challenges but, at the same time, resulted in far
more valuable works of art in that they were totally singular. Then I
became interested in fusing painting and needlework in ways that
would allow the painted areas to show, thereby producing pieces whose
surfaces were quite fragile. Finally, as my understanding of the birth
experience evolved, so did the images, becoming ever more complex,
both technically and aesthetically. The result of all this was that many
of the works were to be entirely unsuitable for casual display.

The underlying problem seemed to be that the art and the democratic impulses are not necessarily the same. The former often leads to ever greater personal investment and, therefore, in the case of visual art, increasingly precious objects, which was what was happening in the *Birth Project*. Democracy would seem to require the opposite: that is, some degree of leveling. Navigating between these two sometimes opposing considerations was something that I was extremely interested in doing.

I decided that one way of accomplishing some greater democratization while also meeting my own creative needs would be to offer the *Birth Project* art for exhibition in a variety of venues, depending upon the nature of the work and the particular site. Instead of becoming a single mammoth work, the *Birth Project* might be better organized as a series of individual pieces of varying character that could be viewed one-on-one while also being monumental in overall concept. As I became fond of saying at this time, if a hundred works were shown in a hundred venues, each to a hundred viewers, one million people would see the *Birth Project* art.

To help develop such an exhibition concept, I turned to my friend Stephen Hamilton, who was an experienced exhibition designer. He agreed to moonlight from his full-time job to work on the *Birth Project*—like most of us, as a volunteer. Stephen brought a very different sensibility to exhibition than that which prevails in the art world. In contrast to the one-time, labor-intensive installations that are done in most galleries and museums, commercial exhibition designers like Stephen tend to think in terms of flexible, reusable systems and presentations that are understandable to a broad range of viewers. His approach was perfect for my purpose, which was to make the art quite accessible, both physically and spiritually.

Over the years, I had noticed that many women tended to underestimate their talents and dismiss their accomplishments as unworthy of note, perhaps having internalized the idea that what women do is not sufficiently important to warrant attention, much less documentation. At any rate, early on I decided that the *Birth Project* would be thoroughly documented, not just the process of creating the art but the nature of the imagery, the needlework techniques employed, the historical conditions surrounding birth, the birth experience itself, and something about the needleworkers' lives.

With this in mind, from the start of the project, we had involved photographers. As my exhibition ideas evolved, so did their role. When we moved into Building 57, we set up a working darkroom and photo archive, which was run by Michele Maier, who moved to Benicia from Houston because of her interest in ensuring that the *Birth Project* would be properly documented. This would involve not only shooting all the finished works after they arrived in Benicia but also recording all the reviews. Later, Sally and I traveled around the country in an effort to meet all the needleworkers and see them in their home environments and Michele went with us to take photographs.

There were some definite rewards in getting to know the needle-workers, and I deeply appreciated the graciousness with which we were welcomed into their homes. I visited some of them many times, some-times to do reviews, other times to meet with them for one or another reason. One thing that was quite striking to me was how many of the women with whom I worked held what would be called feminist values. In fact, it seemed as though many of them had forged lives that reflected a set of human values not dissimilar to my own. It was just that by and large, they had done this in private, behind closed doors as it were, whereas I was struggling to bring these ideals into the world outside.

At the same time, however, I have to admit that entering their worlds was sometimes quite unnerving: for example, the first time I saw a *Birth Project* piece in the middle of a room crowded with toys, right next to a child's rocking horse. Most of the stitchers were insis-tent upon working in the middle of their household environments rather than shutting themselves off in a clean white studio, which of course is what I was used to doing and seeing. In fact, as I used to joke, with a lot of contemporary work, if it weren't in such an envi-ronment one might not be able to even identify it as art.

As work on the *Birth Project* went on and I continued visiting participants' homes, I began to question my own assumption that art needed to be something so apart; perhaps it would be better if it was more integrated into the fabric of existence in both the public and private spheres. In fact, I became convinced that the Romantic and still-prevalent notion of the "alienated artist" only served to further ostracize women from the artistic tradition, inasmuch as so many women (including my stitchers) were quite firmly rooted in domestic life and clearly unwilling to relinquish the many satisfactions it provided them.

Given the thousands of letters of interest we received over the course of our work on the *Birth Project,* it could have probably gone on for years. But by mid-1982, when there were over one hundred needleworks in progress, it became clear that it would be impossible for Through the Flower's small staff to handle any more, which meant that I would have to stop initiating any new projects beyond those that were already promised to waiting stitchers.

All in all, we started about one hundred and fifty pieces, not all of which succeeded. Some ended because the needleworker had boasted of skills she didn't possess or was unrealistic about what she could really do. Others blew up through misunderstanding or unresolved conflicts. A few collapsed because they were badly conceived, and not even the most able needleworker could compensate for my mistakes. But the single greatest reason that projects failed was that the stitcher could not resolve the contradiction between her personal aspirations —in this case, to complete the needlework piece—and the expectations placed upon her by husband, children, and society.

As a result of the *Birth Project,* relationships changed or blew up; friendships evolved or ended; priorities shifted or the piece was returned; the needleworkers learned to stand up for themselves and what they believed in; or they failed to complete the work. Out of the dozens of projects we started, one hundred were what I consider to be victories. Pieces were executed in homes all over America, where they were sometimes worked on for as long as three years. According to many of the stitchers, the presence of these needleworks in progress made their houses the focal points of attention for family, friends, neighbors, and even journalists. Many reported being interviewed for local papers, and by 1985, when the last *Birth Project* piece was com-

pleted, there had been numerous articles in papers all over America
and many of the stitchers were local celebrities. Even now, years later,
a number of the women are still being invited to give lectures about
the *Birth Project* and the process of working with me. Again, this
strikes me as an indication of the potentially empowering nature of
art that speaks to the community.

In terms of the exhibition of the finished pieces, I eventually decided that the needleworks would be best understood if they were
contextualized so that viewers could develop some sense of what lay
behind each image, experientially, aesthetically, and technically. As an
example, some viewers might never have witnessed birth; therefore
they would have no idea whether the images were based upon reality.
Then there was the absence of iconography against which to measure
the art. There was also the fact that many people in the art community
don't consider needlework "art," which suggested that I had best provide some education about the aesthetic potential of an extraordinary
medium too often dismissed as "craft." Most of all, I thought it crucial
to emphasize that each finished work was a triumph of sorts, having
been wrested from lives in which stitching had to be fit into the seams
and cracks of what was often an overwhelming array of responsibilities.

The sum total of my ideas for the exhibition of each piece ended
up in thick folders full of historical information, correspondence, review notes, sketches, notations, translation samples, information about
each stitcher and (if appropriate) her family, and documentation of the
work in various stages, both in-progress and completed. Whenever a
piece was finished (and sometimes even before), Stephen and I would
sit on the floor of my studio and spread out these various and often
disparate materials, searching for the particular "story" each project
seemed to convey. Then Stephen would start to organize what often
seemed like an overwhelming and chaotic amount of "stuff." I always
marveled at his ability to do this, and I learned a great deal from him.

At first Michael Cronan—the father of the baby whose birth I had
witnessed and a skilled graphics designer—worked with us to establish a simple visual presentation format incorporating text and photos
into laminated panels that could be easily affixed to the wall, which
I later decided to supplement with stitching samples, along with some

of my drawings. But it was Stephen who, over the course of several years, would turn the extensive documentation of dozens of works of art into a series of self-contained exhibition units.

Along with the laminated panels and associated materials, each of these would include one or more needleworks contextualized so that the viewing experience might be enhanced for the audience while everyone involved in working on the exhibition unit (artist, artisan, needlework supervisor, designer, photographer) was able to be credited. It was primarily Stephen's incredible talent, combined with his extensive experience in exhibition design, that made this goal achievable and our exhibition system so workable. In addition to Stephen's skills, it was Sally's ingenuity in devising systems for the framing, backing, and packing of the art that made their safe transportation and multiple installations possible. What we eventually came up with was a kind of mix-and-match exhibition program in which we could continually combine the exhibition units in different ways, depending upon the venue.

Even before we opened the Benicia building, we were receiving requests for shows, and we used our own space and some of these early exhibits to try out our installation systems. After a while, we arrived at a process of asking people to submit floor plans of their spaces along with descriptions and photographs of the venue's physical conditions. Based upon these, we would choose the work that seemed most appropriate, and Stephen would do an installation drawing for the show, which we would send out even before we shipped the art. Every needlework was framed, either with fabric borders or, if fragile, in wood. Each of these was placed into a specially designed packing system made of a breathable plastic—designed and fabricated by Sally—and then crated. A second, smaller crate held the panels and ancillary materials, along with installation instructions, condition report materials, brads for hanging the panels, and even white gloves for handling the needleworks.

This approach made it possible to put on shows in many different spaces: museums; university and commercial galleries; hospitals; women's, maternity, and birthing centers; even storefront spaces. No venue was considered too humble as long as the show's organizers could meet

certain criteria, established in relation to the particular characteristics
of the work to be exhibited and the space. For example, a small birthing center with fluorescent lights and no security could be assigned
durable quilts or embroidered multiples, while a gallery with track
lighting and an alarm system might get the more delicate and valuable
art.

Between 1981—when we inaugurated Building 57 with a show
of the first finished pieces—and 1987, when we ended the formal
exhibition tour, Through the Flower organized over one hundred exhibitions. During the height of our exhibition program, between 1985
and 1987, there were sometimes as many as five shows a month. These
were all handled by MR, first alone, then aided by a full-time curator,
Patricia Reilly, and a part-time registrar whose salaries were paid
through exhibition rental fees. Early on we established a sliding scale
in order to accommodate the constraints of different communities.
These fees helped not only to pay salaries but also to defray some of
the costs of organizing this complicated exhibition program.

Although our viewing audience would never attain the goal of one
million, it did reach 250,000, and from the start, the audience response was quite overwhelming. As with *The Dinner Party,* we continuously heard that seeing the *Birth Project* had changed the viewers'
lives. Some show organizers reported large crowds in spaces that had
never drawn more than a few visitors. There were memorable opening
nights such as the one in Minnesota, where, in the middle of a freezing
winter, the gallery somehow lost both its electricity and its heat. Un-
deterred, the opening-night crowd went back to their cars, returning
with blankets and flashlights, determined to see the show, even in the
pitch dark. In Alaska, a large exhibition traveled to both Juneau and
Anchorage. It proved so popular that the sponsors applied for and
received grant funding to send a smaller show to all Alaskan towns
with a population of five thousand or more.

In 1985 we inaugurated something we called our Permanent
Placement Program, aimed at placing *Birth Project* work in institutions
around the country. We would eventually present as gifts or place on
extended loan over forty exhibition units: to museums, university galleries, Planned Parenthood offices, women's organizations, hospitals,

and birthing centers. Sometime later, Through the Flower's board decided to retain a core representative collection, which it intends to offer to an institution for rotating display. Although our Permanent Placement Program would prove extremely effective—in that we were able to introduce a considerable number of pieces into public collections—until recently, we did not have enough staff to properly monitor these placements and thus had no way of knowing if they ended up on exhibit, as was our intention and the terms of the gifts, or were stored away and therefore inaccessible.

The Dinner Party, meanwhile, continued to tour. I missed its opening in Montreal due to illness, but in the spring of 1982 I went to Toronto, where the piece was being exhibited at the prestigious Art Gallery of Ontario. (This was one place where a powerful art critic, in this case John Bentley Mays, embraced the work.) In conjunction with the opening, Natalie Freeman, a journalist and the wife of Jack Austen, a senator serving in then-Prime Minister Trudeau's cabinet, organized a private viewing and supper for a select group of prominent people, including the writer Margaret Atwood and her husband.

Natalie had indicated that Trudeau might possibly join us, though last-minute government business might keep him away. As we were walking around the table, he slipped in without making a sound. I was quite impressed with the prime minister's utter lack of pretension and, at dinner, his unbelievable charm. Howard and Arleen, who had come for the opening and stayed for Natalie's party, ended up in a conversation with him. Apparently Trudeau walked up to Howard and said, "Your family must be very proud of Judy," to which my cousin, with a mischievous twinkle in his eye, replied in a voice loud enough for me to overhear: "We certainly are, particularly since no one in the family ever thought she'd amount to anything." The prime minister roared as I turned beet-red.

In the middle of its Canadian tour, *The Dinner Party* returned to the States for its exhibition in Atlanta. The Atlanta show was presented in an old art deco theater, and was brought there by a now-defunct organization whose director proved to be less than reliable. This was the only venue that was not financially successful, through no fault of the piece. One disaster after another seemed to befall the organizers, including a rainstorm so ferocious that it caused the ceiling of their offices to collapse, thereby ruining their planned 60,000-piece mailing announcing the show. The highlight of the opening for me was that Andrew Young was there. As the mayor of the city, he presented me with a citation. Even better, his marvelous wife, Jean, toured me around the next day, taking me to a restaurant that served the most memorable sweet potato pie. I shall always remember this place, and not just for the food: It was called the Beautiful Restaurant and was run by the Perfect Church.

In June 1982, between the Toronto and Atlanta exhibitions, we held what was called the Big June Review in Benicia, which proved to be something of a turning point for me. More than seventy participants from all over the country showed up. Folks started arriving on Thursday for what were to be three jam-packed days. In addition to reviews, which Sally and I did for many hours each day, there were various other activities, both planned and unplanned, including slide shows, lectures, informal raps, and all-night talk sessions. All in all, there was an incredible sense of sharing in so many ways, not just of the art but of ideas, hopes, and dreams. There was also a strong feeling of community, although once again I felt both part of and separate from it simultaneously.

Loretta Barrett flew in to discuss publishing a *Birth Project* book and to meet Stephen, as I had proposed that he be hired to do the design. Even though he had never done a book, he was so gifted that I felt confident he could design just about anything, and his familiarity with the project would be of great benefit. Somehow, in the middle of all the commotion, the three of us were able to carve out some time to discuss ideas and make preliminary plans. We soon came up with a concept that might best be described as a pieced quilt, like the *Birth Project* itself, made up of disparate parts, preferably with some visual relationship between the book's format and that of the exhibition units.

As energizing as the weekend was, its most salient aspect, at least for me, was seeing so much *Birth Project* art at one time. People pinned their pieces up on every available wall; everywhere one looked, there were needleworks in all stages of completion. For the first time it was possible to see a wide array of images and techniques together; even Sally and I had never seen so much work at once. Because the weekend was so frenetic, it was only afterward that I was able to think about and evaluate what I had seen. One could say that the Big June Review was the culmination of the *Birth Project,* in that I realized that the work we had sent out all over America had definitely taken hold.

However, I felt unhappy about what appeared to be a lack of visual acuity in some of the pieces. Also, I was upset by the realization that once I stopped generating new projects, it was the needleworkers who would enjoy the process I liked the best: that is, the long hours of bringing the images to life. But most important, I suddenly recognized that I was becoming restless with being so focused on female subject matter.

By then I had spent more than fifteen years in what might best be described as a long search for my identity and heritage as a woman. I felt that I had answered many questions about what it means to be a woman, at least to my own satisfaction. Moreover, I was beginning to feel critical of what might be described as an aesthetic fixation upon the female: Men painted women, women painted women—as if the female were everyone's love (or hate) object. I wanted to move beyond this obsession, "beyond the flower" of femininity, as it were. Problem was, the Benicia building was full of the *Birth Project,* and there was no place for me, either psychically or physically, to take up new work.

By the fall I had decided that I would take advantage of the fact that the artmaking phase of the *Birth Project* was coming to a close by establishing a schedule that would allow me to start some altogether new work. I planned to complete the last promised needlework projects; set up a stricter review schedule (I often veered away from it if someone had a piece she wanted seen); do exhibition preparation in short, focused periods; work on the *Birth Project* book at fixed intervals; then go away for a month or six weeks at a time whenever I could. I thought that I might rent a house in one or another town I had visited and especially liked—Galveston, or Port Townsend on the Northwest Coast's Olympic Peninsula—where I could be entirely alone.

By then I was beginning to think about taking up an examination of the gender construct of masculinity in much the same way as I had been investigating what it meant to be a woman. I was once again interested in dealing with ideas I had rarely seen represented in art—specifically, how some women, myself included, perceived men. Over the years, I had listened to women share their fears, rage, and frustration about how men acted both in private and in the world. Yet I had seen few images that presented this same level of truthfulness. I knew that I didn't want to keep perpetuating the use of the female body as the repository of so many emotions; it seemed as if everything—love, dread, longing, loathing, desire, and terror—was projected onto the female by both male and female artists, albeit with often differing perspectives. I wondered what feelings the male body might be made to express. Also, I wanted to understand why men acted so violently.

It seemed fairly obvious that this type of inquiry would not lend itself to a collaborative project, at least not one with married women, who had always constituted the bulk of my volunteers. If their husbands had become upset about their working with me on the *Birth Project,* I could not imagine them taking kindly to images of men that might involve a critical gaze. Two other issues leading me away from collaboration had to do with the points I made about a lack of visual acuity in some of the needleworkers and also my regret about giving away any part of the joy of bringing images to life. Actually, I guess that this was rather a momentous step, after so many years of doing projects with one or another (primarily) women's communities. But I must confess that I did not consciously recognize it as such. In my mind, I was just doing what I had always done, which was to follow my muse wherever it led me—this time, seemingly, back into private artmaking.

In retrospect, it also seems somewhat puzzling that, in starting to formulate my next body of work, I seem to have paid little attention to the issues I had so carefully addressed when embarking on the *Birth Project*: that is, audience and distribution. I have to admit that I made the assumption that the audience I had built would follow me wherever my new ideas took me, not realizing that not everyone was ready to move "beyond the flower." Moreover, even though I was prepared to show whatever I did in the Benicia gallery, I hoped that I was at the point that I would have other exhibition opportunities. It seems important to reiterate my longstanding desire to be accepted by the art community, designing numerous strategies to compensate for its rejection of my work, all the while believing that, eventually, this would change.

In November 1982, I was brought to England for the publication of *Through the Flower* and to present two lectures, one on the *Birth Project* and the other entitled "Women and Society," for an organization called the Blackie, which ran a wonderful community arts program in Liverpool. The title of my second talk was based upon one presented many years before by Virginia Woolf, who was the subject of a week-long celebration. Though far less eloquently, I took up some of the same issues she had addressed in a famous speech, the one that eventually became *A Room of One's Own.*

After my sojourn in Liverpool, I went to London, where I did several interviews, including one with the London *Sunday Times,* then lectured about my work to a packed audience of almost a thousand people. I also met with some folks who were interested in trying to bring *The Dinner Party* to England, visiting several alternative sites because they all said that there was no chance for museum sponsorship, which was disappointing but no big surprise. I also learned that Johanna Demetrakas's film about *The Dinner Party* had aired on television, which increased my recognizability in Europe. It was extremely gratifying to realize that my work was becoming so widely known.

Although I'd been to Europe several times, I'd never been to Italy, where I traveled after England. I met up with MR, and together we visited Rome, Florence, Venice, Naples, and Ravenna. I adored Italy, and particularly the chance to see some of the works I had studied in art history classes. It was fantastic to finally see these images in reality, particularly the Sistine Chapel, the fabulous Raphael Rooms, and the Uffizi collection, which, as I noted in my journal, had more great paintings per square inch than any museum I had ever seen.

I was to be greatly influenced by actually seeing the major Renaissance paintings. Looking at their monumental scale and clarity led me to decide to cast my examination of masculinity in the classical tradition of the heroic nude and to do so in a series of large-scale oil paintings. Though I had used oils in college, I had rather unaccountably hated the texture of the paint and, even more, the smell of turpentine. I was determined, nevertheless, to overcome my aversion, because I was convinced that this was the right medium for such images.

It occurred to me that, along with modern society, the Italian Renaissance had also given birth to the contemporary notion of masculinity, which may be said to date back to the moment when Leonardo configured his version of Vetruvian Man, putting forward the idea of "man as the measure of all reality." Although this particular image was modest in scale, its implications seemed vast, for it presented the male as the center of the universe. I wished to both examine and challenge this construct in a visual form similar to the one in which it had been originally formulated—that is, through a heroic mode.

I returned to Benicia, having made the determination that I needed to hone my drawing skills. (Designing for needlework requires a generalizing of form that seemed inappropriate to what I wanted to do.) I began to work with a male model, finding it absolutely fascinating. It was remarkably different from drawing from a woman, which was what I had done in most of my figure-drawing classes, where there had sometimes been male models, but they were always clothed. When men *did* model, they were required to wear jockstraps, justified by the explanation that, if naked, they might get erections. At any rate, there was a distinct energy, gesture, and attitude in the male body, and also a strange sense of personal power in that I could render the figure any way I wished. At first this scared me, but then I thought: This is a power men have had for centuries—the power to represent women however they wish. If they could handle this, I saw no reason that I could not learn to do the same.

Before long, I found myself thinking about the difference between men as individuals—who as husbands, fathers, or friends could be so kind and loving—and the patriarchal structure of male dominance, which, to my mind, is a global set of values that benefit all men, even those who do not subscribe to these. Curiously, it seemed that most of the men I knew found it difficult to see themselves as members of a gender class. It was almost as if the kinds of insights that women had arrived at through feminism were still entirely foreign to most men, notably that sex-role expectations greatly influence and in fact limit one's options. I was interested in exploring how "being a man" could shape a male, and the seeming relationship between the concept of masculinity and male violence.

I was convinced that one reason men could act so destructively is that in "becoming men," they are required to disconnect from their feelings of vulnerability, a process that begins in childhood when little boys are taught that it is "unmanly" to cry. I wondered about the emotional consequences of such a process and I wanted to examine the connections between this rejection of vulnerability and men's capacity to rape women and molest children (although some women commit sexual abuse, it is predominantly men who are guilty of these crimes). I knew that I myself was entirely incapable of such acts of violence, particularly toward creatures who are entirely powerless, whether small girls or animals. The sheer act of thinking about all this terrified me, because it brought me in touch with my rage at how too many men act. I could still vividly remember my fear when I wrote the "Cock and Cunt" play and worried that I would be horribly punished if I honestly expressed what I believed and perceived.

Given my anxiety, I could only imagine approaching these issues in complete solitude, which was another reason that I had decided to work alone again, thinking to rent places around the country where I knew no one. But then MR suggested that, instead, I might like to use the Santa Fe house, which was unoccupied. Tucked behind a wall that seemed to shut out the world, the house afforded a marvelous sense of privacy. I accepted her offer and made plans to go there early in December.

When I arrived at the Canyon Road house, I set up the small room off the kitchen as a drawing studio and was soon deeply engaged in my new ideas. I was trying to work more directly than was my wont, determined to discard a kind of overcontrol that sometimes happened in my art, in favor of greater spontaneity.

One of the first drawings I did involved a figure shooting a hand/gun, from which spurted blood and tears. This image grew directly out of my revulsion at the seemingly endless depictions of men with guns on TV, in movies, and on billboards. I perceived these almost as a form of terrorism, in that their almost-constant presence caused women to become frightened of men while giving men a fake sense of themselves as overly powerful, an illusion I saw as destructive to both genders. Then I did a drawing that nearly scared me to death. *Crippled by the Need to Control* presents a crippled, blindfolded man riding a woman, using her hair as reins. This image implies that the price men pay for their need to dominate women is that they become blind both to women's suffering and to their own crippled state.

Almost immediately after starting work on these images, I came up against what could only be described as an internalized taboo against depicting men critically, manifested in a ghastly nightmare. One night I woke up with a start, overwhelmed with terror. I was sure that someone was in the house and that I was going to be viciously brutalized or killed. This fear was so intense—and irrational—that I could only explain it as the result of making images about men. Throughout the years I worked on this series, I would have this same nightmare again and again, always awakening in a cold sweat. Each time I would try to reassure myself that surely I would not be so punished; after all, I was only making art.

Over the next five years (the first three while still engaged in the *Birth Project*), I would slowly create a new series of works titled *Powerplay*: drawings, paintings both small and monumental, a suite of tapestries woven by Audrey, cast-paper reliefs, and bronzes. This last technique was one in which I had never before worked, and I found it fascinating, particularly the process of trying to achieve unusual colored patinas. Creating this body of art caused me to take up what turned into longer and longer sojourns in New Mexico.

Before long, I found myself craving the solitude of the Canyon Road compound and the ever-changing light of the Santa Fe sky, particularly the unique pink glow that suffuses the winter landscape.

I also enjoyed being able to walk downtown and do most of my shopping in local stores. But that was before the old Santa Fe was gone, buried under an avalanche of gentrification that has nearly destroyed the very qualities that I and so many other people found there, qualities that were to nurture me and my work for the next decade.

Chapter Eight

If You Don't Have,
You Can't Lose

*I*n mid-January of 1983 I returned to California, where as usual I was quite occupied, juggling *Birth Project* work while continuing to do regular drawing sessions with my male model. Then I attended the opening of the permanent installation of the *Creativity* exhibition at the Seattle Science Center. There I had the opportunity to meet the dancer Merce Cunningham, one of the other artists represented, with whom I had a conversation that was extremely significant to me.

We discussed the need for some type of administrative structure to support and facilitate one's creativity—in his case his dance company, in mine, Through the Flower. Once in place, however, such an organization required at least some degree of attention, which could take time away from one's creative work. As I explained to him, I faced the particular problem of having neither the resources to hire professional level staff nor the kinds of support offered by the art world. Therefore I had to depend primarily upon volunteers, who had varying levels of expertise. Although his situation was not the same, in that he had more traditional forms of support and more qualified personnel, it seemed that he felt just as conflicted as I did about his situation.

Oddly, until this exchange I had not realized that this was actually a rather common predicament for many creative people. When I asked him how I might resolve this dilemma, Merce said that there was no resolution; one simply had to handle the frustrations and go on with one's work. I returned to Benicia with the determination to immediately try to put this advice into practice.

Before very long I was busy again with exhibition preparation and writing. Then I started to experiment with oil paints as preparation for starting to translate some of the drawings I had done in Santa Fe into large-scale paintings. At some point MR had suggested adding a real studio to the Canyon Road house. She had also decided to do some other renovations to the house and arranged for the construction, which she then asked me to oversee. In the early spring I made a short trip to New Mexico to see how the remodeling was coming along.

While there, I met with some fellows who prepared canvas for artists, as I had decided that I would paint on Belgian linen, the traditional artist's canvas. But rather than having the linen primed with a white gesso, as is customary, I asked the guys if they could figure out a transparent coating that would allow the color and grain of the linen to come through while also providing a sealed surface, which is essential for oil paints. I hoped that by using a thin and transparent primer, I might be able to achieve the kind of fusion of color, surface, and form that I prefer.

When I returned to Santa Fe in mid-June, the canvas makers had found a way of preparing the Belgian linen so that its warm and inviting beige surface could show through the primer coat. But they had not yet managed to achieve an even prime coat on the large canvases, so, while waiting, I set to work on a series of small paintings. Using a technique modeled upon Renaissance methods, I first underpainted the images—though in sprayed acrylic rather than the traditional gesso and thinned-down oils—then applied the oil paints. That summer I began a group of works entitled *Maleheads,* which dealt with the way in which some men become disfigured by power. Many of the faces were grotesque, others sad; all in all, they reflected my impressions of the ways in which men's humanity becomes stunted as a result of carrying the burden of power, which must sometimes become onerous.

In terms of this subject matter, one might say that I was involved in an examination of the nature and consequences of power as it has been defined and enacted by men since the Renaissance. As has often been my habit, I decided to do a focused research project into the nature and history of masculinity, thinking to find a body of literature comparable to that existing about the "construct" of femininity. There seemed to be little material, almost as if only women were a gender to be studied and written about. And what did exist seemed not all that insightful (I did this research before Gender Studies was a well-established discipline). I had to depend upon my own sense of truth, working from observation, experience, and, of course, my rage at how destructively so many men seem to act toward women and the world at large.

As I got more deeply involved in a process that MR once described as my "thinking through art," I slowly came to believe that the power that is assumed to belong to all men is, for most, actually a facade. In fact, I began to think that many men actually feel quite powerless, particularly to change a world that they—sometimes even more than women—recognize as both unjust and cruel. I would later come to achieve some greater understanding of how and why men have come to be so violent, particularly toward women. Although this behavior could certainly never be acceptable to me, I would develop a degree of compassion in terms of the seemingly severe consequences of a definition of masculinity that emphasizes aggression and disallows tears.

As soon as the large canvases were ready and lined up in my painting racks, I started on the first of what would be six monumental works, beginning with *Crippled by the Need to Control,* the study for which I had done the previous year. The moment I began tracing the outline of the image onto the canvas, I knew that I had been right; these pictures definitely required the grandeur of this scale. Once the forms were drawn, I began mixing colors in preparation for the spray-painting.

When I airbrush, I work only sections at a time, leaving large portions of the surface taped and covered so that the paint will not bleed. This meant that the overall image was not visible until all of the spraying was done, at which point the male figure not only came to life but practically leaped off the canvas at me. Again, I became fearful of what I'd created, especially after I started applying the oils, which made the forms appear even more powerful. The oil painting took a long time, the process made even lengthier by the fact that I would paint and cover the same area repeatedly. If I let my brush freely express what I felt, I became scared of what I had painted, thinking it ugly and obscuring it, only to paint exactly the same thing all over again.

Powerplay was to be a rather formidable challenge, primarily because of some of the psychological obstacles I had to overcome. Surprisingly, it would turn out that my fear of depicting men critically had historical antecedents, as outlined in the catalog essay that Paula Harper wrote for my 1986 exhibition of this series:

> Images of men as destructive or power mad are not new in the history of art. The grand tradition of figure painting since the Renaissance is populated with powerful and aggressive heroes. . . . But women artists have rarely painted men in an unflattering light. . . . The tradition seems to demonstrate that *women are more willing to portray themselves as victims than men as perpetrators.* [J.C.'s emphasis.]

During the summer of 1983, I spent many weeks alone, immersed in this struggle. Then my friends Stanley and Elyse Grinstein came to Santa Fe. I showed them what I was working on, afraid that Stanley, in particular, might feel uncomfortable with my depictions of men. But if these images disturbed him, he did not make it evident in any way. Rather, he and Elyse were once again entirely supportive, not only of my new ideas but also of my decision to take up individual artmaking again.

With the exception of them (and MR) the only other people I saw that summer were the artist Larry Bell and his longtime companion, the designer Janet Webb, along with the actor Dean Stockwell and his new wife, Joy. I had known both Larry and Dean in the 1960s in L.A., and it was fun to reconnect with them. MR and I asked Jan about assisting Stephen Hamilton with some of the *Birth Project* exhibition work, which was becoming too much for him to do alone. Then Doubleday hired her to do the production on the book, which meant that I would have many occasions to see both her and Larry over the next few years. As to Dean, he had abandoned Hollywood in disgust to take up real estate in Santa Fe, only to have his acting career suddenly spring to life again as soon as he'd moved.

Through Dean, I met the dealer Marilyn Butler, who then ran galleries in both Santa Fe and Scottsdale. By the time I left New Mexico in the early fall, she had asked me to join her gallery and also to have solo shows in both spaces the following year. About this same time I was finally approached by a New York dealer. Through Stephen I had been introduced to someone who had once worked at a gallery called ACA. Indignant that I had no East Coast representation, he immediately contacted the gallery owners, who indicated that they would be extremely interested in handling my work.

In October, after a few busy weeks in Benicia, I went on the road to do reviews and lectures in several cities around the country. When I got to New York I met with Jeffrey Bergen; Jon, his identical twin brother; and their father, Sidney, a short, portly man who had originally taken over ACA from an uncle whose left-wing political persuasions had shaped its once-radical character. In existence for more than half a century, the gallery had retained a decidedly liberal flavor, even though it was then in an elegant brownstone on the Upper East Side, off Madison Avenue. Sidney, whom I instantly adored, was grooming his sons to take over the gallery, a plan that I felt somewhat apprehensive about, once I got to know them. Though already in their thirties, the tow-haired and nearly inseparable twins were altogether boyish and also giddily enthusiastic over just about everything, including all that the gallery was going to do for me. I must say that had it not been for Sidney, I would not have felt at all comfortable signing on.

From the start, he made me feel almost like a member of the family, insisting that I stay with him whenever I was in New York. As he had a fabulous apartment overlooking Central Park, I was delighted to accept his invitation and even more pleased when he announced his intention to be my escort to the next opening of *The Dinner Party,* which he had never seen. Sidney was entirely unfazed by my telling him that it would probably be in London, as Gelon had informed me that it was tentatively scheduled to be shown there in early 1985. Before I left New York, we agreed that my first ACA show would be a small retrospective in the spring of 1984, covering the years 1973–83, with a catalog to be written by a critic of my choice and published by the gallery.

The twins then announced that they wished to see some of my early work, which was (and still is) stored at Cooke's, a huge warehouse in L.A. where I have two bins crammed with assorted artworks, as well as numerous other pieces that are scattered all over the rambling buildings. After a brief stop in Benicia, I met Jeff, Jon, and Marilyn (who had decided to join us) for several days of rooting around, looking at all my stored art. Even though I felt somewhat skeptical of the twins' opinions, after so many years of rejection or indifference by the art community, I could hardly believe my ears when the brothers proclaimed this or that work a "masterpiece." Marilyn chose some representative pieces for her gallery, then left. After selecting work for my retrospective, the twins and I went to see the *Creation* tapestry at Audrey's. She was so excited about the prospect of the New York exhibition that she swore the weaving would be done, even though it had been progressing at a painfully slow pace. Before they left, I told the Bergen twins that I felt somewhat gun-shy after my last New York experience (an understatement), but they told me not to worry, as this time it would be different.

No sooner had they gotten on the airplane home than I experienced the most terrible pains in my side. Although I was convinced that this was just another case of somatizing my feelings—a combination of excitement and anxiety—my suffering soon became so intense that I went to see my longtime internist, Mel Brody. He took one look at me and referred me to a urologist, who said I had kidney stones that needed to be removed immediately. I returned to Benicia, then came back to L.A. for the operation so that I could be under Mel's supervision. Unfortunately, by then I had been afflicted with another attack of the most unendurable nature, as the stones tried unsuccessfully to descend through the ureter, a tiny part of the body definitely not intended for such passage.

As soon as I was able to leave the hospital, MR bundled me into her Blazer and drove me to Santa Fe. I spent some time recuperating, then, as soon as I was able, began to work in the studio again. I stayed in New Mexico for three months, working on another large canvas, *In the Shadow of the Handgun,* a 9'-X-12' painting based upon my *Hand/Gun* drawings of the previous year. Again, I had to struggle to overcome my fright of what was an extremely forceful image, putting in long hours of concentrated work that left me totally exhausted at the end of every day. Almost as soon as I started this picture, I began having nightmares again. Then, almost as if my bad dreams were summoning terrible events into being, I began to be harassed by a man in the alley that ran along the side of the house, who would stand at my window and masturbate.

Calling the police turned out to be an exercise in futility, as they either failed to respond or did so only hours later. By then I had hired a wonderful housekeeper, Mabel Griego, whose family would become very dear to me. Her husband, Manuel, suggested that if the guy showed up again I should call him and he would come right over and "shoot his cock off." As appreciative as I was of his protective gesture, I was shocked to realize that he had a gun, as I knew no one who kept weapons in their house (or so I thought at the time). The Griegos kept telling me that I should get a pistol for protection, and Manuel even offered to teach me how to use one. But the idea seemed so foreign to me that I could not even imagine doing this, even though I was definitely scared. And when MR came for the holidays, she decided to have bars put on the windows, which helped me feel somewhat more secure.

The beginning of 1984 brought with it the sense that I was bringing one phase of my life to an end while opening another chapter, one whose outline was there even though the details were not yet entirely clear. Although I was pretty much finished with my exploration of female subject matter, I still felt engaged in the work of preparing the *Birth Project* documentation panels and the book. These afforded the opportunity to present some of what I had learned from my many years of work with women. The one thing that was worrying me was that Doubleday was planning to send me out on a six-week promotional tour when the book was published, scheduled for the spring of 1985. Given my propensity to break down on the road, I was already fretting about how I'd be able to handle such a long period of uninterrupted public exposure. There was no way that I was *not* going to do this tour, however, as I knew that all the people who had worked with me on the *Birth Project* were counting on me to bring it into the world.

Toward the middle of January, I returned to Benicia to do still more exhibition preparation. While I was there MR and I sent out a letter to the remaining *Birth Project* stitchers, asking that they all finish their pieces by the end of the year so that everything could be made ready for exhibition by the spring of 1985. In conjunction with the publication of the book and the promotion tour, MR and I intended to officially "launch" our formal traveling-exhibition program with simultaneous shows around the country. Both she and I were shocked to realize that some of the needleworkers were upset at the prospect of the *Birth Project*'s being over, as they'd apparently thought that it would go on indefinitely.

By early March I was back in Santa Fe. By then Janet Webb was working steadily on both the exhibition units and the book. Stephen, who loved New Mexico almost as much as I did, was happy to have an excuse for making regular trips to consult with one or both of us. In between his trips, I concentrated on drawings for my next major painting, a huge triptych entitled *Rainbow Man,* which I planned to work on over the summer. In it I wanted to express my own experience with too many men over the years—in particular, their seeming fear of intimacy. In the first image, a male figure holds out a rainbow as if to entice a woman with its beauty, and thereby draw her close. The second painting presents this same man drawing away, as though fearful of the very closeness he had offered initially. In the last picture, the figure becomes violent, threatening to do harm if he is pushed for greater emotional contact.

At the end of March I flew to L.A. because, true to her word, Audrey had put in long hours of work to finish the tapestry just in time to have it blocked and prepared for hanging at my ACA retrospective, scheduled for six weeks hence. Because the weaving had been rolled on the loom during its four years of execution, neither Audrey nor I had had the chance to see the overall image, except in the form of the cartoons I had prepared so long before. Audrey and her husband, Bob, had decided to hold an 'unveiling," setting up a makeshift exhibition space in their living room. It was quite a thrill to finally see the completed weaving, in which my painted image had been transformed and softened through the richness of the wool thread, not to mention Audrey's incredible skill.

I then went up to Benicia for another week of *Birth Project* exhibition work, but not before stopping off to pick up the most fabulous beaded top, made especially for my upcoming opening by the designer Holly Harp, who had become one of my supporters. In early April I returned to Santa Fe, primarily to concentrate on the book, which was soon to go into production. Needless to say, I would have much preferred to spend all of my time in the studio, but I had to content myself with continuing the drawings for *Rainbow Man* in between frantic bouts of writing, as I was already behind on the manuscript. I also managed to expand my tiny circle of New Mexico friends by one: On this trip I had dinner with the potter Rick Dillingham, whom I believe I met through Larry Bell.

I can still recall Rick—an exuberant and quite remarkable man who, unfortunately, later died of AIDS—telling me that he had heard and read so much about me but had never actually seen my work. Therefore, he announced with a flourish, he thought he might fly to New York for the ACA opening, which is just what he did. Another out-of-town artist made a special trip to see the show: the painter Fritz Scholder, who then had a home in New Mexico and who also

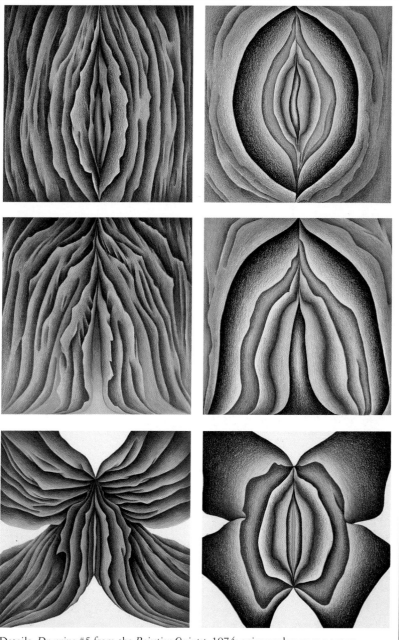

Details, *Drawing #5* from the *Rejection Quintet*, 1974; prismacolor on rag paper.
Collection: San Francisco Museum of Modern Art.

The Dinner Party, 1979; multimedia, installation view showing third wing.

The Creation, 1979; modified Aubusson tapestry, woven by Audrey Cowan, 42" x 14'.

Detail, *The Creation*.

Mother India, EU 69, from the *Birth Project,* 1984; sprayed acrylic, appliqué and embroidery on fabric, executed in conjunction with Judith Meyers, Jacqueline Moore, Judy Kendall, Sally Babson, and a team of needleworkers, 11'2" x 8'.

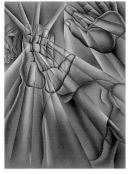

Rainbow Man, 1984; sprayed acrylic and oil on Belgian linen,
9' x 21' (installed).

Detail, *Rainbow
Man;* panel two,
9' x 6'.

Woe / Man: 1987;
multipatinated bronze,
48" x 36" x 5". Collection:
Elizabeth A. Sackler,
New York.

The Fall, 1994; modified Aubusson tapestry, woven by
Audrey Cowan, 54" x 17'6".

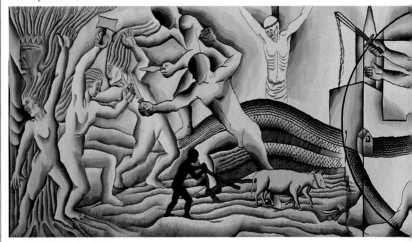

Detail, *The Fall.*

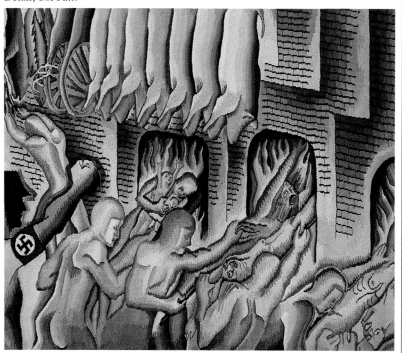

Arbeit Macht Frei / Work Makes Who Free?, 1992; sprayed acrylic, oil, welded metal, wood, and photography on photolinen and canvas, 5'7" x 11'11".

Left Panel #2, *Arbeit Macht Frei / Work Makes Who Free?*

Right Panel #1, *Arbeit Macht Frei / Work Makes Who Free?*

exhibited at ACA. According to the Bergen twins, he came because he wanted to welcome me to the gallery. Sometime during the crowded opening, he invited me to visit him at the house he owned with his then-wife, Romana, in the village of Galisteo, some miles outside Santa Fe.

I could hardly believe how my life was changing; it seemed as though my many years of struggle were finally beginning to bear fruit. As to my retrospective, I thought it looked fantastic and I guess that many people agreed. For the first time in my career, I would actually sell a significant amount of art, thanks primarily to Amy Wolf, a young woman who worked in the gallery and who spent a considerable amount of effort cultivating some major clients. *Heaven Is for White Men Only,* which I had done in the mid-1970s and had never even been shown before, sold almost immediately, as did a companion piece, *Let It All Hang Out.* Over the course of the next few months, the gallery would sell hundreds of thousands of dollars' worth of work (although about half of this was resale—that is, sold by collectors who had bought it from me for a fraction of the 1984 sale price).

However, the one review I read was bad, with the critic going so far as to say that I could not draw. This really upset me, as I prided myself on my drawing skills, which had been perfected by over four decades of practice. I talked to Sidney about it, and he insisted that this was an entirely ridiculous criticism since, judging from the work in the show, he thought that I could draw just about anything. As for the twins, they were awfully sweet. Jeffrey said that he planned to pop himself a huge bowl of popcorn that very night, to which he intended to add plenty of butter and salt, after which he would sit down, put his feet up, eat popcorn, read the article, and laugh while smearing butter on the pages of the magazine.

After the show I returned to Benicia and to the last formal *Birth Project* review; after this final gathering of stitchers, the few remaining pieces would be reviewed through the mail. The impending end of the project had sort of snuck up on me, and even though I was ready for it, it was still somewhat sad. Because I was spending more and more time in Santa Fe, MR suggested that perhaps it was time for me to give up the upstairs studio, an idea that stunned me at first, though I realized that there was really no reason to keep paying rent on a space that was so little used. Even though I was in California less and less, I had not accepted that, in actuality, I had moved away.

MR thought it best to retain the ground floor of the building. It would be useful for art storage, and she needed office space to administer both Through the Flower and the *Birth Project* exhibition program, which she planned to run with a small staff. She soon enrolled in a museum-studies program in the Bay Area with the idea of turning her years at Through the Flower into the basis of a career in arts administration. By then she had her own circle of friends in California, most of whom I did not know, though we continued to feel extremely connected through our shared work and values.

By the end of May I was itching to get back to the Southwest so that I could plunge back into the only life that has ever fully satisfied me: being deep inside myself and creating art. By then ACA had offered to finance a suite of prints. Although I was quite preoccupied with *Powerplay,* there was still something about the *Birth Project* that felt aesthetically unresolved. (It is not unusual for artists to go back to earlier work in order to perfect some of their ideas, which is what I wished to do.) I planned to take some of the *Birth Project* images I liked the best and rework them in order to achieve the level of acuity I desired, intending to find a print shop in New Mexico where I could accomplish this.

I returned to Santa Fe on June 1, and before too long I was hard at work on the *Rainbow Man* triptych, which would take the entire summer to complete. Soon after I had settled in, Gelon called to tell me about European interest in *The Dinner Party*. In addition to a London showing in early 1985, Di Robson, the organizer of the exhibition, had arranged to have it first presented in Scotland—in fact, during this very summer, in association with the annual Edinburgh Arts Festival. Of course, Gelon wanted me to come to the opening in July, but I refused, as I did not intend to give up one moment of my planned four months of painting.

I was slowly becoming more adept with oils, which had been difficult for me at first. The imagery was also gradually becoming somewhat easier for me to handle. As to my fears of being punished for my depictions of men, these weren't helped by my ongoing troubles with the guy in the alley. In fact he had somehow managed to get into the house while I was away, leaving telltale marks of having slept in my bed, which freaked me out. MR and I beefed up the security even more, installing an alarm system.

In early July I spent some time at Unified Arts, a silk-screen shop in Albuquerque that I'd learned about through Larry Bell. Strangely, Judy Booth, who had gone to work with, then become the partner and companion of, Jim Kraft, the owner of the shop, had been a curator at Tamarind when I was there making lithographs in 1972. I had only done one serigraph and that was many years before, but when I visited their shop, I knew that I wanted to do the *Birth Project* suite there, not only because of the wonderful quality of their environment, but because Jim is a technical whiz.

During this summer of 1984 I made several trips to the shop to do tests in preparation for creating a suite of five prints. These were to be completed for my next ACA show, which was to feature *Birth Project* work and be timed so as to be part of the 1985 official "launch." I planned to start the innumerable drawings necessary for the prints toward the end of the year in my Santa Fe studio, then, soon after New Year's, move into the apartment that Jim and Judy kept for artists. I would finish the drawings while doing the proofing (the process of color-testing the prints) in Albuquerque; I intended to remain there until the London opening of *The Dinner Party,* which was scheduled for early March.

Sometime in July, I received a call from a curator at the Fine Arts Museum in Santa Fe who had pried my unlisted number out of Marilyn Butler. Seems she had a group of young male artists in her office who had asked her to contact me because they were organizing an exhibition of New Mexico artists for a Dallas museum and, as the curator put it, it had come to their attention that they had failed to include any women. She wondered if I would meet them for a drink to discuss this problem, which I agreed to do later that week. A few days later I met the "puppies," as I called them at the time, a group of good-looking and frisky artists, all in their mid-thirties, who totally charmed me. They also convinced me to be in this show, despite the fact that—as I kept telling them—my short time in Santa Fe hardly qualified me as a local, which was ostensibly one of the criteria for inclusion.

Summer is the height of Santa Fe's social season, and soon I found myself being invited to this or that art opening or party by these guys and then by their male artist friends. Suddenly I was popular and I loved it, discovering that I liked doing more than working and exercising. What a surprise! I can remember thinking that perhaps I might even find a serious relationship again. I began dating this or that fellow, also hanging out with the puppies, who were great company.

Every year in mid-August, there is something called Indian Market in Santa Fe, when Native American craftspeople from various tribes all over the country present their work in what is the most prestigious show anywhere. Usually there are conjoint exhibitions all over town, along with parties, openings, and festivities of all sorts. Fritz Scholder, as an artist of Indian heritage, was holding a show that was to premiere that weekend. I was invited to the opening and the party afterward at his house in Galisteo. At that time I had not met his wife, Romona, nor had I yet visited the old adobe home that they then shared. I went to the party with one of the "puppies," Jimmy Lowry. We arrived at the party to find that, like many New Mexico dwellings, the house had a wonderful courtyard, which had been set with numerous tables where many boisterous people sat, drinking and laughing within the glowing circle of light that had been created by the careful placement of fixtures and candles.

Although I had not been actually introduced to Romona until that evening, I had certainly heard about her: about her incredible charm and how it was she who had engineered Fritz's successful art career through parties such as this one. I knew that the arrangement of the tables, the quality of the lighting, and the elegance of the atmosphere could probably be attributed to her. When I finally encountered her that evening, I was struck by how handsome she was, and how warm. We exchanged a few words, at which time I discovered that she was a therapist, a fact I tucked away and forgot for a while.

The rest of that summer of 1984 was spent finishing the *Rainbow*

Man triptych and working on the small head paintings that I had started the previous year. Audrey wanted to start weaving again, and I suggested that she do a series based upon the *Maleheads,* though in a slightly larger format. After preparing some photo cartoons from which she would weave, I briefly went to L.A. to work with her in early September. While there, I saw my mother, who was not doing too well. The retirement place where she was living was rapidly going downhill, and we agreed that perhaps it was time for her to move. She surprised me by saying that she had been toying with the idea of applying to the Jewish Home for the Aging in the San Fernando Valley. This place was quite far from where she had lived during most of her time in Los Angeles and, thus, far away from her California friends.

Moreover, given her long-standing lack of interest in anything smacking of Judaism, it seemed somewhat strange that she was thinking about this move. But the home offered high-quality care along with a wide range of activities, which she seemed interested in and I thought sounded good. She was sleeping altogether too much, which I attributed to boredom but was actually a result of her being overmedicated. But this would only become evident after she got into the Jewish home, after a considerable time on their long waiting list.

I returned to New Mexico and another bout of focused work (along with some amount of socializing). At the beginning of October, shortly before my Santa Fe sojourn was to end, the "guy in the window," as I called him, began to show up again. His escapades suddenly became more frequent as well as intense, involving not only masturbating but putting panties on the bars of the windows, knocking on the panes, and making lewd remarks. One day Jimmy Lowry and several of the puppies appeared at my door. I had more than once expressed my fear of this guy—along with my frustration with the police—and they had apparently decided that the time had come for me to know how to protect myself by learning how to shoot a gun. Refusing to take no for an answer, they herded me into their four-wheel-drive vehicle and headed out of town. Before long we were in the foothills of Santa Fe, where there was not another soul around.

The guys had brought a variety of weapons, along with so much ammunition that I told them they could pretty much wipe out everyone in Santa Fe. I could not figure out why I had to learn to shoot with real bullets, nor could I understand what had possessed them to bring—much less to own—an Uzi. "What if I were to blow my foot off?" I asked Jimmy, who assured me that they all knew what they were doing and that I had nothing to fear. "Easy for you to say," I replied, "but I am a middle-class Jewish woman, and in our family, a gun was *unheard* of." He countered by stating that I was now in the Wild West, where many people had weapons—which, at first, I did not believe. Later, when I asked around, I discovered that he was correct.

Although I was scared to death the entire afternoon, my male friends seemed to enjoy themselves immensely, taking turns shooting at various inanimate targets and showing me how to load, unload, and fire the .22, Jimmy's weapon of choice for me to use. I found the guns and the sound of the bullets altogether revolting, while the guys clearly loved the whole enterprise, joking about the phallic shape of the bullets and reveling in the noise and sense of power, particularly that of the Uzi, which they shot again and again. Even though these fellows were all artists and, hence, we had a lot in common, in some ways it seemed as if we were members of altogether different species. Or, as I would later laughingly say: That day, the basis of male dominance was revealed to me. It seemed to boil down to a simple equation between guns and masculinity, or, to put it more baldly, "Shut up or I'll shoot you."

Although I was not at all comfortable having a gun in my home, Jimmy insisted that I keep the .22, which I would repeatedly load and unload, not knowing whether it was worse to have a loaded pistol in the drawer or an empty weapon and bullets rolling around. Nonetheless, some months later, I would be happy that it was there.

Howard and Arleen came to visit me, and I gave them my bedroom in the back for the days they were in town. The "guy" had not been around for some time, nor had he ever shown up when other people were in the house. I was in the front room and Howard was taking a shower, when suddenly I heard Arleen scream. I ran into the bedroom to discover the jerk masturbating in the alley and Arleen shaking with fear. Reaching into the drawer, I pulled out the gun and did just what Manuel Griego had suggested some months before. I pointed the pistol at the guy and shrieked at the top of my lungs that I would blow his cock off if he didn't leave.

Howard came tearing out of the bathroom dripping wet, wrapped in a towel and yelling frantically. He could not believe his cousin Judy standing there with a loaded pistol in her hands, for when it came to weapons, Howard was definitely more like me than like my male artist friends. He kept pleading with me to call the police, though I explained to him that I had done so at least eight times, to no avail, and that I had been given this weapon for just such situations.

Howard was so freaked out that he stayed up all night, guarding the house. But the guy never came back, not then or ever again. Perhaps he got arrested for harassing someone else, or maybe he just disappeared; I do not know or care.

Somewhat unaccountably, this event proved a crucial juncture, in that having that gun in my hand seemed to empower me, which taught me something about every human being's potential for violence. Subsequently, and rather surprisingly, my fear in relation to painting men seemed to subside. Moreover, the *Powerplay* images soon began to evolve, becoming less angry toward men and somewhat more sympathetic. Perhaps this change was a result of this whole episode; I really am not sure. However, when I handed the pistol back to Jimmy Lowry sometime later, I thanked him for having so opened my eyes.

It was during the same fall of 1984 in which I had my lesson in guns that I received a phone call from a former *Dinner Party* worker, Juliet Myers. She surprised me with the announcement that we were now both residents of New Mexico, although I pointed out that I still really didn't think of myself as having actually *moved* from California. She informed me that she certainly had; in fact, one reason she had done so was that she knew I was there. She came to work for me one day a week, bringing with her an extensive knowledge of my art, a familiarity with my network of supporters and friends, and some measure of the quality of assistance and connection I had enjoyed in *The Dinner Party* and *Birth Project* environments, something I had to admit I missed.

As I watched her settle down to work each week, I marveled at how far she had come from the young woman in *The Dinner Party* studio who had dropped whatever she was doing to socialize with anyone who walked by. As this had prevented her from accomplishing much work, I had finally made a big sign to be posted where she sat: "I am working, and if I stop, Chicago will kill me." A photo of Julie and this sign would appear in *The Dinner Party* book, apparently causing some people to conclude that I was extremely dictatorial. To tell the truth, when I spontaneously made the sign and later decided to publish it, it never crossed my mind that it might be so utterly misinterpreted. This lack of self-consciousness is a trait that has been with me all of my life, one that I would soon come to realize was having rather serious repercussions in terms of perceptions (or, more accurately, misperceptions) of me.

In mid-October 1984, I (reluctantly) left Santa Fe for Ottawa, Canada, where I did numerous media interviews in relation to the opening of a drawing show there. But instead of experiencing this press interest as flattering, I found myself becoming extremely uncomfortable. I was also scheduled to present a luncheon lecture, which, I was told, was to be attended by over a thousand people. And according to the sponsors, they could have sold twice as many tickets had they only thought to hire a larger hall. Almost immediately upon hearing this, I suffered an asthma attack, seemingly brought on by the prospect of facing so many people. It was becoming ever more disconcerting to leave the absolute quiet of the studio for the frenzied atmosphere that seemed to surround me whenever I appeared publicly, which I did at intervals of about three months. As a result, I was becoming increasingly prone to such somatized panic attacks.

Moreover, there seemed to be a growing gap between how I saw myself and how others perceived me. Whereas I knew myself to be terribly vulnerable and quite sensitive, many people seemed to view me as someone frightening. Either they became quite aggressive toward me or they approached me with trembling hands. I was also being treated as though I were an extremely successful artist, which is not at all how I saw myself. As a matter of fact, I absolutely refused to take in how much I had accomplished, almost as a matter of principle. If someone complimented me about having done this or that, I would politely thank the person, all the while thinking: All well and fine, but what good will that do me in the studio or on the running path?

The one positive thing about this frame of mind was that it kept me from getting a swelled head. As Stephen used to say, I was one of the few well-known people he'd encountered who weren't jerks. I had certainly made a conscious decision that I didn't wish to become like some of the famous folks I had known (and by then, I had met many) who seemed altogether full of themselves. Instead, I was determined to stay true to something my father used to say: "On the toilet, everyone looks pretty much the same."

Shortly after Thanksgiving, I went back to Santa Fe. As soon as I was reestablished in my New Mexico life, I called Romona Scholder, whom I'd seen socially a few times since our meeting the previous summer. I told her about my escalating problems in relation to public appearances, saying that I was becoming increasingly concerned about being able to handle the upcoming *Birth Project* promotion tour, which at that point was only about four months away. Having decided that it might be a good idea to get some therapy, I asked Romona if she thought that, given our social relationship, it would be inadvisable for me to see her. She thought it would be all right, and it might actually be helpful that she was familiar with the art world.

At my first session, I told her about my propensity to break down on the road and how determined I was that this not occur during the spring tour, particularly because all the needleworkers were counting on me to get the work out into the world. By then, I had begun to realize that some of the roots of my problem lay in my childhood. Over the next few months, I was able to recognize that one way in which I had coped with so much loss was to develop a protective strategy that might best be described, "If you don't have, you can't lose." In fact, it would turn out that this attitude had profoundly shaped my life. I had always marveled at my friends' expectation that their lives would move along in an uninterrupted rhythm and their apparent presumption that they would survive to a ripe old age, something I had never counted on for myself. The death of my father when I was young, combined with so many successive sorrows, had taught me that tragedy could strike at any time. (To this day, whenever I return home I automatically check the street adjoining our house to see if one of my kitties has been hit by a car, an apprehension that has affected most of my adult life.)

More than twenty years earlier, at the time of Jerry's premature death, I had vowed that I would build my life around my own identity and needs. Although this resolution allowed me to forge the life I most wished to lead—one based upon artmaking—I slowly came to understand that it had also insulated me. My fear of loss caused me to be exceedingly mistrustful of others and wary of intimacy. The other side of this was a childlike innocence that left me overly vulnerable, a trait that, Romona pointed out, resulted in my bringing a rather childish desire to be loved into my adult and very public life. She suggested that I needed to learn to better protect myself emotionally, something I had never even thought about. It was as if Romona had to teach me skills that I should have acquired as a child but hadn't, perhaps because my childhood was so shattered by my father's death.

In order to accomplish this education, she asked me to imagine myself sitting in the audience for one of my lectures or as a person attending the opening of one of my exhibitions. "Think how much everyone has heard about you," she said. "They know you've had innumerable shows. They might have read one or more of your books, seen your name in art history texts or magazines; or watched you in a film or being interviewed on TV. They consider you a star, as someone 'up there,' and they are nervous about approaching you, which they evidence through, for example, fawning, animosity, or fear."

To tell the truth, I had never before stepped outside myself and tried to look through someone else's eyes. Starting to do so was a revelation. I began to see what Romona meant, that others viewed me far differently from the way I saw myself. This was understandable in that I had always insisted on staying rooted in my own experience at all times. I had spent so much of my time and energy focused on my studio life, and other than art, the activities I had always preferred were exercise and sex, both of which also seemed to require staying centered in oneself (in the case of sex, of course, while also trying to be sensitive to one's partner's needs).

As I explained to Romona, in terms of my accomplishments, I preferred to approach my life and especially my days in the studio as if I were a blank slate, someone who had never achieved anything. This allowed me to start from scratch again and again, something I have always liked doing. In a somewhat related vein, one that might serve as an example of this pattern, I had never wanted to own any property, insisting that I didn't wish to be tied down. Of course, this decision freed me from the obligation of mortgage payments, but more significant, it protected me from the possibility of losing something that I had. That this is somewhat screwy logic, I certainly would not disagree. It was where I was at this moment in time, however, and was the primary reason for my breakdowns.

I soon came to understand that, in public situations, I would experience a rather dramatic collision between my own sense of self and other people's perceptions, particularly in regard to all that I had done. Because my own accomplishments were so invisible to me, their effect on others was entirely outside of my consciousness. Therefore I could not understand why they treated me the way they did, particularly when they evidenced hostility, with which I have always had difficulty. Also, perceptions of me appeared to be worsening in that they seemed ever further from the level of understanding for which I so desperately longed. My months in therapy could probably be summed up by stating that I was helped to accomplish exactly what I had hoped for. Thanks to my ongoing sessions with Romona, I would be able to successfully accomplish the *Birth Project* tour, primarily because she taught me not to bring this private longing into my public life.

However, I think it essential to point out that what I was suffering cannot be explained merely as a personal dilemma, though there is no question that this represented a significant part of the problem. The art world's ongoing rejection of my work certainly reinforced my own tendency not to internalize the level of my accomplishments. But there was also the issue of the negative manner in which strong and talented women are viewed by society, which I knew both through my research and my own experience. I had of course studied many women who had been depicted in history books in ways that had little to do with who they really were or what they had actually achieved. And over the years, I had met numerous well-known and accomplished women—for example, the artists June Wayne and Louise Nevelson—who had been characterized to me as "bitches." But when I met them, I found them to be not at all as they had been described but, rather, wonderful and complex human beings.

At the end of 1984, while still seeing Romona regularly, I attended a Christmas party at Rick Dillingham's, where I met a poet named Harvey Mudd. He told me he had just finished a long poem dealing with the Holocaust, a topic, he said, that had always interested him. With some shock, I realized that this was a subject about which I knew almost nothing; in fact, it had never even been discussed when I was growing up. I can recall thinking how odd it was that I was so ignorant about an event that had taken place during my childhood, especially in light of our Eastern European Jewish heritage and my father's avid interest in politics and history.

As we were talking, I suddenly experienced something akin to the "click" that so many women have described in terms of an awakening of feminist consciousness. Perhaps I sensed some connection between the Holocaust and my inquiry into male power, suddenly recalling something that Virginia Woolf had written in which she described the rise of fascism and Hitler's march across Europe in terms related to "patriarchy gone mad." Whatever the reason, I found myself rather inexplicably asking to read Harvey's (then unpublished) manuscript, even suggesting that I might like to illustrate it. I certainly had no notion that I was on the brink of a journey of discovery that would occupy me for eight years.

Soon after the first of the year, my cats and I headed for Albuquerque, where we tucked ourselves into the apartment at Unified Arts that would be our home for the next few months. I worked frantically on the *Birth Project* prints, trying to finish them before the London opening of *The Dinner Party*. At the beginning of March I flew to England, and true to his word, Sidney Bergen arrived soon afterward to escort me to the show. Although the installation was in a ratty space in a run-down part of London, the evening was rendered unforgettable by a rousing opening address presented by the writer Germaine Greer.

I returned to New Mexico and some more weeks at the print shop, finishing up and signing the serigraphs so that they could be shipped to ACA. Before I knew it, the long-anticipated (and feared) *Birth Project* tour was at hand. To tell the truth, I ended up having a pretty good time, thanks to my months of therapy and also some advice I received from Dean Stockwell shortly before my departure. I asked him how he dealt with his years of public life. He told me that he looked at each encounter as a fleeting occurrence, thinking at the end of each interview or appearance, Next! This approach really helped me, largely because it allowed me to stop taking everything that happened on the road quite so seriously.

I returned to Santa Fe with a new and unfamiliar feeling of satisfaction. This sense of accomplishment, as I told Romona, was actually a pleasurable sensation, one that I owed primarily to her. "Now if I could only find a real boyfriend," I said. "There must be some men out there who are nonsexist, interesting, and able to deal with me." Even though I had been dating quite a lot, I had been discovering that many guys seemed intimidated by me. Again, I found this difficult to understand, because, as my reader surely realizes by now, in my own eyes I was a pussycat.

Not too long afterward, Romona called to say that there was someone she wanted me to meet, a psychiatrist friend of hers who was about my age. We had been discussing the fact that I had a seemingly irresistible attraction to younger men. She had suggested that perhaps I should try and overcome this and look for someone more mature. Such a man might not feel so threatened by me, she said, and he might be responsive to my desire for a serious relationship. This psychiatrist, David, and I dated throughout the summer, during which time I worked on *Driving the World to Destruction,* another monumental picture. In this image, a man clutches a steering wheel with which he is "driving" the world to its doom. Propelled into madness by the overwhelming "burden of power," he seems incapable of releasing his grip, even though his action foredooms the planet to destruction. Although this is an angry painting, it is also a compassionate one, because it suggests that no person, regardless of gender, could remain sane while wielding such unlimited power.

While reading my journals from this summer of 1985, I was amused to note that despite dating David the psychiatrist, not to mention my promise to Romona, I was still indulging in a quick fling with one or another younger guy. No matter how I tried, I couldn't seem to contain my lust for them, particularly tall, slender fellows in their thirties. I mention this because around the time of my birthday, in late July, David took me to a rodeo (which I found appalling: imagine, grown men tying up baby calves), where I met Donald Woodman. I was extremely drawn to him, and he to me. He was just my type, in his late thirties, tall, rugged, and charming. But he turned me off by asking me if I would like to "see the bulls" with him (he was photographing them), a comment that seemed just too much like the old cliché about seeing "my etchings."

After the rodeo, I forgot all about Donald until the fall, when David organized a picnic supper at something called the Burning of Zozobra. Each September, shortly after Labor Day, there is a fiesta in Santa Fe that could not possibly be less politically correct, in that it celebrates the "reconquest" of New Mexico, when the rebellions of the Native American peoples were finally subdued. Needless to say, the Indians will have nothing to do with this event, which is a big celebration that lasts for an entire week. It culminates in the burning of a fifty-foot-high papier-mâché figure called Zozobra, or "Old Man Gloom." I used to joke that this procedure was a sort of Hispanic Yom Kippur, in that this conflagration is supposed to "burn away" all the woes of the previous year. At any rate, I had never seen this phenomenon until David, the psychiatrist, invited me to the picnic, at which not only this huge paper figure got hot.

I had often admired the colorful fiesta dresses that are traditionally worn to this event and decided to buy one for myself, a flashy pink number that Mabel Griego took up for me so that it was well above my knees. I put my hair up with a series of bright barrettes whose vibrant colors matched the embroidered flowers on my outfit. I arrived at the park and found David and several other friends sprawled out on a blanket right in the front, drinking frosty margaritas and eating chips. I joined them, enjoying the hot, dry air and the rapidly increasing audience, which must have numbered about twenty thousand people.

I can remember the brilliance of the setting sun and the noise of the excited crowd and soon the colorful fire dancers who appeared on the stage at Zozobra's feet and quite near where we were encamped. Just as the music began and the dancers started their frenzied movements, Romona arrived, bringing along her former companion, the artist Patrick Mehaffy, and Donald. As soon as Donald and I saw each other, sparks began to fly, which caused a considerable amount of friction between Donald and David. Before long, the two were vying for my attention, almost as if we were kids in high school. But of course this had never happened to me when I was a teenager, which made it all the more enjoyable.

About this time, Zozobra began to move around in puppetlike motions, emitting strange sounds. Dancing smoke and fire filled the stage; the dancing became more frenetic; the music grew louder; and we all got drunker. When the sun went down and Old Man Gloom was consumed in flames, the huge, noisy crowd began to surge toward the downtown Plaza for more celebration.

The next thing I knew, I was being lifted above the heads of the thousands of people filling the street and carried by Donald on his shoulders the mile and a half to the Plaza. Once there, he put me down, then bought twelve purple balloons (which I had admired at the fairgrounds), tied them around my wrist—and said he had to be going, at which point David breathed an audible sigh of relief. I can still recall the intensity of the attraction between Donald and me. A few days later, he called and we made plans to see each other the following week. Almost immediately thereafter, I wrote a "Dear John" letter to David.

In mid-September, we had our first formal date, dinner at the Santa Café, an elegant restaurant that, as it turned out, was a favorite place for both of us. As we sat across from each other in the courtyard, I found myself thinking that I could marry this man, a thought seemingly so outlandish I could hardly believe that it had crossed my mind. Yet, as I wrote in my journal at that time, if I were to make a list of the qualities that were important to me in a man, Donald would possess most of them. Born in Massachusetts, he was raised in a family somewhat like my own, though less intellectual. And even though there had never been any pressure put upon me to "marry Jewish," I had always felt most comfortable with Jewish men, and in fact all three of my husbands were of this tradition.

From childhood, Donald had never fit in. His father had objected to his youthful aspirations to become a ballet dancer because of the misguided fear that his son might thereby become homosexual. In college, during the days of the Vietnam war, he was a draft resister. Although he had started out in architecture at the University of Cincinnati, he switched to photography because he had a natural talent for it, but also because he discovered that he disliked the profession of architecture. He later became an assistant to Minor White, an important photographer teaching at MIT, which brought him back to Boston. He ended up in the center of Harvard Square during the height of the antiwar protests and in close proximity to the burgeoning Boston Women's Movement, which exposed him to feminist thought.

Strangely, he was in Houston as a returning graduate student when *The Dinner Party* was there. He had been approached to work on the installation (among his other talents, Donald is a mechanical genius with a wide knowledge of construction techniques). In the end, he had been excluded from participating on the basis that he was a man. (Later, I would joke that Donald had to marry me to install the piece.) He had moved to New Mexico in 1972, taking a job at a solar observatory doing photography, then acted as an assistant to the painter Agnes Martin, during which time he lived in a tepee. All in all, he was just my kind of guy: a rebel, a loner, handsome, and incredibly sexy. As avid for physical intimacy as I, after our first night together Donald confided his belief that for each person in the world there is only one other and they are destined for each other; and we were such a pair.

We were inseparable for almost a week, but then, on the weekend after we first got together, I freaked out. Donald had organized a big fortieth-birthday bash for himself, to be held that Sunday at Romona's house, and he wanted me to attend. On Saturday morning, however, as Donald puts it, I "threw him out." I just couldn't accept that I had met someone and fallen head over heels in love like a teenage girl. As I said to my friends: "Things like this don't happen in real life— at least not to me." Donald was heartbroken, but I was convinced that I had done the right thing by leaving him to drown his sorrows at his party while I tried to go on with my life. By Monday I was regretting my decision; by Tuesday I was beside myself; on Thursday I called Romona to say that I had made a "big mistake." She told me that Donald was devastated and that she was sure he'd jump at the chance to try again.

On Friday I broke my usually rigorous work schedule to have lunch with him on my patio, at which time we acknowledged that we simply couldn't live without each other. Soon afterward, Donald suggested that we get married. Though I felt anxious about making such a seemingly precipitate decision, I agreed. As we shared a desire to have a wedding ceremony that reflected our joint dedication to full equality between women and men, we thought we had best turn to a female rabbi, and we found Lynn Gottlieb from Albuquerque. Although Donald and I certainly shared the kind of ethical Judaism in which I was raised, we were both almost equally ignorant of Jewish history and culture. Donald asked Rabbi Lynn not only to prepare us for our wedding, which was to be held on New Year's Eve, but also to help us discover something of our tradition as Jews.

By this time, I had read and decided that I could not illustrate Harvey Mudd's poem, thinking that I would have to make my own voyage into this subject. I had been planning to educate myself about the Holocaust while finishing *Powerplay,* the first step of which would be going to New York to see *Shoah,* the nine-hour film by Claude Lanzmann that was about to premiere there. At one point I told Donald about my growing interest in the Holocaust and my plan to see this movie. He announced that he would like to go with me, which is precisely what we did, in October 1985.

As we sat together, holding hands, we found ourselves utterly overwhelmed; by the film; by our mutual ignorance about the enormity of this tragic event; and by the sudden realization of the preciousness of our shared Jewish heritage and the fact that it had been nearly wiped out. Moreover, this was the first time in my adult life that I felt bonded to another person, not by gender but by culture. After two days of sitting riveted in that dark theater, we began to discuss working on a project together. Neither of us had any idea of what we were getting ourselves into, or of how painful a voyage we were about to take.

Chapter Nine

Why the Holocaust?

*I*n approaching the next period of my life, I am faced with a problem, the same one that deterred me from illustrating Harvey Mudd's poem and that plagued me during the eight years of working on what would become the *Holocaust Project*. Harvey's poem joined together the subject of the Holocaust and his personal problems with women. I found this an untenable association, in that it would seem that everyone's private difficulties pale in the face of the enormity of the tragedy that was the Holocaust. Once I began my own path into this subject, I felt compelled to start a second journal. (Its color was yellow, in remembrance of the yellow stars Hitler forced Jews to sew onto their clothing.) Within its pages, I would record my anguished journey into the dark subject of the Holocaust, keeping my original journal for the documenting of my more subjective vicissitudes.

Had I kept only one written record of these years, I would have been confronted by the same dilemma that appears before me now: how to write about my pained response to viewing *Shoah*, then segue into my—by comparison, trivial—conflict about following my heart and marrying a man I hardly knew. Even then, before my intensive inquiry into this subject, I recognized that the many victims of the Holocaust would have been only too happy to have struggled with such mundane issues as wedding jitters. Instead, so many had been deprived of life's joys through death, while those who survived were probably shadowed by inescapable memories of horrific suffering. And if I felt discomfited by trying to traverse the enormous distance from historical tragedy to subjective reality even in the privacy of my own journal, how much more difficult to do so in this published manuscript?

Yet, the next eight years were lived in the face of Donald's and my struggle to understand and (if ever one can) come to grips with this appalling chapter of history. As hard as we tried to keep these issues separate, we were not always sure when our marital troubles were the result of interpersonal problems or a consequence of the unending turmoil this subject matter caused us. Nevertheless, it would be inexcusable to meld these two separate topics together when discussing these next years. Moreover, the art that resulted from our collaboration, an exhibition called the *Holocaust Project: From Darkness into Light,* is presently traveling and can be viewed by those who are interested. Moreover, the accompanying book, published by Viking Penguin, is readily available.

Also, it would be impossible to summarize in a few brief pages what took eight years to create: a 3,000-square-foot exhibition augmented by an audio tour; a videotape presenting insights into the process by which the *Holocaust Project* was created; and an ancillary show of documentation panels that provides background information. Even if I were to attempt an adequate written description of this complex and layered project (an impossible task, else why choose the vehicle of visual art?), it would crowd out all of the remaining pages of this publication. Also, in structuring both the exhibition and the book about the *Holocaust Project,* Donald and I consciously decided to include some aspects of our subjective experience. These were very carefully selected with the intention of providing a bridge for the viewer or reader by which he or she might approach a subject that we ourselves found entirely daunting. Even so, we were to be criticized for having included anything at all about our individual struggles.

How, then, shall I approach these years in which our personal dilemmas interfaced daily with our efforts to forge images from a tragedy so terrible it is often said to be entirely unrepresentable? Unlike a scholar of this subject, whose approach demands objectivity, creating the images that constitute the *Holocaust Project* required that I continually access my feelings. If my hands stopped translating the myriad emotions this material elicited, the images became flat and inexpressive. Consequently, I could not allow myself the kind of protective distance that seems to afford intellectuals a way of handling long years of study in a topic as heartrending as this. Even now, I become queasy at the very prospect of going over this agonizing terrain once again, because these years were to be the hardest of my life.

It seems best to step back in order to give something of an overview of the *Holocaust Project* and also to discuss how Donald and I came to undertake it. This will mean that, when I resume my personal saga, the reader will have to remember that what I recount about my life between 1985 and 1993 took place against the background of my slowly entering the subject matter of the Holocaust, then becoming entirely occupied with the challenge of translating all that we were discovering into a series of images, whose appearance of simplicity belies their complexity.

When Donald and I saw *Shoah,* it was as if my entire life had led up to the moment at which we spontaneously agreed to work together on this subject matter. An unexpected outcome of our decision was that we would become deeply bonded as a couple by all that we would jointly experience and learn. But why would we spend eight years on such a subject? In the first section of the *Holocaust Project* book, titled "Awakening," I tried to explain some of what motivated me. I described having spent decades exploring my identity as a woman while having neglected a comparable investigation of my Jewish roots, a lack that I became determined to redress. I also pointed out that there seemed to be a rather surprising iconographic void in the contemporary art world on this subject, while at the same time there was a plethora of both art and discourse in the Jewish community. Even now, in most contemporary art museums, it is rare to see art on this subject, one that in other contexts is often presented as a central philosophical dilemma of our time. Just this rather stunning contrast might have provided sufficient reason for my interest, as I have so often been drawn to subjects that are absent from the mainstream aesthetic dialogue.

But even these interpretations cannot really suffice to explain a project that, once initiated, could not be stopped—at least not until we had come to the point at which we saw how the Holocaust related to the larger world. Was it, as so many people in the Jewish community insist, entirely unique and so mysterious as to be incomprehensible? Certainly, the deeper we plunged into the material, the murkier it became. For a while, both of us accepted the argument that it was altogether different in character from all other genocides, mass murders, or historic tragedies. But something drove us to look further and to think ever more intensely about whether this was altogether true.

In terms of the seeming inevitability of my own decision to take up an inquiry into the Holocaust, one could say that issues of power and powerlessness have been central to my work for many decades. When I turned my attention to this subject, it was, in part, an effort to understand the connections (if any) between the small, everyday abuses of power and the larger horrors of the Holocaust. I was also motivated by the realization that most scholars have paid virtually no attention to the fact that the architects of the Third Reich were *all* men. It is true that there were women who participated and who, according to some accounts, even exceeded men in cruelty. But if one were to peruse the list of names of those who actually engineered the Third Reich and the Final Solution, no women's names would appear. Was there some relationship between the Nazi doctrine of masculinity and such wanton abuse of power? Was Virginia Woolf correct in her assessment of Hitler's march across Europe as "patriarchy gone mad"?

As to Donald's reasons, to this day I do not altogether know what motivated him to get involved in this project with me. Certainly, he was interested in collaborating with me because he loved me and would probably have done almost anything I asked him to, largely because that is the kind of person he is. Almost from the beginning of our relationship, Donald began to wrap himself around me and my life, finding many ways to demonstrate his affection. To my surprise, he and I seemed to have complementary abilities, in that he is adept in all things mechanical and technical (areas in which I am seriously wanting), whereas I bring a kind of conceptual strength and emotional directness that are somewhat foreign to him. This intersection of abilities provided us with an unusual basis for the collaboration that would produce the *Holocaust Project*.

Another aspect of Donald's personality is that, like me, he is a risk taker. Both of us were willing to risk everything in order to accomplish this project, including our financial security (we ended up deeply in debt); our future prospects for earning money (who would buy art about such a troubling subject?); and our mental health (which, in my case, was threatened more than once).

Donald was certainly intrigued by my belief that a fusion of painting and photography would be an appropriate method of dealing with the subject of the Holocaust. He had long been dissatisfied with some of the expressive limits of photography and was, therefore, attracted to the possibility of expanding its parameters. I had come intuitively to the notion of uniting these techniques, and seeing *Shoah* reinforced the idea, as did examining drawings by prisoners and survivors. Most of these were not sophisticated images but, rather, sketches and notations done to "bear witness" to the horrific events the artists had either witnessed or experienced. I found these drawings quite compelling, so much so that they validated my feeling that painting could play a potentially useful role in dealing with the subject of the Holocaust.

In the early part of 1986, while completing *Powerplay,* I undertook to educate myself about the Holocaust, trying at the same time to become somewhat more familiar with Jewish history and culture. While I compiled and examined an exhaustive library of books and studied the art that had been made on this subject, Donald pored over photo archives. We also saw many exhibitions, soon discovering that the Holocaust was represented largely through documentary photographs or film footage; of course, what had been photographed was primarily the aftermath of the event. I realized that what I was even more interested in was the living, breathing people—their actual experiences, feelings, and fears. I became determined to try to understand the Holocaust in terms of how such horror could have been inflicted *on* people *by* people. Moreover, even though many students of the Holocaust argue that there is no more suitable way of conveying the scope of this tragedy than through this type of photo-documentation, I found it difficult to relate to pictures of piles of bones or to the somewhat abstract and always overwhelming statistics that characterize so many presentations about the Holocaust.

I soon became totally immersed in my self-guided study program. At first I had to force myself not to fall asleep or just numb out. Before too long, I discovered a way to make a more real connection with the material. For example, to translate what was sometimes rather dryly imparted information about the "liquidation" of a ghetto, I began thinking that, had Donald and I lived in such a community, we would surely have been caught in the Nazi net. By inserting myself and people I knew into the picture, I found that it suddenly became quite vivid to me. This was precisely the role I felt painting could play; that is, it could introduce the *human* story. But it seemed crucial that the images stay rooted in the historic event as a way of emphasizing that this tragedy was something that had indeed happened, and this was the major reason for my decision to combine the two media.

During our years of work and ongoing study, we frequently encountered the argument that the Holocaust is so unique and mysterious as to be beyond understanding; more, that it is not only incomprehensible but totally unrepresentable. I was quite disconcerted by the notion that *any* human event, even one so hideous as the Holocaust, was beyond comprehension. I found it impossible to accept that there was even one aspect of the human experience that could not be dealt with through art. As to the uniqueness issue, what has always seemed to make art so important and distinctive is its capacity to identify the universal in the unique. Art seemed to offer *precisely* what was needed in terms of reaching some larger understanding of the Holocaust—which, from the beginning, was what I was after.

At the beginning, however, our intention was to create a body of art from the same perspective we saw represented in American documentary exhibitions about the Holocaust; that is, with a focus on the

Jewish experience. Then, after two years of intensive research, Donald and I traveled for two and one half months through the landscape of the Holocaust, visiting concentration camps and massacre sites and experiencing the almost deafening absence of Jewish life in Germany, Austria, Czechoslovakia, Poland, and what was then the Soviet Union. Despite our long immersion in the historical record of the Holocaust, we were still completely unprepared for this trip.

As we drove from site to site, following Hitler's footsteps as he set out to vanquish Europe, like some brutal conqueror of ancient times, we were shocked to discover how differently the Holocaust was represented in these countries. Not only was the Jewish experience not the primary focus, as it was in the United States, but in some areas one would have been hard-pressed to understand how many Jewish victims of the Holocaust there had been.

Probably the most significant thing that happened to us was the sense of coming face-to-face with evil (a concept I had never really understood), especially when entering a crematorium for the first time and seeing its oven with a residue of ashes, or in the dank, life-extinguishing slave-labor tunnels in Ebensee, Austria. Until we arrived there, we had known very little about the Nazis' enslavement of millions of people, or of their plans for a permanent slave-labor system. As we pushed our way into an incompletely boarded-up entrance to one of these tunnels—built by prisoners who were worked to death in less than three months—we shook with terror and disgust. How could such unmitigated evil exist in this, the twentieth century? Moreover, we soon came to realize that this evil had affected many millions of people other than the Jews, and had been allowed to spread through the complicity or indifference of millions of others.

Almost immediately upon our return, I began to expand my investigation beyond the Jewish experience of the Holocaust, while retaining a determination to have the art rooted in the enormous tragedy that it represented for the Jewish people. My extensive studies included reading personal testimonies by survivors of other genocidal actions of the twentieth century (described by some historians as the "age of genocide"). I immediately noticed certain similarities between these writings and Holocaust-survivor literature, and then, other narratives like those by former slaves or victims of other historic tragedies. What linked them, of course, was their *perspective,* which was from the point of view of the victim/survivor.

If *The Dinner Party* grew out of my realizations about women's obscured history, one could say that the *Holocaust Project* was the result of my dawning recognition that until quite recently history has not only excluded the experiences of women but those of most of the human race. In fact, what we have viewed as the historic record is actually a chronicle primarily of those few people in power. By examining the Holocaust, I slowly came to pierce this extremely limited record in order to perceive a larger global and historic picture, one in which innumerable—even most—people on the planet might be best described as the "victims" of history in that they have been relatively powerless to shape many of the decisions that impact their lives.

My point here has to do with how few people actually control the destinies of most of those who inhabit the earth (and here I refer to both human and nonhuman life). Gradually, I came to see the Holocaust in the larger context of a global structure of power and powerlessness. Perhaps the Nazis exemplified the grossest abuse of power ever manifested. If so, they demonstrated all too clearly what can happen when such an extreme level of abuse occurs. Given the massive technology of destruction in the hands of those now in power on the planet, if they were to exercise even a similar—not to mention a comparable—lack of restraint, the rest of us would be as utterly powerless as the Jews were to prevent our own victimization and, even more, the utter annihilation of life as we know it.

There is a saying in the Jewish community about how the Jews' position in the world can be likened to that of canaries in a mine, the deaths of the birds signifying the dangerous conditions within the underground shaft. Using this analogy, one might say that the Holocaust of the Jews could be construed not only as a warning but as an omen, one that human beings may *choose* to confront or, at our peril, to ignore. But what, exactly, is this sign telling us, you might ask. The answers that Donald and I came to are best expressed through the art that we created. It is in the exhibition and in the book that we tried to share what we discovered and concluded. But it would seem that in order to learn the important lessons of the Holocaust, people will have to be willing to do just what Donald and I did: *choose* to enter the darkness of the Holocaust (not that I am suggesting our journey as the only path).

I must now come back to the argument posited by so many scholars about the utter uniqueness of the Holocaust, in particular, the Final Solution. Maybe this is true, but if so, why should anyone but the Jews (and Gypsies, who were similarly targeted) care about it? This seems an especially crucial question as the Holocaust-survivor generation dies off and, with them, the *necessity* to remember or to be concerned. In terms of our own journey, as Donald and I became ever more deeply involved in the subject of the Holocaust, its meaning seemed increasingly urgent in terms of contemporary society, which is why we dedicated so many years to this disturbing undertaking.

At one point during the project, while on a Japanese lecture tour, we went to Hiroshima. As we live in New Mexico, the birthplace of the atomic bomb, it was especially distressing to confront—through the photos and film footage we saw there—the ghastly human consequences of the American decision to use the atomic bomb. Moreover, we had to face the fact that we ourselves were engaged in a form of denial not unlike that for which we vehemently denounced the Germans. After all, Donald and I live in a state in which all around us there are weapons and materials of destruction whose potential—either intended or accidental—involves global destruction, which we try not to think about. Nor do we spend our lives working toward the disbanding of this arsenal, even though we have come to comprehend the huge threat it represents.

Certainly, there is an important distinction between the Holocaust, which actually occurred, and that which only threatens. But as Robert Lifton pointed out in the book *Genocidal Mentality,* the process of what he calls doubling and the forms of denial practiced by Nazi doctors and nuclear weapons designers is nearly identical. Which leads me to yet another query: What is the point of studying the dangerous patterns of, for example, the Nazi doctors if we are not going to apply what we learn to change our own behavior today?

My last—and probably most controversial—point concerns the

notion that the Holocaust is somehow mysterious. By the time Donald and I were finished with our inquiry, we had concluded that it was all too understandable. We came to believe that, to put it bluntly, the Holocaust was a manifestation of a world in which power rather than justice prevails. And it is important to stress that I am not speaking about my own concept of power as *empowerment* but, rather, of *power over others,* which seems to be the prevailing paradigm.

But, Judy—I hear my reader protesting—it can't be that simple. My answer is that I believe it is; the problem seems to be a general unwillingness to peer through the window provided by the Holocaust, which actually provides a rather clear picture of the dreadful darkness that now shrouds our planet, as well as our own lack of consciousness. However, I feel compelled to add that another seeming deterrent to looking through this pane of glass is that many questions are raised for which there may not be any adequate answers, at least not at this moment in history.

The goal of the *Holocaust Project* exhibition is to raise these questions, no matter how troubling or unresolvable they may be, which is one reason it took so long to complete. Each of the images, particularly those that combine painting and photography, had to be carefully engineered—philosophically, technically, and visually. Each painting/photo combines/synthesizes an enormous amount of information into a presentation that is elegant and simple—in fact, deceptively so; the purpose is to engage viewers rather than have them close off emotionally or quickly walk by. One task that I set for myself was that the art be intelligible to Holocaust survivors. I wanted it to be not only authentic to their experience—after all, it was their courage in bearing witness that brought this tragedy to light—but also intelligible to them, not so coded that they'd have no notion it was rooted in what they had gone through.

I also hoped that the show might begin to traverse the vast distance between the frequent description of the Holocaust as one of the major philosophical dilemmas of the twentieth century and the near-total silence about this subject in the art world. The *Holocaust Project* is intended to bring some understanding of the extensive scholarship on this subject to a broad and diverse audience, who could be said to be united primarily by the fact that few would be able or willing to spend the many years that Donald and I did on this topic.

The exhibition is structured as a journey into the darkness of the Holocaust and out into the light of hope, paralleling the type of journey—intellectual, physical, emotional, and aesthetic—that Donald and I made. It includes not only a series of painting/photo combines, but also a monumental tapestry, *The Fall*—a visual narrative placing the Holocaust in the "fabric" of Western civilization—and two stained-glass windows.

The last work in the show is entitled *Rainbow Shabbat*. It is a large stained-glass work, a triptych whose center panel extends the Friday Jewish Sabbath meal into an image of international sharing across race, gender, class, and species. This particular work unites my feminism, my Judaism, and my background. The image is specifically based in the Jewish experience of Shabbat, with all heads turning toward the woman, as if to suggest that the structure of male dominance that now oppresses the planet must make room for a profound change, one in which women's voices can truly be heard, along with those of everyone who shares this tiny globe. Also implied, the words "Never Forget"—so often stated in relation to the Holocaust—will never become more than an empty slogan unless many of the world's people (men and women acting together) take up a commitment to the *tikkun* (the healing and repairing of the world) that my father had taught me to strive for.

As to how the work was created, Audrey Cowan wove the tapestry from my cartoon. In addition to Audrey, there were a number of other artisans who worked with us. We all worked without pay and nobody seemed to care. All of us felt engaged in work of a higher purpose, and money seemed almost beside the point, except in terms of getting enough to accomplish the art. The subject matter of the Holocaust was too difficult for Donald and me to expect that anyone other than we ourselves (and maybe Audrey) would be prepared to spend so much time on it. (In fact, Joyce Gilbert, one of the needleworkers on *Double Jeopardy,* an image examining the specificity of women's experience during the Holocaust, confessed that because of the feelings it engendered, she could only work short hours on the piece she embroidered.)

Consequently, it was essentially Donald and I who together created the *Holocaust Project,* united in our effort to first understand and then communicate our discoveries and conclusions.

Our funding came from individual donations, one major patron, Elizabeth Sackler, and a few grants. The *Holocaust Project* was sponsored by Through the Flower, inasmuch as it acted as fiscal receiver for the monies that Donald and I raised. Personally, the two of us came out of it stronger, wiser, and closer, though deeply in debt. I wish to state that the price we paid (on every level) was worth it, if only for the profound responses to the show by the many people who have thanked us, saying that the show moved, inspired, and enlightened them, which is all one can hope that art might do.

*I*would now like to pick up my more personal chronicle. By the time we flew to New York to see *Shoah* we were engaged, which caused a degree of concern among some who knew me, as they were worried about how short a time Donald and I had known each other before taking this rather momentous step. I must confess that I would not recommend such a whirlwind romance to others, as I am sure that, more often than not, these types of relationships do not succeed. I would say two factors worked in our favor. First, we were relatively grown up and clear about what each of us wanted in a mate. Second, both of us had learned to live on our own and thus were extremely self-reliant, something we both believe is critical in forging a marriage, as it prevents overdependency. In addition, I for one was definitely finished with being alone. It was as if a chapter in my life had ended; I turned a page and found the upcoming section filled with a companionship I had longed for but despaired of ever finding.

From the start, one thing about Donald that astounded me was how steadfast he was in his commitment to our relationship. As I am someone who is blown every which way by my emotions, this was startling to me. In all my previous relationships, I had vacillated—sometimes on a daily, if not an hourly, basis—about whether I really wished to be involved with this or that person. I brought this same tendency to my relationship with Donald, but instead of reinforcing my ever-changing feelings with a comparable ambivalence, or by with-drawing or becoming angry, as others had done, he always maintained that what he wanted most was to make a life with me. I would say that this single characteristic of his is what has made our marriage turn out well, and I am grateful that he has had this strength of purpose.

It could not have been easy for him, particularly at the beginning. At the same time that I was madly in love with him, I was scared and anxious about whether agreeing to marry him would prove the biggest mistake of my life. My apprehensions were certainly not less-ened when I met his family, which occurred shortly after we saw *Shoah,* as they live on the East Coast. Donald had been alienated from his parents for many years; in fact, they did not even have his phone number until I came on the scene. Nonetheless, he wanted me to meet everyone: his mother's sister, Aunt Lillian, who lived in New York, as did Rosa, the third sister; Rosa's son, Mark; his wife, Marie; and their son, Brian. Donald's parents, Louis and Bertha, lived in New-buryport, north of Boston. My fiancé and his architect brother, Jona-than, had been brought up in Haverhill, a nearby town. Sometime after Jon settled in Newburyport, their parents moved into a house owned by and right next door to Jon, his wife, Betsey, and their daughter, Kate.

My first inkling of why Donald had become so disengaged from his family came when we had dinner in New York with his aunt Lillian. The oldest of the three sisters, she was a crotchety and rather spiteful woman who greeted us at the restaurant by grabbing my hand and asking if her "dumb nephew" had even had the courtesy to give me a proper engagement ring. Entirely ignoring the beautiful silver-and-turquoise ring on my finger, she pushed this enormous, incredibly ugly opal into my hand.

Before we left New York for Newburyport, I met with the people at ACA, who'd agreed to provide me with a monthly stipend until 1986, when I was scheduled to have my next show with them, which would be the exhibit of *Powerplay.* Given all that seemed to be hap-pening in my career, I felt confident that I would continue to sell art (the Marilyn Butler show had done fairly well), so I was rather blasé about the fact that, as a creative photographer, Donald didn't exactly earn a steady income, something his aunt Lillian had pointed out during dinner in a rather disagreeable manner, as would his brother and sister-in-law.

Newburyport, a small village that has become something of a tourist destination, is about an hour away from Boston. Filled with many restored old buildings and quaint shops, it is near the water, which produces a blustery and chilly atmosphere, especially in the late fall, when we arrived. Having had my own family so torn apart when I was young, I was hoping for a warm relationship with Donald's family. Instead, I was treated to a list of Donald's character flaws by Jon and Betsey. They harped on his financial instability, though never in my adult life had I been supported by a man, nor did I ever entertain this expectation.

I quite liked Louis, Donald's father, a charming though rather mute man. Less educated than his wife, Bertha, he had spent most of his life doing blue-collar work, sometimes holding down two full-time jobs at once. There was something about his manner that reminded me of Donald's, and I could see where my soon-to-be husband had gotten some of his sweetness. As to Bertha, over the years I would come to appreciate her and the active life that she was able to make for herself in the middle of what struck me as a difficult family situation. I also developed a close relationship with Donald's aunt Rosa.

After our Newburyport trip, we stopped in Boston to have dinner with Lois Lindauer, who'd helped bring *The Dinner Party* show there, and her husband, Bill Seltz. By then it had turned cold, and an unexpected early snowstorm had left the streets quite icy. After an enjoyable meal, I slipped on the frozen sidewalk and landed on my right wrist. Although it hurt like the dickens, I refused to think this accident significant enough for medical attention. I wrapped a bandage around my hand and went about my usual exercise stint the next morning. That day we flew home, and I ended up in the emergency room a few hours after we'd arrived in Santa Fe.

I had broken my right hand, which meant that I was out of commission for six weeks in terms of any *Powerplay* work. As I still had the use of my fingers, I contented myself with doing a humorous series of *Cast* drawings, in which I recorded everything that had happened to make me suffer this accident and its consequences, including how smelly the cast became. I also began my Holocaust research and spent time with Donald, working on the many details of our wedding, and studying with Rabbi Lynn. At the end of November we flew to L.A. so that Donald could meet my mother and friends. Everybody adored him, as did my Chicago relatives when we went there in December for my aunt Enid's eightieth-birthday celebration, although Howard was a little standoffish, as he is extremely protective of his "baby cousin Judy" (which is how he refers to me still). But this would not have kept him away from the wedding, and eventually he came around, so much so that he, Arleen, Donald, and I now spend many long and happy weekends together.

On New Year's Eve, 1985, Donald and I were married at Romona's house in Galisteo. Our bonding began with a contemporary version of the ritual cleansing known as the *mikvah*. This is usually performed separately by men and women, but we did it together in a hot tub. After our bath, we went through a rather odd ritual, which involved our facing each other and holding hands while someone circled around us carrying a moonstone. I have to admit that this actually seemed to send energy back and forth between us, until we felt almost as if the wedding knot had been tied right then. (If this sounds rather New Agey, my reader must remember that we lived in Santa Fe, the center of this kind of celestial magic, and also that we were, of course, crazed with love.)

Immediately afterward we separated to prepare for the more formal ceremony, each of us aided by our two "best people." My cousin Arleen, another friend, and I all crowded into one of the bathrooms at Romona's house, primping and giggling like teenagers (a belated activity on my part, as I had never had experiences like this in my teens). My dress was ecru, kind of netlike, covered with pale sequins and beading. In a sweet gesture, Donald's mother had made me a blue garter and also sewn me a lace-edged, ecru chiffon veil. This was designed to completely cover my face during the early part of the ceremony, then be flipped back after the *bedekken* ritual to show both my face and a beautiful crown of flowers that matched the one on Donald's head.

I should explain why, as a twentieth-century feminist, I would agree to incorporate such a rite, which in many traditional societies is associated with some extremely oppressive practices regarding women. By the time of our wedding I had begun my study program, and one of the books I had read concerned Hasidic customs, many of which, according to the author, had been seriously misunderstood. As an example, the *bedekken* ceremony was originally intended to enhance the erotic connection between husband and wife. Whatever its origins, the way in which we enacted this ritual was nothing if not intensely erotic.

I was seated in a small room with our family, closest friends, and Rabbi Lynn. All the rest of the guests were gathered in the living room. After some moments of expectant waiting, Donald entered this antechamber, and when he walked up to me I was trembling. I can still remember the tingling sensation on my neck as he approached me to lift my veil, at which point we beheld each other, transformed from the people we had been only hours before into *bride* and *groom*. Carrying in one hand our ketubah, the marriage certificate we had spent many days working on together, Donald reached out with his other hand to grasp mine, and we walked over to Rabbi Lynn. After reading aloud the vows we had composed outlining our commitment to each other, the ketubah was signed by the two of us, our rabbi, and our witnesses.

Then Donald dropped the veil back over my face and we sat down on chairs. Suddenly we were hoisted into the air and carried into the front room, which was filled with more than fifty of our friends noisily clapping to the raucous strains of a klezmer band. The room was hot from the fire blazing in the huge fireplace, in front of which was the gigantic huppah (marriage canopy) that Donald had built out of logs and pine branches. It was so heavy that our four best people had trouble holding it up during the ceremony, and only Cousin Howard's exertions prevented it from capsizing and covering bride, groom, rabbi, and attendants with the bower of pine needles that constituted the top of this somewhat oversized canopy.

As we faced Rabbi Lynn and she began to chant the traditional Hebrew prayers, both Donald and I felt moved in some deep, unfathomable way. Even though both of us had been married before, neither of us had been married by a rabbi, and somehow we had never felt truly bonded to another person until that evening, at which time Donald told me that this was the happiest day of his life. After the ceremony, there was eating, drinking, and ecstatic dancing, including a wonderful moment when—as though attempting to strengthen their less-than-firmly-knit family bond—Donald, Jonathan, and his father all danced together while everyone else clapped in unison. At midnight, Rabbi Lynn gathered us together for New Year's blessings, at which time she blew the shofar (ram's horn), a sacrament performed each year on Rosh Hashanah to commemorate the Jewish New Year. Many of the guests commented that ours was one of the most wonderful weddings they had ever attended, a sentiment definitely shared by the bride and groom.

We soon settled into married life, Donald taking a part-time job with an architect friend while I returned to my studio and my studies. Before I broke my wrist, I had begun a series of cast-paper reliefs that synthesized the sad and angry male faces of earlier work into a single image, expressing a kind of divided self. Over the next few weeks I worked on drawings for this series, along with doing some sketches of Donald in which I tried to capture his softness along with his strength. While he was modeling for me, he commented that one thing that had always struck him about some of my work was that I had provided alternative images of women, in which they were presented as strong and powerful rather than passive or victimized. He suggested that I try to do something similar, perhaps offering a picture of men as women might wish them to be. I began to ask myself a version of the old Freudian question: What do women really want? My answer was put forth in *Woe/Man,* for which Donald posed. In this large relief, the head is lifted, the throat exposed in a strong gesture that also suggests vulnerability.

One Sunday in January, as was my habit on weekends, I went running on my favorite trail: up the twisting hills of the neighborhood and down upper Canyon Road, then looping back toward the house, where I knew that Donald would probably have a steaming cup of cappuccino waiting for me. We had taken to sitting on the sun porch with our kitties curled up next to us and reading the Sunday papers. I was looking forward to a quiet day. The morning was cold and crisp with the clear, delicious blue sky of a New Mexico winter. As I rounded a turn and started my long downhill sprint, I saw a large, beat-up truck coming up the road. The next thing I knew, I was sprawled out on the ground on my back with an excruciating pain scalding my right side. The old man driving the truck had smacked directly into my hipbone, then sped on.

Several other cars stopped, which caused the truck driver to pause, then back up. Although I didn't know it at the time, he was a myopic eighty-one-year-old who should have stopped driving years before but had been allowed to keep his license thanks to the lax laws of New Mexico. An ambulance was summoned, and I was taken to the hospital. I can remember lying in the back, wondering if I was going to die. Meanwhile, a man who'd been at the scene somehow found his way to my house and notified Donald.

Poor Donald! He rushed to the hospital and must have been terribly shocked to see his wife of less than four weeks lying in a bed in the emergency room. Actually, I was extremely fortunate, because although my pelvis was broken, I needed neither surgery nor a cast, though I was pretty badly bruised; in fact, I had dark red hematomas over one entire side of my body. After three frightening days in intensive care, I spent about a week in the hospital, during which time I had to be transfused because I had lost so much blood from internal bleeding.

I really couldn't take in how badly I'd been hurt. I didn't fully realize that I'd had an extremely close call, and that my body had suffered such trauma that it would take six months for me to fully recover. Donald was wonderful to me, although for some weeks he walked around in a state of shock. Finally we decided to try and deal with our feelings about this upsetting incident by collaborating on a series of images that combined my drawing with his photographs, recreating the accident and documenting the damage to my body. I must admit that it was difficult for me to have my new husband staring straight at my disfigured body through his camera lens, though I was glad for the opportunity to work together in an attempt to transform the raw emotions of the experience and painful photographs of my battered flesh into something resembling art.

It took some time before I was able to resume my schedule of regular hours in the studio, study, and exercise, combined with lectures, openings, *Holocaust Project* research, and other related activities. Whenever we could manage it, Donald traveled with me, which was great; in fact, we would have some of our best times on the road. Gradually our life was taking on a pleasant rhythm. A few months after the accident, we began to make plans to go to Germany. After the London exhibition of *The Dinner Party*, a group of German women had begun organizing to get the piece shown there, eventually convincing Cristof Vitali, the director of the Schirn Kunsthalle in Frankfurt—a "real" museum, thankfully—to mount the exhibition.

This German effort was spearheaded by two women, Dagmar von Garnier and Anne-Marie Gesse, but it eventually expanded to include a vast network of (primarily) women from Germany, Austria, and Switzerland. To build support for and interest in *The Dinner Party*, the organizers were planning something called the Festival of One Thousand Women, to be held at the restored Frankfurt Opera House in June 1986, one year before the scheduled show. Hundreds of people from all over Europe were preparing to assemble there, each costumed as one of the women on *The Dinner Party* table or the *Heritage Floor*. The organizers invited me to come for this gala and to see the museum space, which I agreed to on condition they also bring Donald over to discuss the planned exhibition installation, as he had taken over as installation supervisor.

I had been to Germany only once and then quite briefly, as had Donald. In 1972 Lloyd and I had gone to Europe together and driven through Germany. We sped through the country, because even though I knew very little about the Holocaust at the time, I somehow sensed that I didn't want to spend more than a few moments on German soil. On this same trip Lloyd and I had gone to the Anne Frank house in Amsterdam, where I was quite taken aback by the yellow stars that were displayed there. One could still see the threads with which such badges were sewn onto Jews' clothing, and it had struck me then that, had I been born in Europe, I would have died during the war.

Shortly before leaving for Germany, I traveled around the country for several weeks, going first to L.A. with Donald to view survivor testimony at the UCLA archives and also to celebrate my mother's seventy-fifth birthday, an occasion for which my brother also came to town. At this time Ben and I had another rather difficult conversation, during which he told me that he viewed all my efforts to discuss the problems of our childhood as being "negative," then insisted that he only remembered "good times." I was stunned to realize that we had such entirely different memories of our childhood, although I was tempted to suggest that he was practicing a high level of denial about the reality of his. From there I went to Benicia by myself for a two-day Through the Flower board meeting, which by then had become an annual event. I did a few lectures around the country, then went to New York where, after a few days, Donald met up with me.

John Perrault, the former *SoHo News* critic who had so loved *The Dinner Party,* had become the curator of a small museum in Staten Island, for which he organized a good-sized *Birth Project* show. In another attempt at family solidarity, I invited all of Donald's relatives to the opening, after which Betsey, who had had an art history degree, took it upon herself to write a critique of the exhibit, which she circulated to all her friends. As I told her in my customary less-than-tactful way, I had enough trouble with the art critics without such comments from a member of my new family.

We went on to Washington, D.C., where Donald did some photo research in the National Archives. We also met Isaiah Kuperstein, who became somewhat of a mentor to me. I can still recall sitting in a small coffee shop around the corner from the offices of the Holocaust Memorial Council, where he then worked. Because he was a Holocaust scholar and educator, we wanted to discuss our initial ideas for the *Holocaust Project,* along with our anxiety about the upcoming trip to Germany. Isaiah, who had been born in the German town of Essen, suggested that we might like to visit the old synagogue there, which had been turned into the only museum in Germany then dedicated to the Holocaust. He also advised us to try to keep an open mind about

Germany. This was to be the first of many such conversations in which Isaiah gently steered us away from a somewhat emotional and unthinking reaction and toward a more measured point of view.

Not too long afterward, Donald and I flew to Germany. Gelon, who was living in London, met us in Frankfurt. A day or two later, we arrived at the Opera House for the scheduled festival and found the front of the building draped with a gigantic, blood-red velvet curtain with a small, vagina-like entrance. With some dismay, we squeezed through the folds of the fabric to discover that inside all was tumult. Hundreds of decoratively adorned women mingled, introducing themselves as this or that historic woman, then reciting her biography. After a rousing performance of a piece by Fanny Mendelssohn that had never before been performed (presented by an all-female orchestra conducted by a woman dressed up as the composer), it was time for a performance in which the thirty-nine women dressed as the figures on the table were to assemble a sort of living triangle in the center of the hall.

The person representing Petronilla de Meath, the first woman burned as a witch, was missing, and I spontaneously took her place, encouraging the other women to join hands while we waited for another bout of music to begin. For some reason, never explained, this planned musical interlude did not occur; instead, there was an eerie silence, then a crooning sound seemed to arise as if from nowhere. It was a cross between a moan and a wail, and soon all the women in the room added their voices to this tone. The rhythmic pitch built to a loud crescendo, then abruptly subsided. At the moment when the sound reached its height, all thirty-nine women raised our arms in unison, at which moment it felt as though the very spirit of *The Dinner Party* entered the room. I would be told again and again that this moment was the highlight of the festival.

Later, while I was being interviewed by some major media, the hundreds of costumed women descended from the upstairs hall to the foyer, dancing and passing around a large clay amphora. To some, this large jug apparently represented the ancient Goddess, whose various names were repeatedly invoked. Then, all at once, they began to chant my name louder and louder, until someone came to fetch me. I was immediately hoisted up on many shoulders, whereupon the huge crowd of women surged outside to the plaza, which was thronged with bystanders. Much of the rest of the day was spent in somewhat wild dancing, most of which Donald, Gelon, and I did not witness, as we had had about all of this group frenzy we could take.

One fascinating aspect of the whole German episode regarding *The Dinner Party* was that, on this and our subsequent trip in 1987, my own personal experience was that both myself and the work were well received. And yet, according to Anette Kubitza, a young art historian who has written extensively on the German reaction, my own perspective was once again quite different from that of the art and feminist press. This contrast can probably be explained in several ways. First, I was buoyed as usual by the huge popular outpouring of response, both during the festival and at the exhibition the following year. Second, *The Dinner Party* was the most successful show ever held up to that time at the museum, and I again naively believed that this would count for *something*. Third, I don't read or understand German, and no one ever mentioned that the reviews, according to Anette, were so hostile as to be poisonous. Finally, by the time of the exhibition I would be completely absorbed in the *Holocaust Project*.

As Jews in Germany, both Donald and I were glad that we had taken Isaiah's advice to keep an open mind and also go to Essen. The trip there was quite moving, in that the Holocaust exhibition at the former synagogue chronicled events that had happened in the very streets we could see out of the building's windows. However, the German woman who accompanied us as our translator and guide refused to come into the museum. She told us that she simply could not deal with the Holocaust, as her father had been a police officer during the years of the Reich. Although she and everyone else we met in Germany were very nice to us, her comment gave us a sense of the enormous shadow that lay over the German past.

When we returned from our 1986 trip to Germany for the Festival of One Thousand Women, we decided that we would use the months when *The Dinner Party* was to be in Frankfurt the following year to travel through the landscape of the Holocaust. By then I was negotiating with Doubleday for a book about the project, and I intended to use part of the advance to pay for this next trip. I spent the summer working in the studio and doing research.

Early in September I received a call from my former lover Brian, telling me that Stephen Hamilton had been diagnosed with AIDS and that he was so wretched from the news that he had been unable to tell me himself. Over the next few years I spoke to Stephen weekly and he visited us frequently. But at the end, when he was close to death, I would not be able to bring myself to see him, something I still feel distressed about. But by then several other people close to me were terminally ill and my emotional stamina was terribly strained, especially given the ongoing demands of the *Holocaust Project*. I grieved for Stephen for a long time.

Later that month Donald and I flew to Chicago for a *Birth Project* show at the Richard Love gallery, then to New York for the opening of my *Powerplay* exhibition at ACA. Right after this we went to the Caribbean for our first real vacation, arriving back in New Mexico in mid-October. I left soon afterward for a Through the Flower board meeting in L.A. While there I made another attempt to talk to my mother about what she and my father had known about the Holocaust during the Second World War. My first effort had not gotten me very far, as she had bristled when I first brought up this subject. This time she was somewhat more receptive, and we were even able to talk about why we had celebrated Christmas every year until just after the war. She explained that she hadn't wanted Ben and me to feel alienated from the other kids in the neighborhood, but then she and my father became uncomfortable about this practice once all the facts about the Final Solution were known.

I then went up to Benicia to spend a few days with MR, primarily to follow up on some of the discussions that had taken place at the board meeting. The board had talked about the relationship between Through the Flower and the *Holocaust Project,* agreeing to my proposal that the corporation act as sponsor so that Donald and I could apply for grants and accept donations. MR and I agreed that the administration of the *Holocaust Project* should be done in Santa Fe, where Juliet could provide us some degree of support. MR had her hands full with the *Birth Project* tour, which was then going strong, and she had also begun to take on some *Dinner Party* duties, as Gelon was increasingly occupied with her London law practice. MR indicated that at some point she would like to return to Houston but, given all that was happening, it would be best to keep the Benicia building open somewhat longer.

I went home in late October to discover that there had been almost no *Powerplay* sales at the gallery and, curiously, a near-total silence in terms of articles and reviews, the first time such a thing had ever happened to me. I still don't quite know what to make of this, but I do know that at the time I was worried about the gallery's response. The Bergens were unfazed, however, telling me to just keep working, no matter what. The problem was that, given the lack of sales, my gallery stipend would soon come to an end, which meant that our finances would get extremely tight.

Shortly after the first of the year, MR arranged to buy a small house at the back of the Santa Fe property, which she agreed to rent to me for use as a studio at an extremely modest cost and in exchange for art. I received my advance from Doubleday (when Doubleday was later sold, they let the book contract go, which is how I ended up at Viking Penguin), which would pay for our upcoming European trip as well as renovations on this building. Once these were finished, Donald would take over my former studio quarters in the house, as there was no way we could use the same space.

Throughout the early part of the year we were busy with research, renovations, and preparations for the trip. These were interrupted when my mother was diagnosed with breast cancer and we went to L.A. for the operation, which involved a radical mastectomy. The tests showed that the cancer had spread into her lymph nodes, but we were told by Dr. Brody to take some comfort in the fact that cancer metastasizes slowly in elderly people. Then, within weeks of my mother's operation, Donald's father was found to have colon cancer, and we flew East. Louis's malignancy was localized, fortunately, and his prognosis was good after it had been removed.

In response to these trials, Donald and I set to work on a suite of drawings we called *Coast to Coast Cancer,* in which we could deal with our unhappy feelings in images that combined my drawings with his

photographs. While thus engaged, we went back to L.A. to see how
my mother was doing. When I saw her, I thought about the arrogance
with which the Nazis deemed some people unworthy of life, because
I realized that, given her age and infirmity, my mother would not
have been allowed to survive. My thinking about the Nazi "eutha-
nasia" program triggered an enormous wave of compassion for my
mother.

In mid-April we left for Germany. As soon as we arrived in Frankfurt we went to the museum where the installation of *The Dinner Party*
exhibition was already under way, directed by a handsome young fellow named Hans Werner Pollack. From day one it was difficult to be
in Germany without experiencing a dual level of reality all the time.
For example, the installation crew was incredibly professional, which
was great in terms of *The Dinner Party*; but at the same time this gave
me the creeps as it made me think about German efficiency in the
implementation of the Final Solution. Or when I went running in the
lush park that bordered our hotel, I would pass elderly gentlemen
taking a stroll. They would nod politely and I would smile back, all
the while wondering what they must have been doing during the war.
Then there was the near-constant noise of trains rumbling in the background, as the hotel was close to a train route. This sound, summoning
thoughts of the transports to the concentration camps, would haunt
me throughout the days in which we were there, many of which I
spent curled up in the hotel suite studying writings by Elie Wiesel.

Audrey Cowan and Susan Hill both came to work on *The Dinner
Party* textiles, which needed some repair. Gelon came in for the opening, as did Juliet Myers. It was quite an event, introduced, as in
London, by an opening speech, this time by an art historian whose
words seemed to bespeak an understanding of *The Dinner Party* that
is contradicted by everything reported by Anette Kubitza (no wonder
I get confused). Audrey had indicated that she wished to accompany
Donald and me on some portion of our trip, so shortly after the opening, the three of us set off for France. Our first stop was at the Natz-
weiler concentration camp in Alsace-Lorraine, cold and snowy even in
May. No amount of study could have prepared us for the dank, cold,
humid air; the seven-kilometer road built by the prisoners; then the

crematorium building with its oven and dissecting table; and the nearby hotel and bar, across from which there was an old bathhouse that had been converted into the gas chamber for this camp.

From there we drove back to Nuremberg, site of early Nazi rallies and then the war-crimes trials after the war. We went on to Dachau, a camp that has been thoroughly sanitized, at which point Audrey left us and we continued East into Austria. I wrote Isaiah a letter about our experiences in the slave-labor tunnels of Ebensee that caused him to worry about my sanity. He was justified in these fears, because only two weeks into the journey I was coming undone, as was Donald. There were many nights when we would collapse at this or that hotel, he withdrawing into silence, I sobbing for hours.

We continued on to Theresienstadt in Czechoslovakia, site of a former ghetto, and then to Prague, where I had another epiphany, this time at the old cemetery filled with innumerable Jewish graves and gravestones. There was something about walking among them that created a sense of both pride and despair, as if I finally understood the long and rich tradition of Eastern European Jewry, while at the same time what it meant that so many parts of Europe were now *Judenrein,* or "Jew-free." From there we went to Poland and the very center of hell; Auschwitz-Birkenau, the scale of which astounded both of us.

Everywhere we went I drew and wrote in my journal and Donald took photographs, trying to establish an image base that we could draw upon even before we knew exactly what we were going to do. Whenever we visited a camp or site it seemed to rain; I called the downpours "tears of sorrow." Nowhere was our despondency greater than at Treblinka, which Harvey Mudd had described in his poem as one of the saddest places in the world. Seventeen thousand stones commemorated the murders of hundreds of thousands of people who'd been herded onto trains and brought here tired, hungry, thirsty, and terrified; all were put to death within hours of their arrival.

From Poland we were scheduled to go to Russia. By then it was June, and after a big hassle with the Polish authorities about our visas, we made our way to Leningrad (as it was still called then) at the time of White Nights. The long, oddly lit days were spent visiting dissident Jews, who educated us about the ongoing anti-Semitism there. Our one break was a visit to the famous Hermitage museum.

At one point, we had a screaming fight on the Nevsky Prospekt, watched by Russians who seemed alternately shocked, fascinated, and amused by the sight of two Americans shrieking at each other in the middle of a crowded downtown street. I stomped off, announcing that I was going home—an impossibility, given Russian travel arrangements, and laughable when I think about it, particularly in light of my terrible sense of direction; I probably couldn't have found my way back to the hotel, much less all the way to America. Fortunately, Donald followed me to make sure I got to our quarters safely, by which time I had cooled off. We soon made up and than went on to Latvia and Lithuania. In Vilna—by either miracle or fate, I could not decide which—we found the tomb of my illustrious ancestor, the Vilna Gaon. As I stood inside his mausoleum, I marveled at the journey that had brought me here (along with Donald's insistence). I could not help but wonder what my father would have thought about my determination to reconnect with the family's Jewish roots.

By the time we arrived home in July, we found ourselves transformed by all that we had shared, suffered, and learned. Although we didn't realize this at the time, we had also been more firmly bonded as a couple by what we had been through together. As we would sometimes say later on, if we could get through a trip as grueling as this, there was not too much that could render us separate. Our trip dramatically broadened our understanding of the Holocaust—its scale, scope, and meaning. After almost two years of preparation, I had many ideas, beginning with *The Fall,* the large tapestry that places the Holocaust in the context of Western civilization and examines the historic relationship between anti-Semitism and antifeminism. I worked on studies and then on the cartoon until the end of the year.

By the fall of 1987 plans had been finalized for *The Dinner Party* to go to Australia as part of its bicentennial celebration, scheduled for early 1988. Through the Flower decided to hire Hans Werner, the young man from Germany, to work with the people in Melbourne to set up the space at the Royal Exhibition Hall, which needed considerable renovation; given the demands of the *Holocaust Project,* Donald didn't have the time it would take. Instead, it was agreed that he would go in to handle the actual installation, then I would come for the opening. In addition to the exhibition in Australia, I was also making plans for two gallery shows, one in Los Angeles and another at the Andrew Smith gallery in Santa Fe with Annie Leibovitz, whom I'd seen from time to time since she photographed me in Benicia in 1979.

She and I joked that this exhibit should probably be called "The Queen of Content Meets the Queen of Form," as her highly polished portraits were in stark contrast to what I intended to display: a series of pieces I dubbed "Accidents, Injuries, and Other Calamities." My plan was to exhibit the various works I'd done over the years—some in collaboration with Donald—on the accidents, operations, and other incidents I and other family members had sustained. Most of these pieces were quite direct, even raw, and I hoped that by showing them I might put an end to the many hospital trips I had been forced to make during the previous years.

Toward the end of the year I began to go to therapy with Donald, who'd been seeing a psychiatrist named Donald Fineberg. Early in our sessions, Dr. Don, who'd treated a number of Holocaust survivors, told me that I seemed to have many personality traits similar to theirs. In terms of Donald and me as a couple, Dr. Don was to help us immensely over the next few years as we became increasingly immersed in an artmaking project that caused us both such endless grief. Even though we had become much closer after our months of travel, our marriage still might not have survived the stress the work would cause, primarily because we reacted so differently. Donald's tendency was to shut down emotionally, whereas I became hypersensitive. Dr. Don helped us to build communication skills so that we could cross over these differences in style in order to better deal with the many hurdles, both personal and artistic, that might otherwise have torn us apart.

Shortly after Donald and I celebrated our second wedding anniversary, he left for Australia. I followed him a few weeks later. *The*

Dinner Party was ushered in by a Banquet for One Thousand Women (attended by many more) that mimicked an all-male event held one hundred years earlier in conjunction with the Australian centennial. Once again, the exhibition generated some degree of controversy, but the criticism seemed nowhere near as mean-spirited as that in Germany and New York. The show proved to be such a popular success that a museum in Western Australia asked to mount the exhibition at the end of its Melbourne stay. I refused because by then *The Dinner Party* had been exhibited fourteen times, more than I had originally planned. It was showing considerable wear and tear, particularly the runners, some of which had sustained damage when the roof of the London venue had leaked.

Moreover, I thought—and Through the Flower's board agreed—that it was time to bring the piece back to America. We were under the impression that *The Dinner Party* had triumphed over the resistance that the art world had initially evidenced, as indicated by the fact that the piece was being featured in so many art history books and taught in both art and women's studies classes all over the world. We firmly believed that the work might finally find a permanent home, thinking that, after its demonstrated audience appeal, any number of institutions would be interested in housing it. This assumption was reinforced by what we knew of art history, which demonstrates a trajectory from creation to exhibition to preservation of works of art, at least those viewed as historically important. Judging from its international impact, it seemed that *The Dinner Party* might certainly be so evaluated.

Before leaving Australia, Donald and I traveled around while I did some lectures. We climbed Ayers Rock, a sacred and fascinating Aboriginal site that is, I believe, now entirely closed to visitors or extremely restricted. At one point we stopped in Alice Springs, where we saw many Aboriginal people. Germaine Greer, whom I ran into at our hotel in Melbourne, had described these people as "driven mad with grief" by what she characterized as the Australian genocide. Somewhere in Queensland—in my opinion, one of the most exquisite and ecologically untouched spots in the world—I contemplated her

remarks and thought about the connection between such cultural genocide and the Holocaust.

When we returned to New Mexico, Donald and I set to work
almost immediately on the first series of painting/photo combines. The
months soon settled into the pattern I like best: long, focused periods
in the studio, then breaks for travel—to lecture, do research, and make
presentations on the *Holocaust Project,* which helped us raise funds.

In the early spring of 1988, my mother was finally accepted into
the Jewish Home for the Aging. After her initial surge of interest in
doing this, she had decided instead to move into another retirement
home in the same neighborhood where she had been living. This place
proved as inadequate as the previous one had been, rapidly going
downhill in terms of services and offering no intellectual stimulation
whatsoever, which left her with not much to do but sleep. Ben and I
were both concerned that if she didn't make this move soon, it would
be too late, as the Jewish Home requires that people be in good health
when they enter. Despite the cancer, my mother was still in relatively
good shape physically.

Over the previous few years, things had eased up some between
my brother and me, particularly after I followed his lead and stopped
trying to rehash our childhood. Instead, I concentrated on trying to
improve our relationship by focusing on the present and sharing stories
about our work and respective lives. Ben was becoming established as
a potter, and he and Reiko had two sons, Elijah and Simon. At one
point he offered to come over and help my mother move, a task in
which he was aided by Kate Amend, who had always been fond of
my mom. In addition to her affection for my mother, I believe that
Katie wanted to ferret out and save some of my letters and early
drawings that my mother had squirreled away (I tend to throw out
such materials).

About this same time the L.A. show opened. Even though I and
all my art world friends thought it looked pretty spectacular, the
review in the *Los Angeles Times*—by the same critic who had so hated
The Dinner Party—was scathing, reiterating the opinion that I cannot
draw. Far worse, there were no sales whatsoever from this exhibit,

which ended up costing me money (in framing and shipping) that I could ill afford. On Memorial Day weekend, the show at the Andrew Smith gallery opened with a line down the block. On the day of the opening, one of the largest of my works fell off the wall. Everyone commented on the irony of an exhibit about misfortunes starting off with an accident. No one was injured, fortunately, though the piece was ruined.

Over this summer of 1988, I worked steadily on the *Holocaust Project*. The work was hard, made even more difficult by the fact that by then we were living month-to-month, barely scraping by and not sure how we'd pay the next month's bills. We had started sending out a newsletter, which, with our presentations around the country, brought in donations, but only enough for supplies. In August, a woman named Elizabeth Sackler came to see the *Holocaust Project*. The daughter of art collector Arthur M. Sackler, she visited us as an evaluator for the Threshold Foundation, as the Bergen twins had put us up for a grant.

Meeting Liz was extremely propitious, and we soon became good friends with her and her husband. More important, in terms of the *Holocaust Project* and our strapped finances, she aided us in securing the grant. She also soon became a major patron, helping to sustain us through her art purchases and her contributions to both the project and Through the Flower, whose board she joined for a few years.

In November Donald and I went to Israel, as our research would definitely not have been complete without such a trip. Neither of us had ever been there, and many people had told us that we could not imagine what it would be like to visit a Jewish country. They were right: Here it was the Jews who were the norm while others were the outsiders. Our reactions to Israel were complex, as it is a place of stunning contradictions. On the one hand, I loved the energy of the Jewish people, demonstrated by the way they had made the desert bloom. At the same time, I deplored the sexism that seemed to pervade the country and hated the omnipresent military (while recognizing its necessity). We drove all over, visiting museums, kibbutzim, and Holocaust memorials. One of my favorite spots was the Galilee, so beautiful as to be breathtaking, almost like a picture postcard. While there we managed a dip in the Dead Sea, floating around like corks in the slimy water.

We were home in time to prepare Thanksgiving dinner, to which Howard and Arleen came, along with nearly twenty other friends. Unfortunately, Donald became ill with pneumonia and ended up in the hospital. By early December he had recovered and we were both back in the studio. The first half of 1989 was spent working on the *Holocaust Project*. A short interruption came in April when Donald and I went to L.A. for a tenth-year reunion for *The Dinner Party,* to which more than forty people came (including Gelon, who flew in from London). Before we left for California, Donald and Juliet organized a private celebration at the Santa Café. Julie decorated the table with *Dinner Party* motifs and the chef, Michael Fennelly (who now owns his own restaurant in New Orleans), concocted a series of courses based upon the place setting, my favorite being the "Georgia O'Keeffe chicken wings." The pièce de résistance was an "Emily Dickinson" cake, patterned after the plate, with layers of shaved white chocolate formed like the lace-draped image.

In May we made a short trip to Chicago to meet with the Spertus Museum, a Jewish institution whose curator, Olga Weiss, had written to us after receiving one of our newsletters. It seemed that they were interested in premiering the show, an idea that appealed to Donald and me because, even though we were determined to exhibit the *Holocaust Project* in both Jewish and secular art institutions, we thought it important to start the exhibition tour in a Jewish museum. We believed that this would demonstrate that, although the exhibition definitely broadened the dialogue about the Holocaust beyond the Jewish experience, nonetheless, the art was authentically embedded in a Jewish perspective. Both Donald and I very much liked the (then) museum director, Morrie Fred, with whom we would work on plans for the exhibition over the course of several years.

On July 20, 1989, I turned fifty, and two days later there was a huge birthday party at our house, attended by more than fifty of my friends, all costumed in 1950s outfits, who danced all night to the strains of a band playing 1950s tunes. My friend and housekeeper,

Mabel Griego, prepared a wonderful feast of spicy New Mexican cuisine. Bob Cowan read a poem he had composed about me, culled from interviews with countless friends, that was so funny I fell on the ground laughing. I received gifts and flowers, including a wonderful letter jacket (as they call it in the South) from MR that was emblazoned with my initials and my age. Whenever I wear it I am reminded of this fabulous night, which remains one of the best memories of my life.

The next day, a Sunday morning, Ben called from Japan to tell me that he had been diagnosed as having amyotrophic lateral sclerosis (also known as Lou Gehrig's disease) and had been given less than three years to live, during which time he would become progressively more paralyzed. Whatever difficulties we had had during all our years of alienation dissolved in that one moment when my baby brother reached out to me, his only sibling, in terror and misery. I could not believe my ears; how could this happen? It seemed so cruel. Ben was just getting established professionally; he and Reiko had small boys, and they were planning to buy the house they were renting and were looking forward to a long and happy life together after years of considerable financial struggle.

It was as if time collapsed; my brother was just about the same age my father had been when he died, also leaving two children. The circumstances seemed too similar to be only coincidence. It felt as though our childhood had come full circle, paralyzing my brother physically as a metaphor for what it had done to both of us emotionally. And as we agreed even at that moment of shared torment, we could not tell our mother, since her cancer, though spreading slowly, was terminal. We decided that we would protect her from this sad knowledge for as long as we could. Donald and I insisted upon paying for Ben to come to America immediately for further tests; perhaps the diagnosis was incorrect. We held on to this hope like drowning people, while in our hearts we knew that there was only a slim chance that the prognosis was wrong.

I was exceedingly fortunate that so many of my friends were in town. All day they sat with me while I cried, offering sympathy and loans of money—anything at all. I was desolate—not only for Ben but for my small family, who had suffered so much loss, so much grief. Suddenly Dr. Don's words about my resemblance to Holocaust survivors came back to me. I realized that by the time the *Holocaust Project* opened, I would be the only surviving member of my family, because, in all likelihood, both my brother and my mother would be dead.

Chapter Ten

The Dinner Party
Goes to Congress

*T*he next few days were awful, full of alternate bouts of anxiety, grief, and hysteria. The idea of my brother's body slowly deteriorating until he was unable to move at all was a horrifying prospect. As I am an extremely physical person, the idea of total paralysis was almost more distressing to me than the ultimate outcome of such a diagnosis—that is, his death. Memories of our father's eldest brother, Harry, kept roiling around in my mind. When I was nine I had seen him lying naked on the bed in his home, shrunken and crippled by the lateral sclerosis that would shortly kill him. How would Ben be able to face such a terrible fate? And was it just coincidence that two family members could be stricken with such closely connected neurological illnesses?

A friend of mine, Ginna Sloane, brought over information about ALS, as her father had also suffered from it. It turned out that there was some familial predisposition, though the genetic link had not yet been located. What of Ben's sons? Could they get it? I spent hours on the phone with Mel Brody, asking questions and arranging for medical tests in L.A. I intended to meet Ben there, to be with

him while he went through the battery of examinations Mel was setting up.

I had been scheduled to lecture at the end of July in Norway, at
an international arts conference outside Bergen. Because neither Donald nor I had ever been in Scandinavia, we had thought to enjoy a
holiday while there, as we had been told that the landscape was spectacular. But I couldn't imagine cavorting around the fjords while my
brother was struggling to come to grips with this frightful news.
Moreover, I did not wish to be out of touch with him; I wanted him
to be able to call me at any time, day or night. At first I decided to
cancel the trip altogether. But when I called the conference organizers,
they became quite agitated, saying that people were coming from all
over to hear my speech. Finally Donald suggested that we go but that
we cut the trip short; also, we would stop in Chicago on the way back
so that I could see Howard, which he knew would do me good.

It was definitely helpful to get away for a brief time and also to
talk to Howard, who of all people most understood me and my family
history. We got back to Santa Fe in early August, and the next few
weeks were full of such intense sorrow that it required all my strength
and discipline to get up each morning, exercise, paint, eat, sleep, then
do it again the next day.

In mid-August I went to Los Angeles to spend several days with
Ben, which proved harrowing. On the first day we talked and wept
together for hours. The following morning we went to see the neu-
rologist recommended by Mel Brody. He did not even bother doing
all the tests that had been scheduled but coldly confirmed the diagnosis and said that Ben would probably not survive for more than a
year and a half. I called Donald that evening and begged him to fly
in, as I was desolate. The next day the three of us visited an ALS
center, where we were educated in the care techniques that had been
developed to manage neurological diseases; the methods were far more
advanced than in my uncle Harry's lifetime, at least in the United
States. Along with this information, the people at the center gave
us a degree of hope, saying that in some cases patients are able to
survive far longer than was predicted by the doctor we had seen the
previous day.

At dinner on our last evening together, we discussed some of Ben's fears for his wife and children. Reiko didn't drive and at the moment had no way of making a living. Although she was anxious about doing so she had enrolled in driving school, and Ben said that he was thinking of training her in ceramics so that she could take over his pottery, whose business aspects she was already handling. (Reiko did indeed become a potter and is now supporting herself and her children.) Ben also disclosed his desire for his sons to have the opportunity for some sort of American life, because he was afraid that in Japan their mixed blood would cause them some difficulty. He requested that Donald and I provide for them, should either Elijah or Simon wish to live or go to school in the States, which, of course, we promised to do.

Donald and I went back to New Mexico with the intention of returning to L.A. before Ben left at the end of August. My brother had many friends in America, both in California and around the country. I had encouraged him to share the news about his illness with them, and they responded with great sympathy, many flying in to be with him over the next few weeks, which was a source of great comfort to Ben. During this time he did not contact our mother, although we repeatedly discussed whether we should tell her. Ben felt unprepared to see her and completely unable to confess that he was sick; when the time came that it was unavoidable, he said, he wanted this job done by me. In late August Donald and I went back to the West Coast to be with Ben and to put him on the plane back to Japan. By then my brother was beginning to lose some degree of muscle control. As a result his gait was slightly unsteady, and when we walked him to the gate and said goodbye, he was so scared it broke my heart.

Words cannot express how dreadful I felt. All I knew to do was what I had always done before in the face of life's tragedies: that is, go back to work. I suppose that it was sadly fortuitous that the subject matter of the Holocaust was such an unhappy one, as it provided an apt vehicle for my personal misery, which I struggled to incorporate and transform into visual images of a larger and more historic suffering. Over the next months, while Ben became progressively more paralyzed, I plunged ever deeper into the grim terrain of the Holocaust, immersed both privately and aesthetically in unremitting sorrow and grief.

At first I found it difficult to stay in the studio, and was tempted to leave for any number of excuses, like making a phone call or having a cup of coffee—anything to get away from the distressing feelings, if only for a moment. Gradually I became accustomed to the dull ache of sadness in my heart and the awful reality that my brother was going to die in the near future. I was distraught that he was so far away and I wanted him to return to America, where he would have access to the type of care described to us at the ALS center. In Japan, people with catastrophic illnesses are put into the hospital, where they stay until they die. Ben was adamantly opposed to spending what time remained to him in an institution, but there was no precedent for home care in Kadanji, the small town where he and his family lived. He insisted, however, that he wanted to stay there, feeling that it was his home and that Reiko and the boys were under enough strain without being uprooted.

Ben asked if Donald and I could come to Japan soon, and, though we had no idea how we'd pay for such a trip, we agreed. We were barely scraping by as it was and had borrowed money to pay for Ben's airfare to America and what medical tests had been done. I wanted to arrange some Japanese lectures so that our plane fare and expenses might be covered, so I contacted a woman named Kazuko Koike, who lived in Tokyo. She was the daughter-in-law of an old friend of mine, Dextra Frankel, who had been the director of the gallery where I had long before held my name-change exhibition. Some years earlier, Kazuko had arranged for the publication of *Through the Flower* in Japan and had herself translated the text. She had also organized a traveling show of my work in conjunction with the book's publication. Though I had not been invited over there at the time, I hoped that there might now be some degree of interest in my doing a speaking tour, and, fortunately, there was. Kazuko set to work organizing a series of lectures for the following spring.

Throughout this period and for as long as he was physically able, I spoke to Ben weekly and sometimes more frequently. As usual, I also spoke to my mother on a regular basis and amazed myself by my ability to dissemble with her, something I had never felt comfortable doing with anyone. But because Ben and I had decided to protect her from any knowledge of his illness as long as possible, I felt I had no choice. In fact we hoped that, given her cancer, she might die before he did, as we both thought this preferable to her having to experience such woe.

At this point in the *Holocaust Project* I was working on several images in a series entitled *Banality of Evil,* all done in tones of gray, which seemed an apt hue for my downcast state. Once I was able to force myself back into concentrated work, painting became my only solace other than Donald, who was endlessly supportive. The next months went by as they do when I paint every day, taking on a rhythm that seemed to flow in a steady stream. I spent long hours carefully blending the oil paints in what felt like an almost timeless state, punctuated by exercise and the obligations of everyday life, along with long phone conversations with Ben every Saturday night. Each week before calling him, I became besieged with such fear and anxiety that I began to see Don Fineberg by myself, as I wanted to be there for my brother and needed help in fighting off the depression that threatened to choke me. I can remember Dr. Don trying to comfort me by saying that I was "not clinically depressed but rather, merely responding as anyone would in the face of so much stress."

While I struggled to maintain some semblance of normalcy in my life, Ben began to find ways to deal with what would never again be an ordinary existence. He started building a network of people willing to help him find a way to remain at home as his ALS progressed, eventually organizing an ALS chapter in his region, becoming its president, and opening the way for others so stricken who wished to have home care. Under his direction, Japanese and American friends were preparing to mount an around-the-clock regime as he became more paralyzed, so that he would be able to stay in Kadanji with his family. Before he lost the use of his hands he did some simplified pottery designs based upon his style of ceramics, which he was teaching Reiko to duplicate. He was also making a series of audiotapes for his sons, so that they could retain a sense of their father after he died. Having experienced the loss of his own father at a young age, my brother was acutely aware of how hard it was going to be for them. During this time I began to develop an incredible respect for Ben, who seemed to be mustering spiritual resources that I had never even suspected he had.

In October 1989, MR informed me that she was going to leave Through the Flower by the end of the year. Of course, her timing couldn't have been worse, what with our being in the middle of the *Holocaust Project* (which was taking longer than we had anticipated), in combination with Ben's rapidly deteriorating physical condition. But she had run the corporation for almost ten years and certainly had the right to go on with her life, though I couldn't help but wish she could have hung in there a little longer. She wanted to put everything in storage—the art and the office equipment, slide files, et cetera. I was happy to accept her offer to place the *Birth Project* and *The Dinner Party* in art storage and to pay the costs for a while. But Through the Flower provided a certain level of administrative support that I really couldn't live without.

In fact, one reason that I had been so free to concentrate on *Powerplay* and the *Holocaust Project* was that the constant barrage of requests for information, reproductions, and other materials connected to my career and work (traditionally managed by a gallery) had been fielded by the corporation. The Benicia office also dealt with the various fiscal and organizational responsibilities associated with Through the Flower's nonprofit structure. In Santa Fe, Juliet operated more like a personal assistant, handling only those duties pertaining to me or the *Holocaust Project,* which was still in the artmaking stage and therefore required little in the way of administration.

Even though the *Birth Project* exhibition tour was over, Through the Flower continued to receive occasional requests for shows; we were still involved in the gifting of exhibition units through our Permanent Placement Program; there was the the future of *The Dinner Party* to be concerned about; and there was also the International Quilting Bee, for which Through the Flower was responsible and which by then numbered hundreds of pieces. There were also thousands of slides and photographs of these and others of my works; drawings and studies scattered all over the building; files; archival materials; in fact, the sum total of a career spanning almost three decades. How could we just stuff all of this into storage lockers?

However, as I look back on this period, I find myself wishing that I could have done what MR had suggested, although I am not sure that even now I would be capable of such an act. By then the substantive body of my art was tied up with Through the Flower, and closing it down and putting everything in storage would have meant walking away from all that I had generated and turning my back on its fate. On the one hand, this would certainly have allowed me to just go on making art, but at the same time doing such a thing would have basically involved repudiating my whole life's work. But because I had had little to do with the administration of the corporation over the years, I really had no idea what I was in for when Donald and I decided to move Through the Flower to New Mexico and set up its offices in the front rooms of our house.

Julie and I discussed the possibility of her taking over as the corporation's executive director. But she was not really prepared to work full-time, nor could we afford to pay her. We decided that we would try to figure out some way for her to at least assume some greater administrative responsibility, and she agreed to go to Benicia with Donald and me to help pack up the building. In the middle of December she and I flew to Benicia, where Katie Amend came up from L.A. to meet us. Donald drove across the country at hair-raising speed, joining us soon after the three of us got there. About a week later, Jim Kraft and Judy Booth arrived to help. We had made plans for Julie to fly home and for Donald and me to drive back with them (Jim and Judy), alternating stints in our car and the huge U-Haul truck that would be required to transport the office equipment, photo and paper files, and archives, along with the remaining art, personal possessions, and furniture I had left in Benicia when I took up residence in Santa Fe.

While in Benicia, I again ran daily in the state park, as I had done so many times when I lived there. The park ends on a rocky point abutting the Carquinez Straits, and on my final run, I decided to take a last look out toward the water. As I sat on a rock in the morning fog that characterizes Benicia in January, feeling the damp, chill wind on my face, I ruminated about the fact that closing down the Benicia building at the end of 1989 seemed to mark the end of a period, one that began with the opening of *The Dinner Party* in 1979. There had been so many changes and challenges during these last years; it seemed astonishing that they could all have taken place within a decade. Suddenly and quite uncharacteristically, I found myself praying, asking God that the next ten years of my life might be somewhat easier.

There are many people in the Jewish community who are critical of Jews like Donald and me, those who come back to Judaism through the Holocaust. Whatever the explanation for this recent occurrence—perhaps that sometimes one only comes to recognize something as precious when threatened with its loss—we ourselves made a reconnection this way. Maybe it was the process of integrating something of Jewish observances into our lives that might explain how I came to pray, or maybe it was just the result of my intense grief. Whatever the reason, surprisingly, I felt much lighter afterward. As I ran back the length of the park, I found myself thinking that it might be appropriate to end the *Holocaust Project* with a prayer.

It was at this point that I began to plan *Rainbow Shabbat,* the stained-glass installation that ends the show. "Light is life," I thought as I completed my last sprint, "and the project should culminate in an image that affirms life—along with an invocation." Eventually, I would decide to flank the center Shabbat panel with two side windows bearing yellow Jewish stars, again in a transformational impulse, for these were the humiliating badges forced on Jews by Hitler. Sandblasted into their centers—in Yiddish and its English equivalent—is a prayer based upon a survivor's poem, asking for a better and more just world.

Donald and I got back to Santa Fe on New Year's Eve, in time to celebrate our fourth wedding anniversary. Within two weeks, I did something for which I have never forgiven myself: I fired Juliet. She was so shocked and hurt that she stamped out without even finishing the letter she was typing. My action was provoked by frustration, precipitated in part by the fact that after many days, all the boxes we had moved from Benicia remained unpacked. Although Julie had been coming into the office regularly, it seemed as though she was making no attempt to institute the kind of major reorganization of the office we had agreed needed to be done. I have no idea why I didn't simply sit down and discuss this with her; the only explanation I can come up with is that I was under so much stress. But I shall always regret what I did, which was a function of impatience and near-total stupidity.

With Julie's departure, I lost the last staff person who was familiar with my history as an artist, knowledgeable about and comfortable with my temperament, and experienced in handling the many details of my career. Since then I have gone through one employee after another, not until very recently finding the quality of loyalty and devotion to which I had become accustomed, or the attention to detail that is so essential in an art organization. MR thinks it is because the labor pool in New Mexico is neither as large nor as sophisticated as in, say, Los Angeles or the Bay Area. I do not know if that is the reason, but since Julie's departure, Through the Flower and I have been staggering to keep things together, although we have managed to develop a computerized mailing list (which we never had); more orderly procedures (also formerly lacking); and, finally, the beginnings of a functional administrative structure.

But in order to achieve this, I have had to add organizational work and supervisory functions (for which I am ill-equipped) to my already overburdened schedule. In early 1990, however, I did not realize that this would be necessary; I hoped that it would be possible to quickly assemble a small but competent staff to handle the corporation's ongoing duties and provide me with some adequate level of support. In order to accomplish this, there had to be more financial resources, which I set out to acquire, in part through expanded board membership (which carries with it an annual pledge). Sometime later, I initiated a series of educational programs in Santa Fe that would make Through the Flower somewhat visible in New Mexico, one positive consequence being increased memberships and donations. But my primary reason for instituting such a program was that there began to be a number of art and art history students who expressed interest in interning at our organization. Along with some modicum of skill, they brought with them a near-total ignorance about women's history and the Feminist Art movement, which shocked me.

In fact, one reason they began arriving on my doorstep was that they wished to learn more about my work and that of other women artists. I thought it might be important for Through the Flower to sponsor seminars and workshops to help counter their lack of knowledge. Later that year, we began to show films and videos from our archives and to organize panels of women in the various arts. These were extremely well received, suggesting that the hunger for such information had in no way abated since the 1970s and early 1980s. The only problem was that, given the corporation's more pressing mission—involving the support, exhibition, and care of my large projects—we could ill afford the resources or staff time required for such programming, and within two years we had to cancel it.

Throughout the early part of 1990, while trying to move Through the Flower along, I also worked quite hard in the studio, impelled by the need to complete the *Holocaust Project* and driven to find some relief from my personal anguish about my brother through artmaking. (I remained in continuous contact with Ben, whose paralysis was becoming progressively worse.) In March there was a board meeting in Santa Fe, during which time we discussed a proposal for the permanent housing of *The Dinner Party*. This had been presented to us by Pat Mathis, a Washington businesswoman and former Assistant Secretary of the Treasury under Carter, who was a longtime supporter of my work. The primarily African-American University of the District of Columbia (UDC), of which she was a trustee, was interested in establishing a new and groundbreaking multicultural museum and archive to house the art and papers of a coalition of artists of color, feminists, and others whose life and work were devoted to the struggle for freedom and dignity.

It was the university's intention to turn the Carnegie Library, which they owned, into this type of institution. There had already been an appropriation of funds by the D.C. city council for the library's restoration, which UDC intended to supplement with private donations. Donald flew to Washington to see the space and returned to report that the Carnegie Library was a handsome and historical but deteriorating building located on UDC's Mount Vernon Square campus in Washington's downtown arts district. He was sure that with proper renovations the building could become an appropriate setting for *The Dinner Party*. Also appealing was the fact that the library was not far from the National Museum for Women in the Arts.

The plan that Pat presented to me and the board of Through the Flower involved my donating the piece (then valued at $2 million), which, in combination with the university's existing collection, would form the core of the proposed museum. UDC already owned works by a number of important African-American artists, a collection the university wished to expand. The board was quite excited about this proposal, thinking that it suited the vision of *The Dinner Party*. In fact, Elyse Grinstein was so enthused that she asked the respected black artist Greg Edwards for his help in enlisting other donations of African-American artists in hopes of turning the school's existing collection into a landmark assemblage.

Soon after the board meeting, Susan Grode began working with the university on an agreement for my gift of *The Dinner Party* that would be acceptable to me, Through the Flower, and the university trustees. As UDC intended to impose a ticket charge at the planned museum—and, based upon the financial history of *The Dinner Party* exhibitions, the university anticipated significant revenues at the gate—Susan wanted the contact structured so that the corporation and I could derive some small percentage of whatever profit the university might enjoy. As I was gifting a multimillion-dollar work (instead of its being purchased, as is customary), this plan seemed eminently reasonable; it was a way for the university to obtain a major work of art without buying it and a method of providing me with some modest financial reward for all the years of unpaid labor that had gone into the creation of *The Dinner Party*. And as the caretaking organization of the work, it would seem obvious that Through the Flower deserved to recoup some of the monies expended over the years.

Never thinking that such an arrangement might appear suspicious to people unfamiliar with the conditions under which I have worked —that is, without traditional support, with little financial reward, and forced to create alternative strategies for the creation and distribution of my work—all of us went forward with plans for this new multicultural museum. To prepare the renovation plans, the university engaged an architect who was to work with Donald and Elyse. I stayed pretty much out of all these interactions, focusing on everything else I had to do, though it was understood that I would have final approval of the installation design. The legal contracts were left to Susan, whom I trust implicitly.

In April, while all this was going on, Ben called with the information that his illness, progressing more quickly than anticipated, had already begun to attack the muscles of his throat and chest. He needed a tracheostomy and would be placed on a respirator in order to prolong his life; he would also have to use a voice machine to talk. Up until this time he had been speaking regularly by phone with our mother, but the machine would dramatically change his voice, which meant that the time had come for her to be told about his illness. Donald and I had been expecting that we would go to Los Angeles to inform her, but Ben had decided that this was something he needed to do himself.

As Ben and I had arranged, immediately after he had spoken to her, I called and asked if she wanted Donald and me to fly in to be with her. But my mom said that she just needed some time alone to adjust to the news. For the next few weeks, I talked to her almost every day. Each time she would ask for a little more information, as if she could handle only so much at a time. Several friends had been critical of our decision not to tell our mother for such a lengthy time, insisting that she had a right to know. But as she came to understand how long my brother had been ill, my mom expressed nothing but gratitude that she'd been spared the painful knowledge until then.

In fact, when we came to see her in May on our way to Japan, she made it clear how much she appreciated my having carried the burden of this information on my own shoulders, understanding that I had done so in an effort to protect her from the grief she was now experiencing. By the time we got to Japan, Ben had undergone surgery and was being kept in the hospital. Now totally paralyzed, he was locked inside his body and not yet able to use the voice machine. He

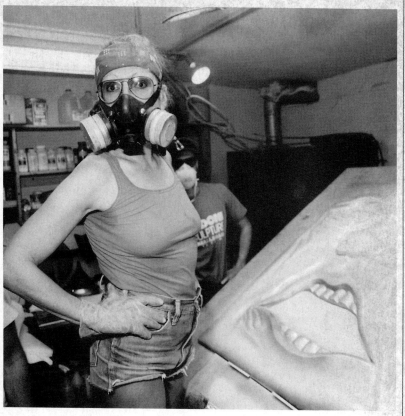

Working on *Doublehead* bronze at the Shidoni Foundry,
Santa Fe, New Mexico, 1986.

Three Faces of Man,
1985; sprayed acrylic
and oil on Belgian linen,
three panels, 54" x 9'
(installed).
Collection: Ruth
Lambert and Henry
Harrison, New Haven,
Connecticut.

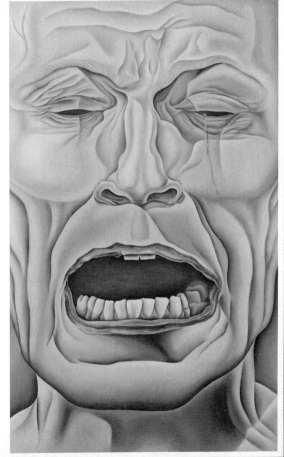

Center panel, *Three
Faces of Man.*

At the tomb of the Vilna Gaon, Vilna, Lithuania, 1987.

Engraving of the Vilna Gaon.

Logo from the *Holocaust Project,* 1992; fabricated by Michael Caudle, Bob Gomez, Flo Perkins, and Donald Woodman; stained glass and barbed wire, 42" x 48½".

With my cousins Howard and Arleen Rosen at my childhood home, 757 Bittersweet Place, Chicago, 1988.

With my brother, Ben Cohen, 1989.

With my mother, May Cohen, 1991.

Center panel, *Legacy,* from the *Holocaust Project,* 1992; sprayed acrylic, oil, encaustic, and photography on photolinen, 54" x 36".

Detail, center panel, *Rainbow Shabbat,* from the *Holocaust Project,* 1992;
painted by Dorothy Maddy from Judy Chicago's design, fabricated by Bob Gomez,
stained glass, 54" x 16' (installed).

FACING PAGE: Congressional hearing, July 20, 1990 (C-Span)
BOTTOM LEFT: Congressman Robert Dornan reading an article from *The Washington
Times* during congressional hearing (C-Span).

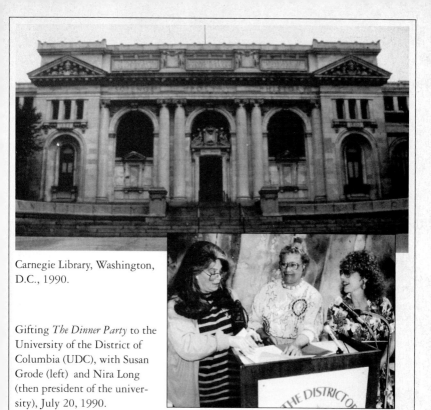

Carnegie Library, Washington, D.C., 1990.

Gifting *The Dinner Party* to the University of the District of Columbia (UDC), with Susan Grode (left) and Nira Long (then president of the university), July 20, 1990.

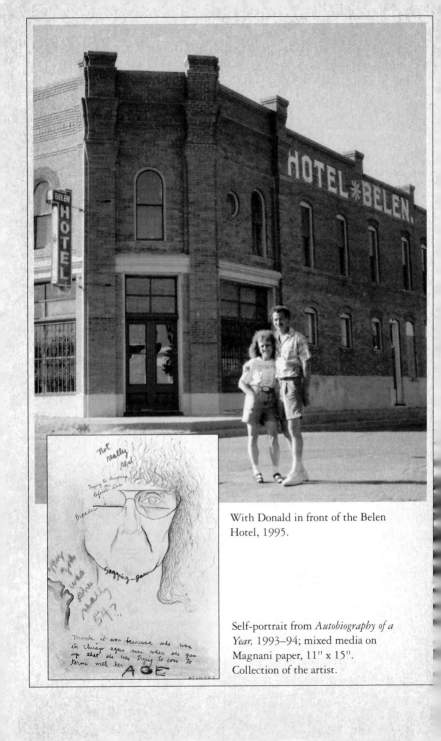

With Donald in front of the Belen Hotel, 1995.

Self-portrait from *Autobiography of a Year,* 1993–94; mixed media on Magnani paper, 11" x 15". Collection of the artist.

Not really red

Trying to disguise Receding line

Broader

Grey Eyes (was she really)

Sagging jaw

54?

Maybe it was because she was in Chicago again now where she grew up that she was trying to come to terms with her AGE later told us that this was the most isolating and horrifying period of his illness, prompting him to say that if he should be rendered permanently unable to communicate, he wished to be helped to die.

When we spoke before the operation, Ben had insisted that we not come to Kadanji until he was out of the hospital and had recuperated sufficiently to be able to master the voice machine, which he said would take some time. In deference to his wishes, I scheduled our visit with him at the end of our Japanese tour. Although I found it exceedingly difficult to do public speaking while my brother lay mute and motionless in a hospital bed, I managed to present four lectures: in Hiroshima, Tokyo, Yokohama, and Kyoto. While in Hiroshima, Donald and I visited the Peace Museum, which is where we saw the horrifying photos and films that attested to the tragic human cost of the dropping of the atomic bomb. Our time there made our work on the subject of the Holocaust considerably more complicated, primarily because what we learned caused us to question the widely held presumption that the evil unleashed during the Second World War had only a Nazi face.

All of my Japan lectures were well attended, and I have to admit that the response was gratifying, particularly in Kyoto. There, numerous women stood up after my slide lecture and, seemingly empowered by the images I had shown, began testifying about their experiences of sexual harassment and rape. This so shocked my translator that all of a sudden my earphones went dead; apparently such public honesty is unheard of there. During this speaking tour I also did a number of interviews, enough that some even reached the small town where Ben and his family lived. Once we arrived in Kadanji, everyone commented about how "famous" I was, but whatever notoriety had followed me was not foremost in my mind.

Ben had arranged for Donald and me to stay in a lovely inn at the Pottery Park, so called because it was at the center of what was a thriving ceramics area, where exhibitions were regularly held. In fact, some of my brother's pots were on display, which gave us the opportunity to see how skilled a craftsman he had become. The inn was only a few miles from Ben and Reiko's house, which turned out to be situated in a stunningly beautiful area, amid rice paddies and immense stands of bamboo. I could see why my brother so loved Kadanji, though its lush beauty made our first exposure to his situation even more excruciating.

I think Ben had known that this visit was going to be very hard for me, which is why he had us stay at the inn. In yet one more example of his spiritual strength, he was concerned—despite his own circumstances—that I have time away from the constant hum of the respirator and the beehive of activity that surrounded him, all that was keeping him alive. Because he was totally paralyzed by then, he was entirely dependent upon the constant attentions of Reiko and his generous network of friends for all bodily functions. Despite the enormous effort it took for him to speak—accomplished in rhythm to the pumping of the respirator—he was insistent upon spending many hours each day in the studio. There he patiently instructed Reiko in the pottery techniques that would allow her to support herself and her children after his death. At every mealtime he wished to be put into his wheelchair and brought to the table, so that he could participate as best he could in the conversation and sample the tasty dishes that Reiko somehow found time to prepare.

His courage was truly amazing and inspiring. But the whole experience was so terribly painful and terrifying for me. Except for the brief time I had spent with my uncle Harry when he was at a late stage of his neurological disease, I had never been around anyone who was so gravely ill. I wish I could say that I rose to the occasion, but mostly I tried to offer what help and comfort I could, spending as much time with my brother as his strength would allow, then returning to our quarters and weeping. Thankfully, Donald was somewhat better able to cope than I.

I also spent a good amount of time with Reiko, something that Ben had asked me to do. Every afternoon we went off together, our conversation facilitated by an American friend who spoke fluent Japanese. We did our best to relate to each other, but the cultural gap was extremely wide. At one point I pushed her to share her feelings about my brother's illness and its emotional impact upon her. Becoming quite frustrated, she said sharply in a tone I understood even before her words were translated: "You Americans, and especially you Jewish people, you always want to know how I feel, but *I don't know*." I suddenly realized that the kind of insight I was asking of her was entirely foreign to her.

I was quite sure that her remark was simply the expression of the bafflement she felt about what I—and, as I was to learn, Ben—had expected from her. During my talks with my brother, he confessed that after he became ill, what was hardest for him was that the level of emotional connection he longed for was precluded by what seemed to be a cultural abyss. Even though Reiko was as devoted and caring as anyone could be, I realized that, romantic ideals aside, the problem of building a life with someone of such a different cultural persuasion must have been difficult. As our translator pointed out to me—and as my lecture experiences reinforced—not every society values such interpersonal intimacy.

Donald and I were able to communicate with Elijah, who already spoke some English and who, since then, has improved his skills. But Simon, the younger son, remains rather unknown to us, as he speaks no English and we no Japanese. (Unlike Ben, who was gifted in languages and taught himself many, I am singularly untalented in this area.) Over the years, Elijah has spent time with us in New Mexico and we have been able to build some sense of connection with him. Should either boy decide to come to America for high school or college, we would of course try to honor our commitment to my brother and provide for him. But as time goes by, it feels as though my nephews are being lost to us, absorbed into an educational system and society that is training them to be more Japanese than American, while certainly not helping them claim their Jewish birthright.

We returned home in early June to discover that while we were gone, Donald's father had suffered a seizure during a rather routine hip-replacement surgery that had put him into intensive care and thoroughly debilitated him. Bertha was flat on her back with an undiagnosed problem, and one of Donald's cousins had died of AIDS. Stephen Hamilton, meanwhile, had been placed in a hospice, as he was going into the final stages of his illness. I fervently hoped that he would still be alive in November, when we were scheduled to go to the Bay Area, as I desperately wanted the opportunity to say goodbye. But there was no way I could fly out there at this time; I could afford neither the airfare nor the emotional energy. And Donald, who had suffered uncomplaining through so many grievous incidents, finally broke down, and for a few days he understandably had trouble getting out of bed.

He soon got himself back into the darkroom, where he started working on the photo panels for *Double Jeopardy,* the twenty-two-foot installation that explores women's experiences during the Holocaust. While waiting for him to finish the photo prints, I began doing research for the next image, this one dealing with children, to be called *Im/Balance of Power.* At the end of June, Bob Gomez, the stained-glass artisan who had volunteered to fabricate *Rainbow Shabbat,* came to Santa Fe for a few days to work with me on the plans.

Meanwhile, preparations for the permanent housing of *The Dinner Party* had been moving along. The gifting ceremony was scheduled for July 20, my birthday, and I was eagerly awaiting this day, as was Through the Flower's board. Many friends, supporters, and board members were planning to fly to Washington for this momentous occasion. The large crowd at the gifting ceremony would also include the founder of the Women's Museum, Wilhemina Holladay. She had been quite enthusiastic when I called and told her about UDC's plan, even offering to establish joint programming with the new museum. She and several others—including Henry Hopkins—sent congratulatory letters that we put together in a small booklet to be given out in Washington.

I'd like to provide some perspective about how I could have been so oblivious to the fact that I and all my friends were about to walk into a hornets' nest. Most of the planning for the new institution that would house *The Dinner Party* was going on within UDC. And while Donald and Elyse had been involved in discussions with the architect, Donald and I were out of the country. As was her habit, Susan had protected me from all legal matters, and if there was trouble in paradise nobody bothered to tell me.

I have already explained how difficult and demanding my brother's illness was for me, and the Japan trip was no picnic. Almost as soon as we got off the plane, I began to suffer abdominal pains at night that kept me awake and sent me to the emergency room. After a series of hideous and futile medical procedures aimed at finding out if I had cancer or was only suffering from stress, it turned out to be a lack of estrogen, but I wouldn't know this for some months. I was also confronted with piles of work—in the office, at my desk, and in the studio. All I wanted to do was get at it—even though my work on the *Holocaust Project* meant that I would be descending almost like Dante into the underworld, into material that was becoming ever darker and more perplexing. As a result I was extremely busy, so busy that I had little time to think about anything but what work I had to accomplish each day.

We still had very little money and living month to month was producing a high level of anxiety for me, particularly because in order to keep going we were getting further and further into debt (Donald would call our financial situation the "Spike Lee Plan," that is, using our credit cards in order to finish the project). The Through the Flower office was occupying the front of our house, which meant that I could never entirely get away from its demands, although I did my best by going into my studio in the back house, where I had no phone, and staying there all day (with my cat Sebastian for company). The corporation was also quite tight for funds, and I was trying to make do with one full-time person and an intern.

In my journal entries throughout the early part of this summer, I scrawled again and again: "MY LIFE IS JUST TOO TOUGH!" The only glimmer of light in what was a pretty dim scene was that *The Dinner Party* was finally going to be housed—which from my point of view made any amount of struggle worthwhile. I assumed that its housing would make my circumstances somewhat easier, if only because with Through the Flower's anticipated percentage of the gate, it might be able to acquire independent quarters and more (and more qualified) staff. As to an increasingly hostile atmosphere surrounding the visual arts in our nation's capital, I am afraid that I and all my friends and supporters were guilty of incredible naiveté. We honestly believed that the controversy about *The Dinner Party* was old hat, that the piece was by now almost an accepted part of art history (which its permanent installation would ensure).

A few days before the gifting ceremony, Donald and I flew to Washington. On the morning of July 18, I went to a local health club to work out. While walking back to where we were staying, I happened to glance at a kiosk displaying *The Washington Times*. There on the front page, in full color, were photographs of both me and *The Dinner Party,* along with the ghastly headline: "UDC's $1.6 million 'Dinner.' Feminist artwork . . . causes indigestion." As I had no change with me, I could not even buy the paper and find out what this was all about. When I finally read the piece, I was stunned by the outright lies about both the art and the terms of the gift. The article incorrectly claimed that *The Dinner Party* had been "banned in several art galleries around the country because it depicts women's genitalia on plates" and that public funds were being spent to buy (and house) the work. It also erroneously implied that monies intended for UDC's operating budget were involved.

This article was my first indication that there were any problems regarding the UDC plan. Throughout the month of June, apparently, rumors had circulated on the campus about an underground sabotage campaign being mounted by some conservative members of the faculty senate who were supposedly unhappy about the trustees' decision to turn the Carnegie Library into a multicultural museum. There was some speculation in Washington that these were the people who had leaked the misinformation to the *Times,* where it seemed to dominate the news for the next few days. I was not at all happy about this negative and distorted coverage, particularly the falsehood that the renovation money for the library was being taken from the university's budget.

Nor was the school "buying" *The Dinner Party*; this was an unqualified fabrication that totally obfuscated the fact that they were about to receive a substantial gift from me, which was to be supplemented by private monies, pledged contingent upon *The Dinner Party*'s permanent housing. University officials dismissed the paper as a "loony, Moony rag" and advised me to put its "right-wing drivel" out of my mind. They promised to hold a press conference the day after the gifting ceremony to set the record straight.

On the morning of my birthday, numerous people and members

of the press gathered in the spacious upstairs gallery of the Carnegie Library. On behalf of Through the Flower, Susan approved the terms of the gift; then it was my turn to sign the document that would formally transfer ownership of *The Dinner Party* to UDC. Afterward, a group of us went to a private restaurant for a lovely lunch, where, as planned, we celebrated this momentous occasion as well as my birthday.

The next morning the university held a press briefing, at which I presented a slide talk about *The Dinner Party*. Several trustees explained the vision of the museum, the terms of the gift, the financial arrangements, and the many expected benefits to UDC, and then we answered questions. This event, which was well attended, resulted in rather accurate articles in both *The Washington Post* and *The New York Times*. As both of these papers are considerably more influential than *The Washington Times,* everyone associated with the university was convinced that these pieces would stem the tide of misinformation being disseminated by that right-wing paper. Donald and I went home feeling reassured and without a clue that the erroneous stories, pernicious rumors, and unspeakably vicious attacks were only just beginning.

On July 26, while recuperating in Santa Fe from yet another wasted surgical procedure, I received a phone call from Cheryl Swannack, a former student of mine at the Feminist Studio Workshop. She had gone to work as a lobbyist for the Gay and Lesbian Alliance, a job that put her on the floor of Congress during the dispute about Representative Barney Frank (concerning an alleged homosexual encounter). She discovered that *The Dinner Party* was about to be discussed by the House of Representatives, and she called to alert us. For the next hour and twenty-seven minutes, Donald and I sat stupefied in front of the televised proceedings on C-Span, while a war of words took place as part of a much longer debate on UDC's budget, which Congress controls.

We still have no idea how *The Dinner Party* ended up in the hallowed halls of the House of Representatives. This was the first such discussion I had ever watched in its entirety, having seen only snippets of other congressional dialogues on the news. I was flabbergasted by the way in which *The Dinner Party* was denounced, excoriated, and eviscerated by men (no women participated) who had never seen the work and basically did not know what they were talking about. As I commented to Donald, "If they understand as little about the other issues they debate and legislate, this country is in big trouble." We watched while distortions, misrepresentations, and even total fictions were read into the *Congressional Record*, thereby convincing even intelligent observers that some sort of hanky-panky was going on, or at the very least an irresponsible financial scheme. Before long the dialogue—if it could be described as such—moved from fiscal issues to descriptions of *The Dinner Party* as pornography.

"We now have this pornographic art," railed California's Robert Dornan, "I mean, three-dimensional ceramic art of thirty-nine women's vaginal areas, their genitalia served up on plates." Holding up *The Washington Times* cover story of July 18, he continued: "Look at this garbage . . . [which was] banned in art galleries around the country . . . and characterized as obscene." The theme was picked up by one of his colleagues, Dana Rohrbacher, another demagogue from Southern California, who carried on for many minutes about how *The Dinner Party* was "weird sexual art." It is true that Pat Williams of Montana and Ron Dellums of Northern California tried to introduce both some reason and perspective into this ridiculous discourse, but to no avail. The House was convinced to support a measure that deleted $1.6 million from the university's budget as a way of punishing the school for initiating the museum plan. This was precisely the amount of money that had been previously allocated for the renovation of the Carnegie Library, to be supplied through city bond funds. No federal funds were involved, though one would have been hard-pressed to know this from the specious arguments.

After the punitive bill passed the House, it went to the Senate, where it was taken up by the Appropriations Committee. They would be convinced to restore the money, the result of an intense lobbying campaign put into action by Susan Grode, and with the help of the Hollywood Women's Political Committee—the largest fund-raising group for liberal candidates in America, which Susan helped to create—educational packets about *The Dinner Party* (emphasizing its position in many art-historical texts) were sent to every senator. Sometime later, MR began a lobbying effort in Texas that effectively dissuaded Phil Gramm from taking the debate about *The Dinner Party* to the Senate floor; this had been urged by Jesse Helms as a way of trying to overturn the decision by the Appropriations Committee. Other grass-roots groups organized around the country, bombarding senators with letters and phone calls. Throughout all this turmoil, the university trustees stood firm in their decision to go forward with the museum, predicting that the Conference Committee (which adjudicates disputes between the House and Senate) would support the decision of the Appropriations Committee and reinstate the funds.

Unfortunately, when the right-wingers realized that they were probably going to be defeated in Congress, they turned their attention to the university campus, where the black religious right got into the act. Charges of pornography and inappropriate federal funding were leveled, and then even blasphemy was suggested. I was called "the Antichrist," and it was rumored that *The Dinner Party* had been in boxes for twenty years because it contained the Devil. Ultimately, events in Congress, coupled with intense right-wing agitation at the university, created a breakdown of confidence in the trustees' judgment among some members of the faculty and the student body, resulting in a disruptive student strike. At the beginning *The Dinner Party* was not the primary issue, but it soon became a symbol for other dissatisfactions felt by the students. By the end of September the protest had escalated, with calls for the cancellation of the planned museum and the trustees' resignation.

The student strike was extremely problematic for me and the board of Through the Flower. It highlighted problems at the university of which we were unaware (for example, a level of unrest on the campus and distrust of the leadership), which made us question the stability of the institution. More important, I did not wish to be in a position of foisting something upon the students to which they were opposed, although I was disconcerted by how easily they had been manipulated into seeing me and my work as "the enemy," when, in fact, the new museum would have brought increased attention and resources to them and their needs. Unfortunately, it seemed as if *The Dinner Party* was becoming a lightning rod for the students' previously unarticulated grievances.

By early October the situation was completely out of control. Throughout the summer and early fall, Donald and I had managed to stay out of the fray, continuing to work on the *Holocaust Project* as best we could. Of course we could not help but notice the irony of being engaged in a project about a moment in history in which the state had turned upon its own citizens while the struggle in Congress was going on. I had found the congressional hearing and the unceasing distortion in many of the media reports quite unnerving, partly because of the work I was doing, but even more because I am someone who is devoted to the truth and cannot bear to see it so utterly disregarded. (The angry faces of the congressmen who had so bitterly attacked *The Dinner Party* conjured up the disfigured images of my *Malehead* series; it was actually uncanny.)

As the student strike intensified, so did press attention and misrepresentations. Our small office was besieged with inquiries, phone calls, and faxes, bewildering the staff. Finally, Donald and I had no alternative but to spend many hours in the office, I answering questions and doing phone interviews, Donald sending out piles of information materials by Federal Express and fax. Reluctantly, I and the board of Through the Flower determined that I had best withdraw the gift of *The Dinner Party,* which I did in a letter to the trustees at UDC and in a press release, stating that the virulent misinformation campaign had "managed to create a division of values where there was none—i.e., between the concept of *The Dinner Party* and the issues that are important to the students." I went on to say that "as my life's work has been dedicated to the [right] of self-determination of all people," I felt that I had no choice but to rescind the gift.

Later, in the only thorough investigative article of these events, published in 1991 in *Art in America,* Lucy Lippard speculated: "Had the student strike not happened, *The Dinner Party*/UDC partnership probably would have survived. . . . [However] the prospect of an alliance [between feminist and multicultural] forces may have set off subliminal alarm systems among those for whom multiculturalism . . . is threatening." Lucy went on to regret the demise of the "proposed center [because it] could have inspired not only exhibitions and art-world attention, but also a much-needed historical analysis of the connections between feminism and the civil rights movement."

Some people have dismissed what happened to *The Dinner Party* in Washington as just another assault on the arts, in particular the NEA (mention was made in Congress of some paltry amount of money provided by this agency for the creation of the work almost two decades earlier), but I do not agree with this analysis. Rather, I believe that what occurred there might be more closely related to everything else that had happened in regard to the piece since it was first exhibited in 1979—specifically, the effort to prevent it from being seen. One way this was accomplished was through the critics' misrepresentation of *The Dinner Party*, which involved focusing almost exclusively on the plates. These were completely decontextualized from the larger intent and scope of the work—that is, the teaching of women's history through art and the honoring of our aesthetic, intellectual, and cultural achievements. I believe that what happened in Washington mirrored this in that once again the plates were the ostensible issue and misinformation the method. Only, this time the stakes were higher, because they involved not a temporary exhibition but a permanent installation in our nation's capital, home to innumerable monuments to men and their history, a history that the presence of *The Dinner Party* might have called into question.

Since the events in Washington, the Carnegie Library has remained unused and, until recently, in the same state of disrepair. As for *The Dinner Party,* there have been no other offers for permanent housing, so it has remained in crates. However, thanks to Henry Hopkins, the loyal "daddy" of *The Dinner Party* who is now the director of the UCLA/Armand Hammer Museum, plans are now under way for a commemorative exhibition. Curated by art historian Dr. Amelia Jones, this show will place *The Dinner Party* into the context of twenty years of Feminist Art theory and practice, its impact finally—and dispassionately—examined by a host of critics and historians, a new generation, most of whom have not had the opportunity of seeing the piece.

In conjunction with this planned exhibit, I have done a new book about *The Dinner Party* that features an extensive color section demonstrating that the plates are but one element in this multilayered symbolic history of women in Western civilization. In that manuscript, I dealt with an issue I would now like to explore more fully: why *The Dinner Party* remains unhoused.

Let me begin by addressing the fact that some of my readers are surely thinking how wonderful it is that *The Dinner Party* is to be shown again. Perhaps they're already intending to travel to L.A. to view it if they missed it the first time around; maybe they're planning to bring their daughters or friends if they themselves were among the many viewers who stated that *The Dinner Party* changed their lives. As happy as that would make me, I feel compelled to ask: How many of you are pondering how you can help to ensure that this same life-changing experience will be available to future generations? I can probably answer this question for most of you: This is not uppermost in your mind.

In raising this issue I am not trying to make you feel guilty, particularly if you are a female reader, for women know enough of guilt. Rather, I am attempting to deal with the question that is so often put to me about why *The Dinner Party* doesn't have a permanent home. The unhoused state of the piece illuminates two important issues, both involving *absence*. Since the UDC debacle, there have been no other offers for permanent housing, the simple explanation for which is that there is apparently an absence of institutional will regarding women and women's art. I had intended *The Dinner Party* as a historic test of the art system, which, overall, has been found seriously wanting in terms of providing appropriate exhibition and preservation opportunities for this work.

After Washington, I and the board of Through the Flower concluded that, given the virulent resistance demonstrated by the art institutions and then the United States Congress, *The Dinner Party* would surely be lost if we did not undertake its permanent housing ourselves. Since that time, we have repeatedly stated that we intend to accomplish this, most recently with the idea of using the UCLA/Hammer show as the impetus for the launching of a capital campaign.

But if truth be known, we are but a small group of dedicated women, none of whom have the resources to accomplish this goal. Unless some museum or university intent upon demonstrating that I am wrong about the absence of institutional will—or a group of wealthy people, or even an individual of great means—comes forward, this dream of permanent housing, born with *The Dinner Party* many years ago, will die stillborn.

I am often asked if I myself am going to house *The Dinner Party* —as if this were something I could accomplish alone or with my paintbrush. Although I was somewhat unrealistic in my ambitions when young (or how could I have had such large dreams?), now that I am more mature, I am also more humble, recognizing that I cannot single-handedly alter a world that continues to devalue women's accomplishments. Nevertheless, I have managed to create a work of art that can act as a wedge in the effectuation of some modicum of change. But who will take up this wedge? That is the question. If the institutions that normally preserve art won't provide housing for *The Dinner Party*, who will?

This raises another issue: What will it take for women to turn their attention to the honoring of our own history and achievements? Women do not yet understand that they must financially support the work that speaks to them. And do not argue that women are too impoverished to do this, because even if this is true for many, I have personally witnessed the raising—and in some cases the gifting—of millions of dollars by women to every cause but our own. During my years of work on the *Holocaust Project*, I had many occasions to observe the Jewish community. Basic to the ongoing existence of Jewish culture is the understanding that it is through the existence of its institutions that a culture is maintained. Why, then, is it so difficult for women to understand that in order to preserve *our* heritage, *our* art, *our* perspective (in all its variety), we must create institutions to accomplish this, or change those that exist so that they *include* us in significant ways.

To come back to the UCLA/Hammer exhibition, if once again thousands of viewers see and become empowered (or reempowered, as the case may be) by *The Dinner Party*, after which it returns to a musty storehouse and an uncertain or bleak future, I will of course be desolate. But, more significant, a crucial opportunity will have been lost in that *The Dinner Party* represents a unique historic challenge, basically because it contains within it the chance to empower future generations through its very existence. (I *must* emphasize that it is not enough to read about it; it must be seen.) The question is, Can those who have been empowered by it use it as a wedge in a process of such ongoing empowerment?

Achieving permanent housing for *The Dinner Party* would require that many people make this goal a priority, putting aside efforts (worthy though they might be) on behalf of all those institutions, hospitals, churches, temples, and other organizations that are neither woman-centered nor interested in female empowerment, at least until the piece is successfully housed. How difficult a commitment this would be for most women to make illuminates another absence underlying the unhoused predicament of *The Dinner Party*—that is, the absence among too many of us of such a firm, abiding commitment to ourselves and the needs of women. As a result, *any* missions—even those that entirely exclude women or include us only peripherally—are almost always seen as infinitely more important than our own.

Even as the story of *The Dinner Party* shows us how hard it is to change the institutions, it challenges us to change ourselves. Most of us are prevented from making such a commitment, not by laws—these have all been altered, at least in the West, thanks to our foremothers who made *our* rights *their* priority—but by something equally binding: fear, guilt, and, most of all, a deep-seated belief in our own lack of worth. My own story exemplifies some of this. I have explained how I came to view my power as frightening and, as a result, how long it took me not to be bullied into feeling that there was something wrong with me and/or my art. In terms of guilt, I was lucky: I was raised differently from other women in that I was not made to feel guilty about pursuing my own needs, though I consistently (and confusedly) collided with everyone else's expectation that this was what I should do. Certainly, I had to deal with feelings of shame about my body and my sexuality and could not become fully empowered until I had overcome these feelings, primarily because self-worth emanates from self-acceptance, and one's self occupies a physical body with essential needs.

From my perspective, however, the tale that I have been relating about my own struggle has little meaning unless it helps provide the basis of growth for others. Similarly, all of the efforts that went into creating and exhibiting *The Dinner Party* will be rendered hollow unless it is permanently housed. One important lesson I derived from my study of the history of women's achievements was that if other people could do it, so could I. In discussing how I slowly overcame my fear of my own power, I was by implication urging my readers to do the same. In explaining how I was able to stand up to all the demands upon me and carve out time for my own needs without feeling guilty, I was trying to provide a path for others.

But foremost in my tale, in my estimation, is the importance, the price, and the rewards for taking risks. One might say that I have probably taken too many and, consequently, paid too high a price in terms of having provoked so much hostility (an entirely unanticipated result) and having altogether sacrificed financial security (a difficulty for me, especially now that I am older). At the same time, I have been rewarded in many other ways. Yet as much as I enjoy standing ovations and fan letters, I would like to express my impatience with those many people who seem to stand on the sidelines and cheer me on or admire me from afar. I would rather that their appreciation be expressed by active participation in achieving those goals of mine that are shared by them.

To those who are fearful of making this kind of commitment, allow me to say that there is some pleasure, even fun, in rushing headlong into life and in taking on large challenges. I firmly believe that both true satisfaction and real achievement require taking such risks. And my story is not the only one that can serve as inspiration; the lives of many of the women represented at *The Dinner Party* provide an array of models to be followed. In fact, the housing of *The Dinner Party,* which is so essential precisely because it will allow future generations to have access to these many inspiriting examples.

Moreover, *The Dinner Party* directly contravenes the lack of self-worth experienced by too many women, in part through an esteeming of our bodies, as conveyed through the imagery of the plates. It is no wonder that male art critics (and those women who have internalized their loathing of all things female) and congressmen alike focused on the plates and their vulval forms. Rippling out from their tiny centers is the insistence that female sexuality is to be celebrated and embraced, not hidden away, purchased, excised, or despised. In life, as in art, from the base of self-acceptance all else issues. In the case of *The Dinner Party,* it meant filling a gigantic room with symbols of some of what we have done and suggesting how much we might become. In terms of ourselves, it means replacing the *absence* of commitment to ourselves and each other with a new *presence,* that of self-love and the honoring of the feminine.

When I stated that *The Dinner Party* presents a historic challenge, in addition to all that I've outlined, it also presents the opportunity to break the cycle of history that condemns each generation of women to grow up ignorant of their heritage and thereby be condemned to continuously repeat the stages of development described in this book or embodied in the 1,038 stories (symbolic of many more) of the women on the *Dinner Party* table and *Heritage Floor.* This is exactly the cycle that *The Dinner Party* was intended to interrupt but—if it remains unhoused—will only reiterate. I must confess I have no idea whether the time for this change—or this beginning—is at hand. Nor do I know what I will do with *The Dinner Party* if, at the end of its Los Angeles showing, there is no place for it to go.

However, since I cannot resolve this issue, I shall, instead, now return to the everyday events of my life. By the fall of 1990, while the UDC events were unfolding, my brother was going through a terrible depression, brought on by his decision to go on a respirator (his alternative would have been to die right then). This meant that for the rest of his days he would be attached to this machine, and he was obsessing about whether he had made the right choice. At this time I wrote him a long letter to report on all that had transpired, explaining why I had been somewhat remiss in my attentions to him. Ben immediately called to reassure me that he understood and to offer his sympathy and his support, a gesture that, given his own condition, was so generous that I burst into tears.

Fortunately, my brother's spirits were improving. He told me that he had some goals he wished to accomplish, including completing his tutelage of Reiko, finishing the tapes for the boys, and purchasing the house in which they lived, which he believed could be done through sales of his pottery. Before becoming completely paralyzed, he had worked furiously in the studio—aided by several assistants—to create a large body of work. He was now unable to attend his shows, so Reiko was going in his stead. Happily, his last pots were some of his best and were eagerly swooped up. Ben said that once all these plans were concluded, he would be ready to die, an eventuality he was coming to be at peace with. I fervently hoped that our mom would be able to handle it as well.

Throughout that summer and fall of 1990, I was working on the women's image, *Double Jeopardy,* a huge painting/photo combine that —with research, drawings, scale model, and final painting—involved several years of effort and would occupy me for quite some time. That fall, while engaged in it and in the midst of the UDC debacle, I enrolled in a weekend glass-painting seminar in Albuquerque because Bob Gomez, the glass fabricator, had told me that the only way to achieve the face details in *Rainbow Shabbat* was through hand-painting. My glass-painting teacher was a woman named Dorothy Maddy, an experienced painter, whom I asked to be my adviser, as I had never done any painting on glass.

Some months later, in early 1991, Dorothy was diagnosed with lung cancer and told that she had only a short time to live. Although she had painted glass for many years, she had never had the opportunity to work on anything in the scale of *Rainbow Shabbat*. As I told her at the time of her diagnosis, if she wished to bring all her experience and talent to bear on this piece, it was hers. In a testament to the power of the human spirit and in keeping with the nature of the *Holocaust Project* itself, Dorothy decided to use her remaining time and energy in a final burst of creativity. Working from my full-scale shaded drawing, she painted the innumerable pieces that make up the center panel virtually single-handedly. Sadly, she would never get to see the piece put together, let alone installed.

That fall I went to L.A., where I was given a Vesta Award by the

Women's Building. At the last minute I decided to present my mother with the award, which I did at the crowded ceremony, to which I had taken her in hopes of giving her some pleasure. As we stood side by side on the stage in our matching Holly Harp dresses (made especially for the occasion to show off our similarly shapely legs), I handed the medal to my mom with thanks for her having sent me to art school, which produced a big round of applause for her. Sometime later, Howard and Arleen came for a quiet, private Thanksgiving, which was wonderful. The rest of the year was spent tucked away in the Canyon Road compound, working in the studio, exercising, and hanging out with Donald and the cats, which was about all I wanted to do.

On New Year's Eve, Donald and I celebrated our wedding anniversary in our customary way: at home and at the Santa Café. The early part of the year was busy with painting, working on the stained glass with Bob and Dorothy in Santa Fe (this was shortly before her diagnosis), and trying to move the *Holocaust Project* along. At the beginning of April, Donald and I went to L.A., where I held an eighteth-birthday party for my mom at Audrey and Bob Cowan's. Upon our return, I set to work on *Im/Balance of Power,* an image dealing with the treatment of children during the Holocaust and today, which occupied me until July, when I began the research on slavery that would result in *Arbeit Macht Frei/Work Makes Who Free?* This large, multipanel installation explores the slave-labor aspect of the Holocaust in relation to American slavery, which, I feel ashamed to admit, I knew less about than I should have. One interesting aspect of this inquiry was that once again I stumbled upon an iconographic void: that is, a relative lack of images about the American slave experience in both photography and visual art.

That summer, Donald and I indulged in the purchase of a tandem mountain bike, an extravagance but one that provided us with a welcome escape from the troubling work of the *Holocaust Project*. By this time we were finding it difficult—and exhausting—to socialize. Moreover, we weren't the most desirable dinner guests; we referred to ourselves as "Ms. Doom and Mr. Gloom; invite us to dinner and get depressed." It was almost impossible to put aside the work when visiting with people, and it was uncomfortable—for them as well as us

—to have to discuss it. Instead, we took up mountain-biking, going for long rides and looping downhill at breakneck speeds. I sat in the back and pedaled steadily with my eyes closed, shrieking with fear and delight as Donald steered us around mountain precipices. Actually, biking together became another measure of the growth of our marriage in that, like the making of the *Holocaust Project,* it required that we cooperate in order to get anywhere.

We were anticipating that we'd finish the art early in 1993, then take another six months to produce all the ancillary exhibition materials. The opening was set for October of that year at the Spertus Museum in Chicago. I liked the idea that the premiere was to be held in the town of my birth, as it seemed fitting to return there with a project through which I had become reconnected with my Jewish heritage. Other institutions were expressing interest in the show, and we were working on putting together a tour that would span Jewish and art museums around the United States, hoping that at the end of its American travels, the exhibition would travel out of the country.

Throughout the course of the project, Donald and I held private viewings of the finished pieces in our respective studios. At the end of 1991, when *Rainbow Shabbat* was done, Donald set it up in his space. Among the invited guests was David Turner, at that time the director of the Santa Fe Fine Arts Museum, who peered admiringly at the illuminated windows, then turned to me and said, "It's really wonderful, but what's Shabbat?" Evidently the prospect of crossing over from the Jewish to the art communities was going to be more of a problem than I had originally thought. Once again, therefore, I began to think hard about how to span audiences. Whenever we held these types of viewings, people would ask many questions about the imagery and its historic underpinnings. After receiving the desired information, they seemed to want to be quiet and just look. Observing this same pattern at every one of these showings led us to the decision to incorporate an audio tour, which could provide such knowledge while also assuring a rather silent and contemplative viewing atmosphere, given that everyone would be listening to the tape.

Working with Isaiah Kuperstein and a company called Thwaite (which produces such tours), Donald and I spent many months developing an audio component that could provide a bridge for multiple audiences into a project whose subject matter (it seemed to us) could overwhelm the most sympathetic viewer, particularly if the person knew as little about the Holocaust as, for example, Donald or I had when we began. I have to say that it never occurred to any of us that someone would be offended by the notion that they might need some education in order to understand and appreciate the art. In yet another example of my naiveté (maturity may have mellowed me but it has obviously not changed my fundamental nature), I assumed that everyone would be glad for whatever help they could get in dealing with a subject matter that—in my opinion, anyway—was humbling, to say the least. However, I would discover with some shock that art critics in particular find it insulting to have to don headphones, presumably feeling that this reflects badly upon their supposed expertise in all art concerns.

In retrospect and despite their displeasure, I would still have made the decision to make the audio tour an integral part of the exhibition because the *Holocaust Project* grows out of an amalgamation of experience, knowledge, and scholarship that is largely unknown to most people outside of the Jewish and academic communities. Moreover, from those to whom the show is addressed—that is, the broad audience—who are not so arrogant as to think that they are not in need of guidance on this topic, we would hear again and again how valuable the audio was for them.

By the early part of 1992, Donald and I were beginning to talk about where we would live after the *Holocaust Project* was done. MR had generously agreed to extend the lease on the Canyon Road house until we were finished, but then, it was understood, we would leave. We had been looking around at various places in this area that we both might like, although I was not at all sure that I wished to stay here. But Donald really feels rooted in New Mexico, and therefore I agreed to consider remaining in the Southwest, though not in Santa Fe. First off, it was becoming too expensive for us, particularly because Donald expressed his ongoing—and abiding—desire to own a place. Moreover, the town had changed so much during the years of my sojourn, I just couldn't feature spending the rest of my life in a place overrun with tourists. Sightseeing buses often passed by our front door, and sometimes when I took out the garbage I would find people peering over the adobe wall.

Sometime earlier, we had found and—thanks to Donald's ingenuity—actually bought a building, an old, dilapidated but imposing Victorian hotel, built in 1907, in Belen, a small and unpretentious town thirty miles south of Albuquerque. The structure's strong, masonry-ringed, seven thousand square feet of space appealed to both of us. We thought that it would allow Donald and me large studios, ample living space, and the delicious quiet of a small New Mexico town, the kind of peace I had found in Santa Fe when I first started going there. Donald had swung a deal by which, with a combination of art and an unexpected and modest lump-sum inheritance (via his aunt Lillian, who had passed away), we could make the down payment. My mechanically inclined husband thought he could slowly work on renovating the hotel while we completed the *Holocaust Project,* even thinking that by the time the show opened we might be moved in.

Unfortunately, things didn't work out quite as we had planned, and we soon ended up giving the hotel back to the owners because of some serious problems that would have been expensive to rectify. Although they returned the art that had provided part of the down payment, it turned out that they had used all the money. They offered to repay these funds over the course of some months with a balloon payment due at the end. As it turned out, the owners would disappear, leaving us with another chance at buying the building, though at a greatly reduced cost.

In mid-February we received the news we'd been dreading for so long: Ben had died. Donald and I immediately flew to L.A. to tell my mother, which we did in the office of a sympathetic social worker at the Jewish Home. I can still see my mother—who by then was quite weakened by the cancer that had already metastasized to her bones—sitting on the couch. When we told her, she took the news like a body blow, crumbling into herself with a pained grimace on her face, then pulling herself erect as if to brace herself for the waves of grief. That Sunday we held a memorial service in the lovely garden of Audrey and Bob's house, to which Howard and Arleen came. Although I was deeply pained by Ben's death, I was also relieved that his ordeal was finally at an end. But before too long, it would become evident that even though his suffering was over, my mother's was to be intensified.

When we returned to Santa Fe, I began work on a large triptych entitled *Legacy of the Holocaust,* which explores the survivor experience and which would be positioned just before *Rainbow Shabbat* in the exhibition. The juxtaposition of these two works leads viewers back to the Jewish experience of the Holocaust: what the survivor experience might have to teach the larger human community, and then how the Jewish Shabbat ceremony might be regarded as a metaphor for a global healing and sharing. Working on *Legacy,* I struggled to achieve a level of integration of all that I'd learned and been through that, in some small way, might be likened to what was required of Holocaust survivors.

This image was to present some significant problems in terms of bridging the gap between audiences, as the Jewish community possesses an understanding of the Holocaust-survivor experience that is utterly lacking in, for example, the art world. Here, my commitment to creating art that was authentic to this experience would be put to the ultimate test. Could I come up with a painting that suggested how much could be learned from survivors that would be intelligible to viewers who knew little about the Holocaust and/or the array of responses evidenced by survivors?

This was problematic for a number of reasons. First, let us go back to the story I told about the museum director who didn't understand the word "Shabbat." The Jewish Friday-night ceremony is not exactly arcane, and at least a minimal understanding of it would seem to be desirable in order to relate to *Rainbow Shabbat.* However, there is little precedent in the art world for art with openly Jewish content (Chagall's work being the outstanding exception). Thus the question, By what standards should such art be measured? In terms of art—in particular, that dealing with the survivor experience—are the images to be evaluated according to their authenticity? By their formal properties? By how they fit into the canon of modern art? How much of a problem this was to be did not become apparent until after the opening of the exhibition.

In terms of working on *Legacy,* my personal and aesthetic lives would merge in that my grief about the worst that people could do to each other—manifested in such catastrophes as the Holocaust—came together with my private sorrow. Creating this image caused me to traverse a path that might be best described as trying to achieve spiritual survival—and some level of integration—after my long descent into the darkness of the Holocaust, during which time I seemed to have been accompanied by an inordinate number of personal tragedies. As I painted the center panel—which presents two survivors, a woman leading a male figure out of the hell that was the bombed-out crematoria of Birkenau—I thought about Terrence Des Pres's book *The Survivor*. In this amazing (and extremely slim) volume, he argued that it was in the camps that the need to bear witness was born, that "if all else failed, one must scream." Each day as I struggled to bring the figures alive, I thought that this mandate might actually describe my own life.

Chapter Eleven

Lost in Albuquerque/
Found in Belen?

I worked on *Legacy* until the end of the summer of 1992, alternating intense periods of painting with finishing the *Holocaust Project* book. In the intervening months since my brother's death, the Belen saga had inched along. I was quite ambivalent about this enterprise, but Donald was intent upon going ahead with it if at all possible. I knew that I would get some money as soon as I turned in the manuscript and agreed that, if Donald could work it out, we would use some of it for what would be an extremely modest purchase price. In retrospect, it seems clear that undertaking this venture would not be the wisest thing I'd ever done, but it was incredibly significant to my husband. Given the way he had stood by and supported me through the years of our marriage, it seemed fair that he should have the opportunity to pursue something so important to him as achieving a place of his own.

However, I had never been involved in a building project and had no idea what we were getting into. First, there was the problem of financing. Donald had tied our buying the hotel to obtaining renovation monies, an effort I got tired of after being turned down by a few banks. Not Donald; he patiently applied to one lending institution after another until he had pretty much exhausted all the options in New Mexico. (In the process, we learned why so much local development is done by outsiders: The banks are not exactly supportive of regional enterprises.) At one point Donald thought he'd found an interested lender and was trying to convince them of the importance of saving the hotel, which had been put on the Historic Register by a former owner. He asked if I would phone the head of the State Historic Preservation office for a letter of support because I had met the man before; he and his wife had stopped to help me when I was hit by the pickup in 1986.

When I called, I asked if he remembered me. "How could I forget?" he said. "We had quite a memorable meeting." He expressed some eagerness when I told him why I was phoning and explained that there were monies available for projects involving old buildings, a fact that I promptly reported to Donald. Eventually we received renovation funds from both the state office and the National Trust for Historic Preservation, a private organization that tries to save valued buildings from destruction. Unfortunately, it would turn out that these funds were insufficient for the remodeling of a building that needed everything: new mechanical, electrical, and plumbing systems; a new roof; restored windows and brickwork; and what continues to be a seemingly endless stream of additions, subtractions, alterations, and adjustments. It would have been a lot smarter to get through the *Holocaust Project,* get ourselves out of debt, and then try to buy or build a place. But I suppose that everybody could acquire a Ph.D. in hindsight.

At any rate, while these negotiations dragged on, we decided that we would move to Albuquerque as soon as the artmaking was done so that Donald could be closer to Belen, as he would be doing most of the renovations (with a small crew). Albuquerque is cheaper than Santa Fe—which was definitely important, since starting a building project would mean that we'd be stretched very thin financially. We would be extremely fortunate to find a rental property that, though quite inexpensive, was situated on an acre of land, which would provide our bevy of cats room to roam. The building itself is of modest size, but I figured that I wouldn't need a large studio to do the exhibition work—which would occupy me between the time of our moving and the opening of the show—or to write, which is what I planned to do, at least for a little while. Moreover, I thought ("dreamed" would be a better verb) that it would not be long before we could move into the hotel, where we'd have ample space.

During this same period my mother was failing and had to be moved into another wing of the home, where she could have more care. This was very upsetting to her, as it meant she would have to give up her private room. She had prized these quarters, which were filled with my art, Ben's pots, and her favorite records and books. In addition to reading and listening to music, she had availed herself of the many classes that were offered there and had made a whole new group of friends, including several men who paid her court on a daily basis. I used to joke that she was so busy I would have to make an appointment to see her or even to speak to her on the phone. But after Ben's death she seemed to slowly recede into herself, a process accelerated by the spreading cancer.

Donald and I went to L.A. to pack up her things and move what little she was allowed to take into her new environs, where she'd be afforded greater care. When we returned home we soon became absorbed in working out *Four Questions,* the last and most complex piece in the *Holocaust Project.* Its title is based upon the traditional ritual of asking the same four questions every year at the Passover seder, queries that were once quite significant but have now become somewhat blunted, both by repetition and the passage of time. Not so the issues raised in this image, which represents some of the most perplexing ethical problems raised by the Holocaust, problems that as I suggested earlier, might not be solvable at this point in history. Four slatted panels entirely blur the distinction between painting and photography as a visual metaphor for how "blurry" and unresolvable these dilemmas appear to be.

In November Louis had a massive heart attack. Donald flew east with the idea that, if it looked as if his father would not recover, I would immediately follow. Although Louis pulled through, he never fully regained his strength, which was to prove terribly difficult for him, as he had always lived a very physical life. This affected my husband more than I would have anticipated. Given all we had been through during the previous years, I was surprised to realize that Donald had never before really confronted mortality, his own or his parents'. As I have lived with this type of knowledge for most of my life, I was astounded to realize that this was not true for everyone my age.

While Donald was in Massachusetts, I sprayed *Four Questions* with acrylic to establish the basic tonal ranges of the four panels, whose facing sides are done in color opposites so as to reinforce the contrast between past and present realities, which are presented on the opposing sides (Holocaust events on the left, contemporary situations on the right). When he returned, we began hand-coloring the panels, a tedious process and one with which I was unfamiliar, as photo oils— the medium we were using—is more a photographer's than a painter's method of applying color. We had chosen to employ these because of the fineness of the pigments and the transparency of the colors, which seemed to suit the nature of these particular images.

Our seventh anniversary brought with it a sense of approaching transition, in that the conclusion of the *Holocaust Project* was in sight. Finishing the project would usher in a new period for Donald and me, one that we both felt somewhat anxious about. There had never been a time in our marriage when we were not working on the project. Consequently, we could not help but worry whether there would be life after this intense collaboration and, if so, what it would be like. It seemed altogether appropriate—and also reassuring—that we would finish the *Holocaust Project* as we had started it years earlier, when we had sat in the movie theater watching *Shoah*: that is, side by side.

Until February 1993, Donald and I spent long hours together in my studio, carefully manipulating the photo oils with cotton balls and Q-Tips, after which I would apply the final coats of oil with tiny brushes. Even as we suffered together over the disquieting nature of these pictures, we took considerable pleasure in the ease with which we worked in concert (something we had not always been able to do), seeing in this shared activity a measure of the strength of the relationship we had wrought. This gave us confidence that our marriage would not only survive the end of the project but might even thrive once we were out from under the ongoing stress the subject matter caused us.

Once the painting of this image was completed, we had one more hurdle before we could celebrate, with kisses and champagne, the culmination of our long struggle: the silk-screening of the letters onto the slatted panels that would communicate the questions to be raised. The only people to whom we would have entrusted such a task were Jim and Judy of Unified Arts, because there was absolutely no room for error. Eight passes of the squeegee blade would either make the words or irreparably ruin the finished work. I had to turn away each time Jim drew the squeegee across the screen because I was so nervous; but of course, they accomplished the job with no mistakes.

Once the artmaking phase of the project was completed, I became occupied with all the logistics involved in preparing the exhibition. In addition to consulting on the framing and crating, I worked intensively with my friend Ginna Sloane on the documentation panels. Ginna had worked as our graphics designer throughout the course of the *Holocaust Project,* pro bono or in trade for art. While I was writing the text for the panels and working with her on their visual format, Donald was printing the many photographs that would help to create a short chronicle of our journey for viewers at the show; he also began dealing with some of the mechanical details of the installation. I spent many weeks working on the audio tour including some time with Michael Botwinick, now the director of a museum in California, who would provide the art-historical narration. The videotape that would introduce—or, in some venues, end—the show was being put together by Kate Amend. After *The Dinner Party,* she had gone on to become a successful film editor; she had volunteered to bring her considerable professional skills to bear on the making of this thirty-minute video. It was a joy to work with her as she supplemented and edited footage that had been shot by a local filmmaker, who had been documenting the project for a TV show on art.

The music for both the audio and video was done by a composer named Lanny Meyers, a fellow with whom I'd gone to college, during which time we had considered each other "soulmates" (which, in the 1950s, meant being close but never having sex). We had stayed in touch over the years, and as it turned out, just at the time I asked him for help, he had begun exploring his own Jewish roots. Doing the music for the *Holocaust Project* provided him the opportunity to explore some traditional vocal and musical traditions, and he produced a hauntingly beautiful score. Then, thanks to another one of my cousins, Alan Schwartz, who is a TV producer, Katie was provided with excellent post-production facilities.

Everyone who came forward during this period demonstrated yet again how indispensable support is in accomplishing an ambitious project such as this one. And even though I have spent much time in this manuscript lamenting my ongoing problems with inadequate levels of support, I must acknowledge and rejoice in the generosity of those numerous persons whose magnanimity ensured the completion of the *Holocaust Project* (and, in some cases, sustained me for many years). However, in terms of the preservation of the art I have created, such individual support is insufficient unless, of course, it is offered by patrons of vast wealth or power. But most of my network is made up of people of more modest means and position—a structure that has been demonstrably adequate for the creation and even the exhibition of my work, but not yet able to guarantee its future.

This is the problem that the board of Through the Flower has been discussing, specifically in regard to *The Dinner Party* since the congressional debate and the consequent blocking of its permanent housing. In March 1993, we held a board meeting in New York, during which much time was devoted to this topic. As I have tried to explain, the women on the board have come together over the years largely out of their desire to support me in my artmaking. I doubt that any of the board members could have predicted that they would end up responsible for *The Dinner Party*, the International Quilting Bee, the *Birth Project*, and, now that it was done, the *Holocaust Project*. (The last is being toured under the auspices of the corporation, though most of the responsibility is being handled by Donald and me. For a while it had seemed that the tour would be coordinated by the Spertus Museum, but this fell through.)

At this time Donald and I had no thought of keeping the exhibition intact, although we had come up with an installation plan in which the individual pieces would fit into a larger whole. We had hoped to sell each of the works to museums, so we were quite surprised after the show opened to hear numerous viewers say that the various parts belonged together permanently. But if we pursued this idea, it would only exacerbate the problem that Through the Flower's board was already addressing, which was what to do with *The Dinner Party*. As to what will happen to the *Holocaust Project* at the end of its exhibition schedule, neither Donald and I nor the board is ready to take this issue up.

At the March meeting the board continued its discussion about *The Dinner Party*'s permanent housing, a conversation that centered on the notion of trying to build a museum in Santa Fe. Sometime later, after the inception of the plan for the 1996 exhibition at the UCLA/ Hammer Museum, the board's focus would shift to California and a more modest goal, one that involves trying to find and forge a partnership with an existing institution, either on the West Coast or in another part of the country. As I said earlier, institutional interest is something that so far has not been exactly forthcoming. However, this show, which promises to both contextualize and demonstrate the importance of *The Dinner Party,* might serve to change that stance. If so, even such a concept—though less ambitious than the building of a museum—would still require a major fund-raising effort, undoubtedly involving millions of dollars. Like many small, nonprofit arts organizations, Through the Flower has always been a seat-of-the-pants operation, primarily geared toward supporting my participatory projects. These could be accomplished with volunteers, grass-roots organizing, and a loose administrative structure.

As we all recognized at this board meeting, building a museum would involve a different type of operation (along with experienced staff), and that at that moment the corporation was entirely unprepared to launch a capital campaign of any size. In order to do so, it seemed apparent that we would need a type of infrastructure that we did not have. Consequently, the board decided to set up an independent administrative office, whose function would be the strengthening of the organizational base and also the preparation of a major fund-raising campaign. The idea was to restructure the corporation in order to entirely concentrate upon the preservation of the art for which it is now responsible, notably *The Dinner Party*.

Given Through the Flower's limited resources, the plan would require that the priority for expenditures be this effort, which meant that I could not look to Through the Flower for support of future artmaking projects, at least for some time to come. Several board members brought up this issue, to which I responded by saying that not only did I not intend to do any more major projects but I was thinking of giving up art altogether in favor of working solely for the permanent housing of *The Dinner Party*. I explained that I was beginning to question the point of making any more images if the work I had already created was in such jeopardy.

Through the Flower did in fact open an administrative office in Santa Fe. Under the leadership of Judith Sherman Asher, the board president, and Beth Parisi, our dedicated comptroller, this space would function for several years, its small staff slowly forging a stronger organizational structure. I wish that I could say that we are now ready to undertake a capital campaign, but, as of this writing, this is still unclear. We have moved forward in fits and starts, impeded by the fact that board members are spread around the country. More significant, it seemed that as soon as we undertook the restructuring of the corporation, the board was plunged into a period of confusion, unrest, instability, and insecurity from which we have still not fully emerged.

Perhaps this can be explained by the fact that everyone is being asked not only to make *The Dinner Party*'s permanent housing a priority but also to raise funds beyond what most of us have imagined ourselves capable of doing. One could say that we are between a rock and a hard place in that few of the board members seem willing to assume the level of responsibility involved, and yet no one, myself most of all, wishes to see the piece lost. Maybe the problem is fear of what seems like an overwhelming task, particularly the money involved. Over the next few years, we would be instructed by various development directors (who volunteered their time) in how to ask for a "lead gift" of a million dollars or more, something that all folks knowledgeable about capital campaigns insist is essential in order to succeed. At successive board meetings after these training sessions, we would all joke about going into the closet to practice making such a request, most of us admitting how difficult it was to get the words out of our mouths without getting the giggles or having panic attacks.

I found myself asking numerous men who were the presidents or trustees of various museum boards how they were able to raise the many millions of dollars involved in their planned building projects. Although I often heard how much they hated fund-raising, nonetheless the men did not seem troubled about the prospect of raising such large sums, something that has been quite overwhelming to most of my board. Overcoming this feeling would seem to be another aspect of the empowerment process, one that would seem essential if we are to be able to accomplish our stated goal. Perhaps we ourselves are at the forefront of a change, one that will allow us and women like us to rise to the historic challenge of housing not just *The Dinner Party* but also taking responsibility for seeing that the rich abundance of creative objects produced by women throughout the centuries will no longer be relegated to the dustbin of history but will, instead, have a place as part of a treasured cultural heritage. In order for this to happen, however, many women will have to do what Through the Flower's board is attempting: that is, move into what is, for most of us, uncharted and frightening territory.

After the rather significant March 1993 board meeting in New York, Donald met me and we went to Newburyport to visit his parents. We especially wanted to see Louis, who was in a terrible way, his physical strength diminished and his emotional state one of pure rage. Hardly speaking to us, he openly took his anger out on Bertha, though she was certainly not to blame for his debilitated condition, which had been brought on by illness and age. After this disheartening visit, we returned to Santa Fe and the task of packing up and preparing to move, store, sell, or throw away the accumulation of ten years of living and working in the large, sprawling Canyon Road compound. We moved on Memorial Day weekend, leaving a hauntingly empty series of rooms where once there had been a bustling domicile.

Almost immediately, Donald began going to Belen every day, leaving me completely alone in a small house with our cats. The solitude was interrupted only when my assistant at the time, a young artist named Jessica Buege, came to work part-time in the small separate building on the property that we had set up to house Through the Flower's art office. It was barely adequate for the cabinets full of slides that were suddenly the only reminder of my lifetime of work. Most of the *Holocaust Project* was off being framed and crated, and what was not to be in the show (preparatory drawings, studies, and photographs) was stuck away in flat files or yet more storage bins. As I looked around at our new quarters in the semirural and funky South Valley of Albuquerque, there seemed no evidence that we had ever even done such a project, as if the previous seven and a half years had been a dream.

I felt lost, as if my accomplishments—not just the *Holocaust Project* but my total thirty-year career—were dissolving before my eyes. This was before the plans for the UCLA/Hammer exhibition of *The Dinner Party* were finalized. The piece was in storage, awaiting the outcome of the board's decision to undertake the building of a museum in Santa Fe. Although Through the Flower had placed numerous *Birth Project* works in public collections, these seemed to have disappeared into the cavernous basements of the institutions that had promised to display them, and the rest of the exhibition units was in crates. The remainder of my work was scattered in warehouses and storage lockers around the country, the total bill for which was over $1,600 per month. A good part of this was paid for by Through the Flower, but it was all too clear that if I and the board became unable to make these combined payments, my entire body of work would instantly become jeopardized.

At this time I began to be plagued by the memory of Anaïs's nightmare; her fright about the insubstantiality of her achievements was becoming my own. Looking back, I can see that my despair was the result of many factors, one of which was the shock of having traded in my spacious quarters in Santa Fe for this humble house. And even though I could not bear what had happened to the so-called City

Different—which had gone from being a charming and livable small city to an Aspenized retreat for rich people—I missed the landscape, the sense of community, and the continuity of my life there.

Moreover, even though I had told my board (and other people as well) that I saw no sense in continued artmaking, still, creating art had defined my life for many decades. The prospect of not doing so deprived me of a sense of purpose—and of joy. I desperately missed the long, uninterrupted days in the studio, and my impulse to create would not subside. For no reason except my intense need, I began a series of small drawings, the "Autobiography of a Year," on which I would work whenever the urge to put marks on a page became overpowering. I would not draw for long hours—as had been my habit —but, rather, in short bursts, sometimes doing the same image again and again until I located the desired aesthetic impulse, then expressed it as directly as I could. Over the next year, I would do 140 drawings, which I have never shown. Instead, they sit in two archival boxes in my study/studio, evidence of that painful year in which I was convinced that I was reenacting Anaïs's nightmare in my own life.

In retrospect, it seems somewhat odd that I should have felt this way just prior to the opening of a major exhibition. Not only was the *Holocaust Project* going to premiere the following October, but Donald and I had managed to put together a respectable museum tour. This should have given me some sense that I was making progress, especially because, unlike the exhibition of my earlier projects, this tour involved no alternative spaces—some small indication of greater acceptance of my work. Maybe I was suffering something that had never happened to me—that is, postpartum blues. Previously, I had always been immersed in another undertaking by the time a major project was done. But I had promised my board that this would not happen, and without Through the Flower's support, there was no way I could take on any more large-scale work.

When I think back upon this period, I realize that I was considerably more worn out from the *Holocaust Project* than I knew at the time. In fact, I am only now recovering my zest for life, something that has been quite lacking during much of the last few years. But even my exhaustion does not explain my mood over that summer of

1993, which was so dark as to have made suicide seem an attractive way out. In fact, I found many journal entries from these months concerning ways of "offing myself" while Donald was in Belen. One thing that stopped me was that I could not bring myself to inflict upon him the level of grief this would certainly have caused. Ultimately, it was writing this book that would help me understand the primary reason for my depression, which basically comes down to my fear for my body of art. Even now that my prospects seem somewhat improved, my situation is fragile, dependent upon so many factors out of my control. This was something I would have to come to terms with, which is what writing this book has allowed.

In July Louis died, and Donald and I flew east for the funeral, after which my husband went through a really bad period. Then, in August, my mother died; as I had anticipated, I was the last survivor of my immediate family at the opening of the *Holocaust Project*. Donald and I went to L.A. for a memorial service at the Jewish Home, to which Howard came, as did Cousin Alan and his older brother, Julian. One amusing note was that during the memorial service, all my cousins revealed that they had each considered themselves my mom's favorite. But other than this one moment of shared laughter, the rest of the day was pretty dismal and sad. As I write this, I hear my editor asking, "But Judy, how did you *feel* about your mother dying?" The answer is that maybe I had gone through so much pain during the years of the project—both my life and in the studio—that I was numb. After distributing her ashes in a rose garden as she'd requested, I came home and opened a bag I had retrieved when we'd moved her to the nursing section of the Jewish Home. I had thought that these were her limericks, funny poems she had written over the years; but instead, they were letters to several friends who had apparently saved them and sent them back to her. While reading them, I became quite choked up because I discovered an aspect of my mother I had not known, a part of herself she had kept from both my brother and me.

These letters spanned the period from when she first moved to California until she retired, an interval of fifteen years, during which time her exhaustion and her loneliness were apparently far greater than she had ever let on to me. I was angry that she had refused to share this part of herself, while at the same time I admired her determination to keep her problems from intruding in her children's lives. It was this fierce pride, however, that had prevented us from ever achieving the closeness I had so desperately needed when I was young. And while reading these letters, I realized with a start that she had passed this same pattern on to me. For I, too, have hidden behind a facade of strength when my heart was breaking, a facade that writing this book seems to have entirely broken down.

My intention was to begin work on *Beyond the Flower* in Chicago, where we planned to go in the early fall of 1993. As the *Holocaust Project* had never been assembled, Donald and I had no idea how long it would take to install, so we wanted to leave ample time for any unanticipated problems. We arranged to rent an apartment where I could write (and draw) when I wasn't needed at the Spertus, where Donald would be supervising the installation. The place where we would be staying, overlooking Lake Michigan and up the street from Howard and Arleen's, was not far from where I had grown up. The Spertus Museum is located on Michigan Avenue some blocks south of the Art Institute, where I had spent so many happy days during my childhood.

Shortly before we left for Chicago, I had received word that my new publisher, Viking Penguin, would be working with the publicists hired by the museum and that *The Village Voice* was sending a reporter to cover the opening. I was particularly happy with the paper's choice. Though I had never met her, I knew that she was an experienced art writer and also a friend of a number of my close friends, including Lucy Lippard. I knew her to be sympathetic to feminism and, I thought, to my work. Moreover, she had been assigned by an editor who happened to be the longtime companion of John Perrault, who had written such a positive piece about *The Dinner Party* and later had organized a *Birth Project* show.

I can recall thinking that finally people with attitudes similar to my own were in positions of influence in the New York art media, and thus I felt as though I had no reason to fear this reporter. Given that there was (in my opinion) so little art of merit in the museums on the subject of the Holocaust, at the very least I expected to have the project accepted for the integrity with which we had approached this subject matter, not to mention the length of time we had devoted to it. And both Donald and I presumed that the uniqueness of the ways in which we had combined painting and photography would earn us some respect. Actually, I was far more worried about the Jewish press than the art press, because—even though the *Holocaust Project* was rooted in the Jewish experience—we had departed from the way the Holocaust is traditionally presented in Jewish institutions.

The opening was to take place, oddly enough, almost eight years to the day after that momentous viewing of *Shoah*. Numerous events were scheduled over that October weekend, beginning with the opening of our joint exhibition of drawings, studies, and photographs on Saturday afternoon at the Joy Horwich Gallery. That evening, Through the Flower was planning a gala banquet to celebrate the completion of the *Holocaust Project,* to which people would be coming from all over the country; everyone who had a particular interest in the show had been invited. The next morning there was to be a private viewing, inaugurated by a specially composed prayer and then a ribbon cutting. Sunday afternoon, the Spertus had scheduled the opening activities, which included time for its trustees and constituency to see the exhibition, then its huge annual fund-raising dinner, at which I was to be presented with an award.

Prior to the weekend I had several busy days of interviews, book signings, and a press conference on Friday. I guess I should have become suspicious when the *Voice* reporter arrived at the end of this press event wearing an army flak jacket, which she never took off all weekend, even during the Saturday-night festivities, which had been billed as requiring cocktail attire. When I met her she appeared friendly, expressing appreciation that we had consented to her being present at all the events surrounding the opening (the Saturday-night dinner was a strictly private affair). After seeing the show, she interviewed me at my hotel apartment, an interchange that was quite unsatisfactory in that I felt that we were unable to make any real human connection, something I always try to achieve with reporters in order to break through the impersonality of interviews. On top of this, I felt some-what let down because I had looked forward to a stimulating exchange at this session.

Her first question baffled me, for she began by asking me about my "agenda." In retrospect, I realize that she was actually telling me something about herself, which I didn't pick up on. She had probably already made her assessment of both me and the show, and neither my answers that afternoon nor her witnessing the incredible audience response to the exhibition on Sunday would have any effect on the ax she'd apparently come to Chicago to grind. On Saturday night, more than 125 people assembled at a hotel for our celebration banquet, another one of the memorable evenings of my life. Isaiah Kuperstein acted as the master of ceremonies for a joyful, exuberant event that sometimes seemed more like a bar mitzvah than the prelude to a serious art opening. There were toasts and tears throughout the night, along with dancing to the music of a klezmer band; at one point Lanny Meyers joined in for a special musical moment dedicated to Donald and me.

In attendance that evening were some of my oldest and dearest allies; in fact, there were faces in that room that I had seen at the opening party after the San Francisco Museum of Modern Art opening of *The Dinner Party* in 1979. But it is essential to emphasize that what linked most of these diverse folks was a belief in the importance of my art. No matter how much love they might have felt for me, they had come to Chicago for the same reason they had gone to San Fran-cisco and stood by me for so many years: their commitment to my work. But because there was so much history between us, everyone felt safe to "hang it out there," as the saying goes, for my part, with no thought of my public persona. And given the varied credentials of the people in that room, they had every right to expect that both they and their opinions would be respected. Unbeknownst to any of us, we were all about to be openly ridiculed.

On Sunday morning, the exhibition was officially opened with a moving invocation. Donald and I waited anxiously during the hour or more it takes to see the show, because it was this group of people whose opinions we valued most of all. I shall always remember Stanley

Grinstein emerging from the exhibition with tears in his eyes, folding me into his arms and saying, "I'm so proud of you!" In all the thirty years I've known him, I have never seen Stanley cry—and certainly not at any art opening. One after another, individuals or small groups emerged to embrace and extol us; one museum director was so overwhelmed he could hardly speak.

"Go into the show," everyone urged, "people are crying in the exhibition"—which was somewhat hard to imagine. Although I have repeatedly expressed my belief in the potential power of art, it was difficult to imagine such unrestrained emotion in a gallery setting. But it was true: Everywhere Donald and I looked, people were weeping—a response so gratifying it was, as I said to Donald, beyond my wildest dreams. Throughout the morning, the *Voice* woman stood around watching these reactions, which are hardly the usual ones at art shows. Although she didn't say anything to me or to Donald, I was sure that she would at least comment upon this remarkable effusion of response. Instead, she wrote a piece so hateful it was hard to believe we were at the same opening.

By the time it was published, Donald and I were home, trying to get settled back into the routine of our lives after an absence of more than a month. We felt quite good about the initial reception of the work. And even though the exhibition would not draw the huge crowds that some of my previous shows had, it would still prove to be one of the more successful exhibitions at the Spertus (and subsequent institutions), reportedly stimulating an unusual amount of dialogue, along with ongoing expressions of gratitude from many viewers. Although I certainly did not expect unanimous critical acceptance, I must admit that I was quite taken aback when the Viking Penguin publicity people called to say that the *Voice* piece was "horrible" and they were faxing it to us so we could read it. At first glance, it seemed to be just another example of the New York art world's negative stance toward me; it was the "same old same old," as I described it to my publishers. But I was nevertheless surprised that, after so many years, this position seemed not to have changed one whit.

To tell the truth, I did not read the article all that carefully, having surmised from its title and tone that it might be best not to take it too seriously, though I was somewhat concerned about the fact that the art press often picks up on earlier writing (as had happened with *The Dinner Party*), especially that emanating from the East Coast. But this particular piece of writing was to have a far more detrimental effect on me than any before or after it. And this despite the fact that the reporter confessed that she had always felt "squeamish" in Jewish institutions, an announcement that would seem to ensure that any intelligent person would realize that such an admission would render the writer incapable of an objective opinion about the show.

The article, which featured what appeared to be a deliberately unattractive photograph of Donald and me, was entitled "Planet Holocaust: From Feminism to Judaism," as if to imply that I am someone who jumps on bandwagons. Much of the piece was devoted to disparaging our private party; the distinguished people gathered there were dismissed as nothing but a bunch of "fans." She critiqued my outfit, the color of my hair, the way I interacted with Donald, my lack of a sense of humor, even the sauce on the hotel chicken dinner. Only in the last third of the review did she even take up the subject of the art, describing it as an "aesthetic travesty," an odd phrase and one that reminded me of Hilton Kramer's labeling of *The Dinner Party* as "grotesque kitsch." The rest of the review fell into the old New York cant about how I make bad art. But in a gesture so malicious as to seem below contempt, she played Donald and me off each other by suggesting that my inadequate painting skills had "ruined" his wonderful photographs.

I tried to blow off the article, as I had done so many bad reviews. But it was not easy to maintain my usual cavalier attitude, given that the phone started ringing off the hook with people voicing their outrage, particularly over having their sincere outpouring of feelings publicly denounced as nothing but the gushings of a fan club. Then I received a phone call from Arlene Raven, who also wrote for the *Voice*. Shortly after the opening weekend, she had been in Chicago and had gone to see the show, which she had greatly admired. When she returned to New York, she read the review and asked the editor (the same one whom I had mistaken for a friend) for the opportunity to present an opposing, more positive perspective, a request that was categorically denied. Arlene asked Donald and me to write letters in response to the article, something that I had never done in all the many years of my career. But Arlene insisted, saying that everyone who had been calling to express their indignation should do the same.

I think she hoped that such an effort might convince the editor to let her write another piece, a strategy that proved unsuccessful. In fact, sometime later, Arlene was fired from the *Voice,* but not before the newspaper received dozens of letters of protest, including one in which the writer sent a Fleet enema to the reporter, along with the humorous advice that she might consider using this offering to cleanse herself of the vile temperament evidenced by her review. In preparation for writing my letter (one of the very few of this group to be published), I had to read the piece again, far more closely; I almost wish I hadn't, largely because its seemingly gratuitous viciousness caused me to suffer for a long time. I guess I was in no shape to handle such hostility at this particular time.

Allow me to make it clear that I am in no way suggesting that my work could not do with some good criticism or that the *Voice* reviewer was not entitled to her opinion of the art. It is just that— as in this instance—what has too often been put forth in regard to my work has been vitriol rather than a thoughtful critique. As a result, I have frequently felt forced into a position of having to throw out the baby with the bathwater, unable to accept any possible critical insights because they have usually been couched in such rancor.

As I look back upon this whole experience, I believe that I see revealed one of my most fundamental problems. In my mind, I see a different world, one far less cruel than that in which we live. By spending so much time in my studio, I had been able to believe that the world I could so clearly envision and tried to express through my art existed outside of my imagination and the personal, educational, and artmaking environments that I have created. Whenever I left these environments, I would be stunned. Then I would return to the alternative reality that I had constructed in order to forge yet another body of art in the belief that eventually my work and values would be apprehended and appropriately recognized.

When I read the *Voice* article carefully, I realized that basically nothing had changed despite decades of work; it seemed that I was as misunderstood as I had ever been, maybe even more so. Also, I truly could not reconcile what appeared to be a vast abyss between my own perception of the *Holocaust Project* as my finest achievement and the evaluation that the work was utterly devoid of any quality at all. This was particularly distressing, because one reason I thought the project especially excellent was that I had seemingly brought together the various aspects of my identity—that is, artist, writer, woman and feminist, Jew, and student of history. Now, for the first time in my life, I began to doubt my abilities as an artist as well as my own perspective. If I had been in low spirits before the opening, I found myself shattered afterward, even more lost than when we first moved to Albuquerque. It was with this mélange of emotions that I took up the writing of this book.

One might say that since the Spertus opening I have felt myself to be in a state of suspended animation, waiting to see if the life I had previously led will resume. That existence would be best described as a large one, defined by big projects and lofty aspirations. To go on with such a life, I would again need a large studio such as that which Donald and I hope to have in Belen. But it would also require some greater level of support than I have now. And if the art world remains so dead set against me and Through the Flower has become unable to provide the framework out of which I have worked these last two decades, in what terms am I to be an artist? As I mentioned, for a while I contemplated giving up artmaking entirely—my state of mind when I began this book. But since then I have discovered that I am absolutely unable to do so, nor am I able—or willing—to relinquish my vision of a different world.

In early 1994 I turned to those few needleworkers who had previously worked with me and who had expressed an interest in continuing to do so. I had an idea for a series of needleworked and painted images based upon traditional proverbs, to be reinterpreted in a contemporary context. Called *Resolutions for the Millennium,* this series is intended to present images of a world transformed into a global community of caring people. Though quite modest in scale, these works will provide a basis for teaching values through art, both through the images themselves and a (planned) book that will include instructions for parents interested in teaching their children needle skills while also transmitting hope for a better world.

For this undertaking, I went back to the idea of joint ownership of the finished pieces. From the outset, I was determined to avoid any increase in my already significant storage bills and thus came up with a contract stipulating that future responsibility for the work would also be equally shared by myself and the needleworkers. In this instance, I was grateful for the slow pace at which most of my stitchers tend to work because—what with writing both this book and the new one on *The Dinner Party,* along with the ongoing demands of the *Holocaust Project* tour—I had to work on these pieces in what was for me an atypical manner—that is, on and off, in what I sometimes refer to as "needleworker's time."

About the same time as I initiated this small project, Donald and I returned to Chicago for the installation of *The Fall* tapestry, which had not been finished in time for the premiere (I had shown the full-scale cartoon in its stead). While there, we were asked to take Richard Francis, the head curator of the Museum of Contemporary Art (MCA), through the *Holocaust Project.* (I joked that he would thereby avoid having to don the audio headphones). He was a pleasant chap who, amazingly enough, had attended the opening of *The Dinner Party* in London; in fact, he informed me, he had gone to school with Germaine Greer (who, I might remind my readers, had delivered the opening-night speech). After touring the exhibition, we began to discuss why so many people in the art community seemed to hold such a negative opinion of my art. He said that these people had no context for my work and that it raises numerous issues that make them uncomfortable. When they dismiss the art as "bad," they avoid having to deal with it seriously in any way. No sooner had we had this conversation than another review appeared in an alternative but influential Chicago paper. Headlined "The Banality of Bad Art," the piece demonstrated precisely what Richard had suggested: The writer described the work in such a negative way as to let himself off the hook in terms of providing any real critical analysis.

Although Richard's explanation was to be very helpful to me, as

I thought about our discussion I realized that there is and always has been a context for my work. But what our conversation made clear was that in the case of both my earlier work and the *Holocaust Project,* their respective contexts were unknown to the art community at the time the art first appeared. The *Holocaust Project,* for instance, grew out of Jewish history and values, the survivor experience, and Holocaust scholarship, especially that of the recent period. As this project is still touring, it is too soon to know whether this context will become evident to the art world, at which point I would hope for some better discourse than that with which the show was originally met.

The Dinner Party and the *Birth Project* arose from the context of women's history and experience, their creation and distribution fueled by the activism of the Women's Movement. Much to my surprise and relief, it would turn out that a number of young art historians and critics—notably Amelia Jones, the curator of *The Dinner Party* exhibition—were beginning to examine this period. Amelia is an expert in Feminist Art of the 1970s and thus possesses precisely what Richard Francis had described as being lacking in the art world's approach to my work—that is, a thorough understanding of the context from which my early work, in particular, had emerged. In the spring of 1994, she came to New Mexico to go through my slide files and archives. Here was someone well versed in art history looking at and appreciating what I had created—not just *The Dinner Party* and the *Birth Project* but also works of art from those years that had, in some instances, never even been shown.

After spending many days peering at slides and rooting through piles of articles and archival material, Amelia said that in her opinion, most of what had been written about me and my work was not true, and that she intended to *pierce* the misrepresentation that has surrounded me. As I recall this moment, I cannot help but laugh. Amelia was almost nine months pregnant then, and this statement was accompanied by a determined thrust of her very large belly. However, given what I've been saying about my depressed state of mind, I am sure my readers can imagine how much these words meant to me. In addition to lifting my spirits, they also gave me hope that eventually my whole body of work might come to be understood.

But this can only happen if I can make sure that it does not all disappear or grow mildewed in some musty warehouse space. I had anticipated that as soon as the Belen hotel was finished and we were moved in, I would try to bring all my work there, to slowly organize and catalog it. But at the moment, even this plan is in danger of not being able to be accomplished, primarily because of money. In the summer of 1994, Donald and I ran out of funds, which threatened to shut down the building project altogether. We were extremely fortunate that Donald's mother, Bertha, gave him a substantial gift, which she dubbed an "early inheritance." But even this generous amount would not be enough, though we did not realize it at the time.

In September, shortly before the opening of the *Holocaust Project* at its second venue, the Austin Museum of Art at Laguna Gloria in Texas, I went to Colorado to begin to rework this manuscript. My editor, Mindy Werner, had helped me to see that there were many things about myself and my life that I needed to explain to my readers, something that was exceedingly hard for me to do. In my previous books, I had focused primarily on my art or just described what I had done. It had never occurred to me that who I was, how I had lived, and what I believed were not self-evident. But judging from Mindy's comments, along with the many misunderstandings and misrepresentations that have swirled around me over the years—not to mention Richard Francis's insight—it seemed that I was wrong. In fact, as I was to later tell Lucy Lippard, the only positive result of the *Voice* article was that it served as a wake-up call. If someone presumably sympathetic could get me and my intentions so wrong, perhaps it would behoove me to try to convey more clearly what I am all about.

Of course, I realize that doing so in no way guarantees that anyone's perceptions will change; but at least I will have made the effort to set the record straight. Moreover, working on this book would force me to publicly reveal myself more than I'd done before. It would also cause me to think about many aspects of my life I had never really reflected upon—most crucially, how I had come to a point at which I was thinking about putting down my paintbrush. Writing and rewriting *Beyond the Flower* has been a very painful process, which was one reason I wanted to go off by myself, at least for a while. I was able to do so because of Audrey and Bob Cowan, who own a vacation house in Beaver Creek, outside Vail, Colorado, which they made available to me for many weeks in the fall of 1994.

Each day I spent many hours at the typewriter, then went outside to breathe in the delicious fall air and to push my body in long runs over the hills and valleys of this mountainous retreat. The leaves of the aspen trees that dot the hills were beginning to turn brilliant hues of gold, and I inhaled their color and watched the soft pink light of the late afternoon bathe the mountainsides. Some days I wept while I typed, recognizing that although I had in some ways recognized how hard my life had been, I had also distanced myself from this realization by working all the time, taking all my emotions—the rejections, the disappointments, and the many sorrows—and transforming them into painted images. But the day of reckoning had come. As I forced myself to honestly describe myself and my feelings to my readers, I also came in touch with all of this myself.

So now where am I, one year later, as I finish this book? Donald and I are still in the Albuquerque house, and for the moment the Belen hotel project is shut down, as we have again run out of funds. Donald is working as a foreman at a small construction company that does remodeling, a job he seems not to mind, though I keep asking him how he can bear not doing photography. He responds by saying that he will do anything to complete Belen; he is working at this job to meet the mortgage payments and the associated costs of the building. Meanwhile, I am continuing to support us while trying to slowly cut away at the debt we accumulated while doing the *Holocaust Project* so that in the future we might qualify for the bank financing we will need to maintain the hotel. I hope that together we will be able to earn enough money so that we can finish the building. If this happens, I will be able to move out of this suspended state in which I have been these past several years and into the next chapter of my life.

What might this be like? I have already described my desire to get my body of art out of storage and into a safe place. Then perhaps someday there will be another young woman who feels angry and conflicted—as I did—by what she encounters as she tries to make her way in the world. Who knows? Perhaps she will stumble upon my storehouse and find images there that empower her, that help her know that there is nothing wrong with who she is or what she wishes to be. Perhaps she will be able to stand on my shoulders, as I have stood on those of my predecessors. It comforts me to know that I found them—even if their work was not adequately displayed in the museums; even if their faces were not carved in granite or imprinted on coins, even if their names were not highlighted in the history books. And it will be enough for me if I can assure that this young woman can find me.

Achieving this seems like a realistic goal, one that I might attain in my lifetime. More than that, I am not at all sure I can do, not without support or money far beyond what I have right now. As I have stated, even this aim is higher than my arrow can reach right now, no matter with what strength I may "woman" this particular bow. As to my artmaking life, after being away from it for over two years, I am clear once again that it is still what is most important to me. Perhaps Merce Cunningham was right in what he told me years ago: that there is no resolution to many of these problems and one must just go on. And this is precisely what I have decided to do.

For some time, I have been pondering the fact that there is such an unequal distribution in art; some people seem to have too much while most have not enough in their lives. If I have the opportunity to address this in some way, I surely will. But mostly, I just want to pick up my paintbrush and dip it into color, then stroke the paper to discover what comes forth. Maybe I shall mind Emily Dickinson's admonition, outlined in one of her poems, and once again "take my power in my hands and go out against the world," though precisely what form this might take is still unclear. Certainly, I intend to never again be persuaded that it is time to put aside my art, for it has made my life worth living.

Writing this book has allowed me to pull myself out of a hole into which I had never imagined I would fall. For I can now see that during these last few years I finally succumbed to that pernicious idea, the same one that continues to disempower so many women: that such creative power as I have evidenced is somehow unseemly when it exists in a female body. Upon considerable and anguished reflection, done in the pages of this manuscript, I have been able to realize that the underlying message of most of those nasty things that have been said and written about me over the years comes down to just this wrong-headed and fearful notion. I am grateful to those readers who have hung in there with me as I have made this excruciating journey through my life and out of the temporary immobilization that I have suffered. I hope that what I have described, especially what I have gone through in the last few decades, might be useful to you. Whatever the benefit of my tale to others, for whatever time remains to me, I plan to subscribe to the old adage: "It's not over till it's over." And even though I continue to be acutely aware of my mortality—and hence the fact that this condition could change at any time—for the moment, I'm still here. If maturity has brought me anything, it is surely the wisdom that one never knows what the future might bring.

Acknowledgments

The artist/author wishes to thank:

My husband, best friend, and extraordinary photographer, Donald Woodman.

The board of Through the Flower, the organization that has sustained and supported me for nearly two decades and also provides me with a fine small staff.

Viking Penguin, which gave me the opportunity to tell my story.

Mindy Werner, who made me tell the truth.

My stellar design and production team, especially Kate Nichols, Dolores Reilly, and Susan VanOmmeren.

My wonderful publicist, Ron Longe.

The "dream team" in publicity and marketing, Maureen Donnelly and Marcia Burch.

Copyeditor fantastique Bob Castillo, who cleans up my often messy act.

My agent, Loretta Barrett, who found me such a good literary home.

Phyllis Sullivan, who endured and typed endless revisions of this manuscript.

The thanks be to Grandmother Winifred Foundation, which provided
    me with a grant for this book, along with a much appreciated
    level of enthusiasm for my work.

My cousins, Howard and Arleen Rosen, who have demonstrated what
    family is all about.

Gelon, who changed my life.

MR, who stood by me for a long time.

Susan Grode, who has never failed me.

The Grinsteins, my first and long-suffering patrons.

The Cowans, for letting me so disrupt their lives.

Henry Hopkins, who premiered and renewed *The Dinner Party*.

Amelia Jones, who came to visit just in time.

To future generations of women, to whom I offer my shoulders to
    stand on with the hope that they may climb out of the terrible
    cycle of repetition that is too much of women's history.

Index

FOR THE BEST IN PAPERBACKS, LOOK FOR THE

Don't miss these other great books by Judy Chicago

☐ **THE DINNER PARTY**

This lavish volume, now updated in a new edition, is the spectacular companion to the 1996 commemorative exhibition of *The Dinner Party*, Chicago's controversial, vastly popular "icon of feminist art" (*Art News*).

       ISBN: 0-14-024437-9 (pbk)   *0-670-85957-5 (hc)*

☐ **HOLOCAUST PROJECT**
From Darkness Into Light

Chicago's searching evocation of the Holocaust is a stunning work of both art and autobiography, chronicling the genesis and creation of one of the most provocative exhibitions of our time.   *ISBN: 0-14-015991-6*

☐ **THROUGH THE FLOWER**
My Struggle as a Woman Artist

In this classic in the literature of women and the arts, artist, author, teacher, and feminist Chicago details with charm and candor how she survived personal tragedy and professional ostracism to become an influential and internationally known artist.   *ISBN: 0-14-023122-6*

☐ **BEYOND THE FLOWER**

Twenty years after the publication of *Through the Flower*, Chicago lifts the veil of the international public person she has become to reveal the intimate story of her life and the effect upon her ongoing struggle as an artist and feminist in late twentieth-century America.   *ISBN: 0-14-023297-4*

FOR THE BEST IN PAPERBACKS, LOOK FOR THE

In every corner of the world, on every subject under the sun, Penguin represents quality and variety—the very best in publishing today.

For complete information about books available from Penguin—including Puffins, Penguin Classics, and Arkana—and how to order them, write to us at the appropriate address below. Please note that for copyright reasons the selection of books varies from country to country.

In the United Kingdom: Please write to *Dept. JC, Penguin Books Ltd, FREEPOST, West Drayton, Middlesex UB7 0BR.*

If you have any difficulty in obtaining a title, please send your order with the correct money, plus ten percent for postage and packaging, to *P.O. Box No. 11, West Drayton, Middlesex UB7 0BR*

In the United States: Please write to *Consumer Sales, Penguin USA, P.O. Box 999, Dept. 17109, Bergenfield, New Jersey 07621-0120.* VISA and MasterCard holders call 1-800-253-6476 to order all Penguin titles

In Canada: Please write to *Penguin Books Canada Ltd, 10 Alcorn Avenue, Suite 300, Toronto, Ontario M4V 3B2*

In Australia: Please write to *Penguin Books Australia Ltd, P.O. Box 257, Ringwood, Victoria 3134*

In New Zealand: Please write to *Penguin Books (NZ) Ltd, Private Bag 102902, North Shore Mail Centre, Auckland 10*

In India: Please write to *Penguin Books India Pvt Ltd, 706 Eros Apartments, 56 Nehru Place, New Delhi 110 019*

In the Netherlands: Please write to *Penguin Books Netherlands bv, Postbus 3507, NL-1001 AH Amsterdam*

In Germany: Please write to *Penguin Books Deutschland GmbH, Metzlerstrasse 26, 60594 Frankfurt am Main*

In Spain: Please write to *Penguin Books S. A., Bravo Murillo 19, 1° B, 28015 Madrid*

In Italy: Please write to *Penguin Italia s.r.l., Via Felice Casati 20, I-20124 Milano*

In France: Please write to *Penguin France S. A., 17 rue Lejeune, F–31000 Toulouse*

In Japan: Please write to *Penguin Books Japan, Ishikiribashi Building, 2–5–4, Suido, Bunkyo-ku, Tokyo 112*

In Greece: Please write to *Penguin Hellas Ltd, Dimocritou 3, GR–106 71 Athens*

In South Africa: Please write to *Longman Penguin Southern Africa (Pty) Ltd, Private Bag X08, Bertsham 2013*